Balanced Literacy
Through Cooperative Learning & Active Engagement

by Sharon Skidmore
& Jill Graber
in consultation with Dr. Jacqueline Minor

Kagan

Kagan

© 2011 by **Kagan Publishing**

This book is published by **Kagan Publishing**. All rights are reserved by **Kagan Publishing**. No part of this publication may be reproduced or transmitted in any form by any means, electronic or mechanical, including photocopy, recording, or any information storage and retrieval system, without prior written permission from **Kagan Publishing**. The blackline masters included in this book are intended for duplication only by classroom teachers who purchase the book, for use limited to their own classrooms. To obtain additional copies of this book, or information regarding professional development in cooperative learning or multiple intelligences, contact:

Kagan Publishing
981 Calle Amanecer
San Clemente, CA 92673
1 (800) 933-2667
www.KaganOnline.com

ISBN: 978-1-933445-07-6

Balanced Literacy
Fourth Grade

Introduction

Do you remember when you learned to ride a bike? You watched the neighborhood kids zooming down the street on their bikes. You knew you wanted to join them. You watched and listened carefully as your parents demonstrated and explained how to start and stop. Getting on the bike was a little scary at first. However, training wheels, the reassurance of supporting hands, and encouraging words gave you the confidence needed to successfully practice your new skill. With each practice, your ability grew and parental support was gradually withdrawn. Your new skills soon allowed you to ride your bike independently and successfully as you zoomed down the street with your neighborhood friends.

Just as learning to ride a bike requires a series of supported steps, literacy requires guiding the learner through scaffolded instruction. The balanced literacy components provide the framework for developing deep thinkers and strategic readers. Balanced literacy increases teachers' effectiveness as they explicitly instruct through varying degrees of demonstration and practice, teacher feedback, and ongoing assessment.

> *[Effective teachers provide] just the right amount of support that allows the learner to assume increasing control of the task. It's a gentle dance that requires careful leading, following, and occasionally sidestepping. Gradually, as students become competent, we reduce the amount of support we offer. Intrinsic to this belief is allowing enough time, support, and feedback.*
>
> — Regie Routman

Fourth Grade Book Organization

In this book we have provided lessons and activities to support the balanced literacy components of aloud, shared, guided, and independent practice to strengthen national standards in comprehension, word study, vocabulary, fluency, and writing. Research emphasizes that learners need to acquire skills in these areas to be proficient readers and writers. Activities appropriate for fourth grade students have been developed for each of the four sections in this book, incorporating Kagan Cooperative Learning Structures.

As educators ourselves, we understand the limited time teachers have to develop student materials to support the literacy outcomes for their particular grade level. One of our goals for this book was to develop teacher-friendly materials. Therefore, you will find blackline masters (cards, spinners, cubes, and mats) designed to support the activities in each section. These are located directly behind the direction page for each cooperative learning structure. You may want to consider copying these pages onto cardstock for durability. Blank templates have been included for some of the activities giving you the flexibility to tailor activities to closely match specific literature or skills for your individual class.

The five national literacy standards of comprehension, word study, vocabulary, fluency, and writing are addressed in separate sections of this book, with the exception of vocabulary, which is included in both the Comprehension and Word Study sections.

Section 1: Comprehension

Section 2: Word Study

Section 3: Fluency

Section 4: Writing

Fourth Grade
A Note to the Reader

The ideas for this book are drawn from our combined experiences in the elementary classroom and as literacy coaches. As educators we are always striving to maximize learning and make every moment count as we endeavor to educate our students. It is our intention that this book will be a resource for you as you systematically think about literacy: What are the needs of my students? How can I best deliver instruction? What is the most effective use of instructional time?

When we combine balanced literacy and Kagan Cooperative Learning, our classroom practices become more purposeful and connected resulting in increased student performance. We hope that this book will be a guide as you strive to improve instruction and enhance student learning.

A special thanks to Dr. Jacqueline Minor, our former Assistant Superintendent of Curriculum and Instruction and the present Director of Curriculum and Instruction for Kagan Professional Development, whose vision and knowledge continues to challenge us professionally. It has been with her involved guidance and encouragement that the ideas for the lessons and activities were organized for this book. Because of Jackie, this book has now become a reality.

Appreciations:
- **Illustrations:** Erin Kant
- **Graphic Designers and Layout Artists:**
  Kellee LaVars
  Alex Core
  Becky Herrington
- **Copyeditor:** Kim Fields
- **Publications Director:** Miguel Kagan

Fourth Grade
Table of Contents

Introduction iii
Book Organization iv
   A Note to the Reader v

Section 1
Comprehension

   Comprehension Overview 2
   Table of Comprehension Resources 3
   Table of Comprehension Activities and Lessons 5

Comprehension Resources

   Metacognitive Awareness Resource/Materials Descriptions 10
   Metacognitive Awareness Definitions 13
   Metacognitive Awareness Posters 14
   Metacognitive Awareness Student Bookmark 27
   Metacognitive Awareness Student Tally Sheet 28
   Metacognitive Awareness Student Page Response 29
   Student Clarification Checklist 30
   Metacognitive Awareness Student Rubric and Response 31
   Metacognitive Awareness Lesson Planning Form 32
   Book List for Metacognitive Awareness Shared Read Alouds 33
   Text Types and Text Structures Resource Descriptions 35
   Four Text Type Resource Pages 37
   Text Structures Resource Page 39
   Four Text Types & Five Text Structures Resource Page 40
   Figurative Language Resource Descriptions 41
   Figurative Language Definitions 42
   Figurative Language Student Record Sheet (Alliteration, Idiom,
      Onomatopoeia, Hyperbole, Metaphor, Simile) 43

Comprehension Activities and Lessons

   Metacognitive Awareness Shared Read Aloud—*Lou Gehrig
   The Luckiest Man* 46
Showdown Activities and Blacklines 50
   Comprehension Showdown 50

Metacognitive Terms and Definitions 51
Text Types—Author's Purpose 55
Text Structures—Definitions, Signal Words, and Graphic Organizers......58
Text Structures and Paragraphs 65
Text Structures and Paragraphs Answer Key..68
Text Structures—Signal Words 69
Fact or Opinion 76

Quiz-Quiz-Trade Activities and Blacklines......................................83
Comprehension Quizzes 83
Text Types—Definitions..84
Text Types—Author's Purpose 88
Text Types—Examples 96
Determining Author's Purpose and Text Types from Titles..................103
Text Structures—Definitions, Signal Words, and Graphic Organizers....112
Text Structure Passages..119
Cause-Effect 124
Text Features 132
Homophone Definitions 136
Figurative Language 143
Homophone Sentences 149
Word Meanings..157
Possessive Nouns 164
Present-Past Tense Verbs 171

Numbered Heads Together Activity and Blacklines......................179
Which Definition?...179
Vocabulary Definitions..180

Fan-N-Pick Activities and Blacklines 182
Pick a Card, Any Card..182
Fan-N-Pick Mat..183
Metacognitive Awareness Strategies 184
Text Features 186
Story Elements (Fiction) 189
Previewing Before Reading (Nonfiction) 194

Talking Chips Activity and Blacklines 196
Comprehension Cubes 196
Nonfiction Comprehension Question Cube (Before Reading) 197
Nonfiction Comprehension Question Cube (Reflection).....................198
Fiction Comprehension Question Cube (Reflection) 199
Questioning Cube..200
Metacognitive Cube (After Reading)..201

Fourth Grade
Table of Contents *Continued*

    Literature Circle Discussion Cube #1 (After Reading) 202
    Literature Circle Discussion Cube #2 (After Reading) 203

RoundTable Consensus Activities and Blacklines 204
    Spinning Vocabulary 204
    Vocabulary Spinner 205
    Sentence Cards for Vocabulary Spinner 206
    Blank Sentence Cards for Vocabulary Spinner 207
    Comprehension Puzzles 208
    Retelling (Fiction) Puzzle Pieces and Puzzle Mat 209
    Retelling (Nonfiction) Puzzle Pieces and Puzzle Mat 211
    Text Feature (Nonfiction) Puzzle Pieces and Puzzle Mat 213

Solo and RallyCoach Activity and Blacklines 215
    Anticipation Guide 215
    Anticipation Guide Samples 216
    Anticipation Guide Student Form and Blank Student Form 219

Listen-Sketch-Draft Activity and Blacklines 221
    Sketching for Comprehension 221
    Listen-Sketch-Draft Sample Form 222
    Listen-Sketch-Draft Form 223

Timed Pair Share Activity and Blacklines 224
    Story Predictions 224
    Prediction Mat 225
    Blank Story Element Cards for Prediction Mat 226
    Story Element Cards for Prediction Mat 227

Jot Thoughts and Sorting Activity and Blacklines 228
    Sort It Out 228
    Recall Mat 229
    Sorting Mat 230

Traveling Heads Together Activities and Blacklines 231
    Idioms and Morals 231
    Idioms 232
    Idioms Answer Sheet 235
    Fable Morals 236

RallyCoach Activity and Blacklines 238
    Idiom Meanings 238
    Idiom Mat and Cards 239

Find-the-Fiction Activity and Blacklines 242
    Idiom Cards—True or False? 242
    Idiom Cards 243

Section 2
Word Study

Word Study Overview 248
Table of Word Study Resources 249
Table of Word Study Activities and Lessons 250

Word Study Resources

Word Study Resource Descriptions 254
Word Study Spelling Strategies 255
Word Study Prefix and Suffix Word List 256
Word Study Contraction List 258
Word Study Homophone List 259
Word Study Homograph List 262

Word Study Activities and Lessons

Partner Word Study Activities 264
Team Word Study Activities 268
Class Word Study Activities 272
Making Words Lesson Plans 273
RallyCoach Activity and Blacklines 274
   Making Words Lesson 1: *Yourself*—Activity 1: Making Words 274
   Words to Make from *Yourself* 275
Find My Rule Activity and Blacklines 276
   Making Words Lesson 1: *Yourself*—Activity 2: Sorting 276
RallyCoach Activities and Blacklines 277
   Making Words Lesson 1: *Yourself*—Activity 3: Transfer 277
   Making Words (*Yourself*) Teacher Transparency Form 278
   Making Words (e, o, u, f, l, r, s, y) Student Form 279
   Making Words Lesson 2: *Rainforest*—Activity 1: Making Words 280
   Words to Make from *Rainforest* 280
Find My Rule Activity and Blacklines 281
   Making Words Lesson 2: *Rainforest*—Activity 2: Sorting 281
RallyCoach Activities and Blacklines 281
   Making Words Lesson 2: *Rainforest*—Activity 3: Transfer 281
   Making Words (*Rainforest*) Teacher Transparency Form 282
   Making Words (a, e, i, o, f, n, r, r, s, t) Student Form 283
   Making Words Lesson 3: *Relationship*—Activity 1: Making Words 284
   Words to Make from *Relationship* 284

Fourth Grade
Table of Contents *Continued*

Find My Rule Activity and Blacklines 285
    Making Words Lesson 3: *Relationship*—Activity 2: Sorting 285
RallyCoach Activities and Blacklines 285
    Making Words Lesson 3: *Relationship*—Activity 3: Transfer 285
    Making Words (*Relationship*) Teacher Transparency Form 286
    Making Words (a, e, i, i, o, h, l, n, p, r, s, t) Student Form 287
    Find My Rule Mat for Making Words 288
    Making Words Planning Form 289
    Making Words Student Form 290
Find Someone Who Activities and Blacklines 291
    Who Knows? 291
    All About Prefixes! 292
    Skill Review #1 293
    Skill Review #2 294
    Skill Review #3 295
    Find Someone Who Form 296
Quiz-Quiz-Trade Activities and Blacklines 297
    Partner Word Study Practice 297
    Contractions 298
    Silent Letters 305
    Letter Patterns (ar, er, in, or, ur) 312
    Letter Patterns (au, aw, ou, ow) 319
    Letter Patterns (ie, ei) 327
    Prefixes (anti-, dis-, ex-, non-, under-) 334
    Prefixes and Suffixes 342
    Their, There, They're 349
RallyCoach Activities and Blacklines 356
    Coach Me 356
    Prefix Cube (anti-, dis-, ex-, non-, under-) 357
    Prefix Worksheet (anti-, dis-, ex-, non-, under-) 358
    Prefix Answer Sheet (anti-, dis-, ex-, non-, under-) 359
    Suffix Cube (-ful, -en, -less, -ment, -ness) 360
    Suffix Worksheet (-ful, -en, -less, -ment, -ness) 361
    Suffix Answer Sheet (-ful, -en, -less, -ment, -ness) 363
    Antonym-Synonym Cube 365
    Antonym-Synonym Worksheet 366
    Antonym-Synonym Answer Sheet 367
    Contraction Spinner 368

Contraction Worksheet 369
Adding Endings Spinner (-ing, -ed, -s) 370
Adding Endings Worksheet (-ing, -ed, -s) 371
Adding Endings Answer Sheet 372
Sorting Mat (Hard g or Soft g) 373
Word Cards (Hard g or Soft g) 374

Showdown Activities and Blacklines..377
Word Study Showdown 377
Word Cards—Prefixes (anti-, dis-, ex-, non-, under-) 378
Word Cards—Antonyms, Synonyms, and Homophones................................382

Numbered Heads Together Activity and Blacklines..389
Word Wall Spelling 389
Fourth Grade Word List 390
Fourth Grade Word Wall Cards 392
    Fourth Grade Additional Word Wall Cards..398
    Fourth Grade Blank Word Wall Cards 405

Section 3
Fluency

Fluency Overview 408
Table of Fluency Resources 409
Table of Fluency Activities 410

Fluency Resources

Fluency Resource/Materials Descriptions 412
Fluency Bookmarks 413
Fluency Graphics/Note Taking 414

Fluency Activities

RallyCoach Activities and Blacklines..416
Fluency Scoring 416
Expression Rubric and Graph 417
Phrasing Rubric and Graph 418
Accuracy Rubric and Graph 419
Rate Rubric and Graph 420
Fluency Continuum 421

Poems for Two Voices Activities and Blacklines..422
Fluency Poems 422
Tropical Rainforests 423

Fourth Grade Table of Contents Continued

Human Body Riddles 425
Blank Form 427
Quiz-Quiz Trade Activity and Blacklines 428
Fluency Sentences 428
Fluency Sentence Cards 429

Section 4
Writing

Writing Overview 438
Table of Expository/Writing Resources 439
Table of Expository Writing Activities 440
Table of Persuasive Writing Resources 442
Table of Persuasive Writing Activities 443

Expository Writing Resources

Expository Writing Resource Descriptions 446
Expository Writing Model 447
Expository Writing Steps 448
Expository Writing Six Trait Checklist 449

Expository Writing Activities

Expository Writing Stages 452
Prewriting Activities
Inside-Outside Circle Activity and Blackline 453
Prewriting Circles 453
Prewriting Question Cards 454
Jot Thoughts Activity and Blackline 455
Brainstorming Ideas 455
Brainstorming Mat 456
RoundTable Consensus Activity and Blackline 457
Sorting Ideas 457
Sorting Mat 458
Writing Activity
Solo Activities and Blacklines 459
Paragraph Writing 459
Sample Topic Sentence Form 460

Sample Detail Sentences Form 461
Topic Sentence Form 462
Detail Sentences Form 463

Editing and Rewriting Activities

Editing & Rewriting Activities
RoundRobin Activity and Blacklines 466
  Improving Details 466
  Six Ways to Improve Details 467
  Detail Improvement Form 468
CenterPiece Activities and Blacklines 469
  Word Choice Practice 469
  Word Choice—Powerful Verbs 470
  Word Choice—Powerful Adjectives 472
  Word Choice—Similes 474
  Word Choice—Describing a Noun 476
  Word Choice Form 477
RallyCoach Activity and Blacklines 478
  Sentence Writing Practice 478
  Sentence Mechanics 479
  Revising Sentences 481
  Revising Sentences Form 483
Team Stand-N-Share Activity and Blacklines 484
  Hooks and Endings 484
  Hook Examples 485
  Ending Examples 486
  Hook & Ending Form—Sample 487
  Hook & Ending Form 488
Peer Feedback Activity
Two-Partner Edit Activity 489
  Six Trait Feedback 489
Sharing Activity
Mix-Pair-Share Activity 490
  Sharing Final Drafts 490

Persuasive Writing Resources

Persuasive Writing Resource Descriptions 492
Topics for Persuasive Writing 494
Persuasive Writing Model 495
Persuasive Writing Model Form 496

Fourth Grade
Table of Contents *Continued*

Student Persuasive Writing Plan (Form A) 497
Student Persuasive Writing Plan (Form B) 498
Student Persuasive Writing Plan (Form C) 499
Student Persuasive Writing Plan (Form A—Example Sheet) 500
Student Persuasive Writing Plan (Form B—Example Sheet) 501
Student Persuasive Writing Plan (Form C—Example Sheet) 503
Persuasive Writing Six Trait Checklist 505

Persuasive Writing Activities

Persuasive Writing Stages 508

Prewriting Activities
Inside-Outside Circle Activity and Blackline 509
   Prewriting Circles 509
   Prewriting Question Cards 510
Corners with RoundRobin Activity and Blackline 511
   "For" or "Against" Sentence Writing Practice 511

Writing Activities
RoundTable/RallyTable Activity 512
   Reasons for Opinion 512
RoundRobin Consensus/RallyCoach Activity and Blackline 513
   Supporting Details 513
Solo Activities and Blacklines 514
   Restatement of Opinion and Main Reasons 514
   Adding an Ending 515
Jot Thoughts Activity and Blackline 516
   Hook Examples 516
Inside-Outside Circle Activity and Blackline 517
   Choosing a Hook 517
Solo Activity 518
   Final Copy 518

Revising Activity
RallyCoach Activity and Blacklines 519
   Transitional Words 519
   Transitional Word List 520
   Transitional Word Passages 521

Peer Feedback Activity
Two-Partner Edit Activity and Blackline 523
   Six Trait Feedback 523

Sharing Activity
Mix-Pair-Share Activity 524
   Sharing Final Drafts 524

Index of Structures for Balanced Literacy 525

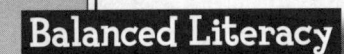

Balanced Literacy

Comprehension ✓
Word Study
Fluency
Writing

Comprehension

Comprehension

Comprehension research as reviewed by the National Reading Panel (NICHD, 2000) suggests that students learn best when teachers are explicit in their instruction. This is most effectively accomplished when teachers tell students what they are expected to do and model their own thinking processes for the students (aloud). As students are encouraged to ask questions, discuss possible answers, and apply other comprehension strategies, active engagement increases (shared, guided, and independent).

Comprehension provides the purpose for all reading. Proficient readers are aware of their own thinking processes making conscious decisions to apply different comprehension strategies as they read (e.g., awareness of text organizational patterns [text types and structures], figurative language meanings, vocabulary clarification, and metacognition deepen comprehension).

Table of Comprehension Resources

Balanced Literacy

Page(s)	Resources	Aloud	Shared	Guided	Independent	Literature Circles
Metacognitive Awareness						
10	Metacognitive Awareness Descriptions					
13	Metacognitive Awareness Definitions	●	●	●	●	●
14	Metacognitive Awareness Posters	●	●	●	●	●
27	Metacognitive Awareness Student Bookmark	●	●	●	●	●
28	Metacognitive Awareness Student Tally Sheet	●	●	●	●	●
29	Metacognitive Awareness Student Page Response	●	●	●	●	●
30	Student Clarification Checklist	●	●	●	●	●
31	Metacognitive Awareness Student Rubric and Response	●	●	●	●	●
32	Metacognitive Awareness Lesson Planning Form (Shared Read Aloud)	●	●			

Table of Comprehension Resources (continued)

Balanced Literacy

Page(s)	Resources	Aloud	Shared	Guided	Independent	Literature Circles
33	Book List for Metacognitive Awareness Shared Read Alouds	●	●			

Text Types and Text Structures

Page(s)	Resources	Aloud	Shared	Guided	Independent	Literature Circles
35	Text Types and Text Structures Resource Descriptions					
37	Four Text Types—Text Type Resource Page	●	●	●	●	●
39	Text Structures—Text Structures Resource Page	●	●	●	●	●
40	Four Text Types and Five Text Structures—Resource Page	●	●	●	●	●

Figurative Language

Page(s)	Resources	Aloud	Shared	Guided	Independent	Literature Circles
41	Figurative Language Resource Descriptions					
42	Figurative Language Definitions	●	●	●	●	●
43	Figurative Language Student Record Sheet	●	●	●	●	●

Table of Comprehension Activities and Lessons

Page(s)	Activities/Lessons	Blacklines	Aloud	Shared	Guided	Independent	Literature Circles
46	**Timed Pair Share**						
46	Metacognitive Awareness Shared Read Aloud Comprehension Lesson	• Comprehension Lesson	●	●			
50	**Showdown Activities**						
51	Metacognitive Terms and Definitions	• Team cards • Student cards		●	●		
55	Text Types—Author's Purpose	• Team cards • Student cards		●	●		
58	Text Structures—Definitions, Signal Words, and Graphic Organizers	• Team cards • Student cards		●	●		
65	Text Structures and Paragraphs	• Team cards • Student cards • Answer Key		●	●		
69	Text Structures—Signal Words	• Team cards • Student cards		●	●		
76	Fact or Opinion	• Team cards • Student cards		●	●		
83	**Quiz-Quiz-Trade Activities**						
84	Text Types—Definitions	• 4 pages of question/answer cards			●		
88	Text Types—Author's Purpose	• 8 pages of question/answer cards			●		
96	Text Types—Examples	• 7 pages of question/answer cards			●		
103	Determining Author's Purpose and Text Type from Titles	• 9 pages of question/answer cards			●		
112	Text Structures—Definitions, Signal Words, and Graphic Organizers	• 7 pages of question/answer cards			●		
119	Text Structure Passages	• 5 pages of question/answer cards			●		
124	Cause and Effect	• 8 pages of question/answer cards			●		

Balanced Literacy • Fourth Grade • Skidmore & Graber
Kagan Publishing • 1 (800) 933-2667 • www.KaganOnline.com

Table of Comprehension Activities and Lessons (continued)

Balanced Literacy

Page(s)	Activities/Lessons	Blacklines	Aloud	Shared	Guided	Independent	Literature Circles
132	Text Features	• 4 pages of question/answer cards			●		
136	Homophone Definitions	• 7 pages of question/answer cards			●		
143	Figurative Language—Alliteration, Idiom, Onomatopoeia, Hyperbole, Metaphor, Simile	• 6 pages of question/answer cards			●		
149	Homophone Sentences	• 8 pages of sentence cards			●		
157	Word Meanings	• 7 pages of question/answer cards			●		
164	Possessive Nouns	• 7 pages of sentence cards			●		
171	Present and Past Tense Verbs	• 8 pages of sentence cards			●		
179	**Numbered Heads Together Activity**						
180	Vocabulary Definitions	• 2 pages of Vocabulary Definitions		●	●		
182	**Fan-N-Pick Activities**						
184	Metacognitive Awareness Strategies	• Fan-N-Pick Mat 2 pages of cards		●	●		
186	Text Features	• Fan-N-Pick Mat 3 pages of cards		●	●		
189	Story Elements (Fiction)	• Fan-N-Pick Mat 5 pages of cards		●	●		
194	Previewing Before Reading (Nonfiction)	• Fan-N-Pick Mat 2 pages of cards		●	●		
196	**Talking Chips Activity**						
197	Nonfiction Comprehension Question Cube (Before Reading)	• Question Cube		●	●		●
198	Nonfiction Comprehension Question Cube (Reflection)	• Question Cube		●	●		●
199	Fiction Comprehension Question Cube (Reflection)	• Question Cube		●	●		●

Balanced Literacy • Fourth Grade • Skidmore & Graber
Kagan Publishing • 1 (800) 933-2667 • www.KaganOnline.com

Table of Comprehension Activities and Lessons (continued)

Balanced Literacy

Page(s)	Activities/Lessons	Blacklines	Aloud	Shared	Guided	Independent	Literature Circles
200	Questioning Cube (Who? What? When? Where? Why? How?)	• Question Cube		●	●		●
201	Metcognitive Cube (After Reading)	• Question Cube		●	●		●
202	Literature Circle Discussion Cube #1 (After Reading)	• Question Cube		●	●		●
203	Literature Circle Discussion Cube #2 (After Reading)	• Question Cube		●	●		●
204	**RoundTable Consensus Activities**						
205	Vocabulary Spinner	• Spinner (Vocabulary) • 1 page of Sentence Cards • Blank Sentence Cards		●	●	●	●
209	Retelling (Fiction)	• Puzzle Pieces • Puzzle Mat		●	●	●	●
211	Retelling (Nonfiction)	• Puzzle Pieces • Puzzle Mat		●	●	●	●
213	Text Feature (Nonfiction)	• Puzzle Pieces • Puzzle Mat		●	●		
215	**Solo and RallyCoach Activity**						
216	Anticipation Guide "Reptile Safari" "Saving Saigas"	• Anticipation Guide Sample • Anticipation Guide Student Form • Blank Student Form	●	●		●	●
221	**Listen-Sketch-Draft Activity**						
222	Listen-Sketch-Draft	• Listen-Sketch-Draft Form • Example Page	●	●	●	●	●
224	**Timed Pair Share Activity**						
225	Prediction Mat	• Prediction Mat • Blank Story Element Cards • Story Element Example Cards	●	●	●	●	●

Table of Comprehension Activities and Lessons (continued)

Balanced Literacy

Page(s)	Activities/Lessons	Blacklines	Aloud	Shared	Guided	Independent	Literature Circles
228	Jot Thoughts and Sorting Activity						
229	Recall and Sorting Mat (After Reading)	• Recall Mat • Sorting Mat			●	●	●
231	Traveling Heads Together Activities						
232	Idioms	• 3 pages of idioms • Answer sheet	●	●	●		
236	Fable Morals	• 2 pages of fable morals	●	●	●		
238	RallyCoach Activity						
239	Idioms	• Idiom Mat • 2 pages of cards			●		
242	Find-the-Fiction Activity						
243	Idioms	• Idiom cards			●		

Comprehension Resources

Metacognitive Awareness Comprehension

Resources/Materials Descriptions

How do we, as teachers, help our struggling readers improve their comprehension? We can show them how to build up their sight words, build their book list, and build time to practice reading. All of these activities are valuable but won't improve comprehension until we help students build a bridge . . . a bridge between their brains and the text.

Years of research have provided teachers with a list of comprehension strategies that good readers use while reading. Good readers are actively thinking while they read. They are aware when meaning has broken down, and they stop to fix the confusion. These strategies (Clarifying, Connecting, Deciding What Is Important, Evaluating, Inferring, Monitoring, Predicting, Prior Knowledge, Purpose Setting, Questioning, Responding Emotionally, Retelling/Summarizing, and Visualizing) become the thinking tools needed for bridge building.

Metacognitive awareness means that the reader is aware of his or her thinking during the reading of various types of texts. Through metacognitive awareness lessons, students learn to apply self-monitoring comprehension strategies. The components of balanced literacy become the avenue for the teaching and strengthening of these metacognitive comprehension strategies. Students are supported as they hear the teacher explain and use the strategies (aloud); observe the teacher use the strategies with text and participate at specific points (shared); practice the strategies with direct support and feedback (guided); and own the strategies through additional practice opportunities (independent).

Resources/Materials Descriptions (continued)

Metacognitive Awareness Definitions (p. 13)
- The teacher should have the students read a text or passage and be aware of what they are thinking about or doing as they read. Have them make a list of their reading behaviors or the questions they ask themselves as they are reading.
- Hold a class discussion and make a student-generated list of different reading behaviors used. Use discussion questions such as "Why did you ____?" and "How did it help you while you were reading?"
- Distribute the Metacognitive Definitions list to each student and guide the discussion to help students make connections between their reading behaviors and the list of strategies. The Metacognitive Awareness Definitions list can be kept in reading notebooks or journals for students to refer to while reading.
- Now that students are aware that good readers think while reading, the teacher should model these strategies by stopping at various points during read aloud, explaining what she or he is thinking.
- Use this activity with different text types (narrative, expository, persuasive, and technical).

Metacognitive Awareness Posters (p. 14–26)
As the teacher reads aloud, one strategy poster can be displayed or referred to at a time helping to focus the students' attention on the one strategy being modeled and explained. For convenience, the strategy posters can be three-hole punched at the top and then put into a notebook. The notebook will easily stand on a hard surface next to the teacher and she or he can flip to each individual Metacognitive Awareness poster as it is modeled and discussed.

Metacognitive Awareness Student Bookmark (p. 27)
During the learning phase of teaching students about metacognition, students should have a bookmark that sits beside their reading material as they independently read. This not only reminds the students to use the strategies, but is also helps attach a strategy label to their thinking.

Metacognitive Awareness Student Tally Sheet (p. 28)
As the teacher reads aloud, students can tally each time the teacher models a strategy. Students can also write notes, thoughts about the strategy, or specific questions that the teacher asked herself or himself aloud while reading. This activity will help the student identify the strategy that was used, attach a label to it, and think about how it helped with comprehension.

Resources/Materials Descriptions (continued)

Metacognitive Awareness Student Page Response (p. 29)
While reading and preparing for guided reading groups or literature circles, students can use the Metacognitive Awareness Student Page Response sheet to record page numbers and identify passages where they used comprehension strategies while reading. These recorded selections become discussion points as the students share their thinking with the group. The purpose of this activity is to help the students understand that readers use multiple strategies while reading and that each reader might use different strategies.

Student Clarification Checklist (p. 30)
Good readers have a repertoire of strategies to use while reading. The Student Clarification Checklist will remind the students of strategies to use when decoding a word, understanding the meaning of a word, or understanding an idea. The goal is not only to help students know the clarification strategies, but to realize when another strategy should be tried.

Metacognitive Awareness Student Rubric and Response (p. 31)
After students have observed repeated modeling of the use of metacognitive strategies during teacher read aloud and shared read aloud, the Metacognitive Awareness Student Rubric and Response page can be used to scaffold the students toward independent use of the strategies. The rubric gives the students specific feedback that is necessary for improvement.

Metacognitive Awareness Lesson Planning Form (Shared Read Aloud) (p. 32)
As the teacher continues to model the metacognitive awareness strategies, the Metacognitive Awareness Lesson Planning Form can be used to preplan specific, targeted comprehension strategies.

Book List for Metacognitive Awareness Shared Read Alouds (p. 33)
The book list is a resource for teacher read aloud, shared read aloud, or student literature circles that will focus on metacognitive awareness strategies.

Metacognitive Awareness Definitions

Clarifying	What words or ideas don't I understand?
Connecting	What does this remind me of? • Text to self • Text to text • Text to world
Deciding What is Important	What is most important to remember?
Evaluating	What do I think about this text? How can I use this information?
Inferring	Why do things happen? What does this probably mean?
Monitoring	Which parts are confusing? What fix-up strategies could I use?
Predicting	What might happen next?
Prior Knowledge	What do I know about it?
Purpose Setting	Why am I reading this? Why did the author write this?
Questioning	What questions do I have?
Responding Emotionally	How does the character feel?
Retelling or Summarizing	What was this text about?
Visualizing	What pictures, smells, sounds, tastes, and touches come to my mind?

Metacognitive Awareness Poster—Clarifying

Clarifying

What words or ideas don't I understand?

Balanced Literacy • Fourth Grade • Skidmore & Graber
Kagan Publishing • 1 (800) 933-2667 • www.KaganOnline.com

Metacognitive Awareness Poster—Connecting

Connecting

What does this remind me of?

- Text to self
- Text to text
- Text to world

Balanced Literacy • Fourth Grade • Skidmore & Graber
Kagan Publishing • 1 (800) 933-2667 • www.KaganOnline.com

Metacognitive Awareness Poster—Deciding What Is Important

Deciding What Is Important

What is most important to remember?

Metacognitive Awareness Poster—Evaluating

Evaluating

What do I think about this text? How can I use this information?

Balanced Literacy • Fourth Grade • Skidmore & Graber
Kagan Publishing • 1 (800) 933-2667 • www.KaganOnline.com
17

Metacognitive Awareness Poster—Inferring

Inferring

Why do things happen?
What does this probably mean?

Balanced Literacy • Fourth Grade • Skidmore & Graber
Kagan Publishing • 1 (800) 933-2667 • www.KaganOnline.com

Metacognitive Awareness Poster—Monitoring

Monitoring

Which parts are confusing? What fix-up strategies could I use?

Balanced Literacy • Fourth Grade • Skidmore & Graber
Kagan Publishing • 1 (800) 933-2667 • www.KaganOnline.com

Metacognitive Awareness Poster—Predicting

Predicting

What might happen next?

Balanced Literacy • Fourth Grade • Skidmore & Graber
Kagan Publishing • 1 (800) 933-2667 • www.KaganOnline.com

Metacognitive Awareness Poster—Prior Knowledge

Prior Knowledge

What do I know about it?

Balanced Literacy • Fourth Grade • Skidmore & Graber
Kagan Publishing • 1 (800) 933-2667 • www.KaganOnline.com

Metacognitive Awareness Poster—Purpose Setting

Purpose Setting

Why am I reading this?
Why did the author write this?

Balanced Literacy • Fourth Grade • Skidmore & Graber
Kagan Publishing • 1 (800) 933-2667 • www.KaganOnline.com

Metacognitive Awareness Poster—Questioning

Questioning

What questions do I have?

Balanced Literacy • Fourth Grade • Skidmore & Graber
Kagan Publishing • 1 (800) 933-2667 • www.KaganOnline.com

Metacognitive Awareness Poster—Responding Emotionally

Responding Emotionally

How does the character feel?

Balanced Literacy • Fourth Grade • Skidmore & Graber
Kagan Publishing • 1 (800) 933-2667 • www.KaganOnline.com

Metacognitive Awareness Poster—Retelling or Summarizing

Retelling or Summarizing

What was this text about?

Balanced Literacy • Fourth Grade • Skidmore & Graber
Kagan Publishing • 1 (800) 933-2667 • www.KaganOnline.com

Metacognitive Awareness Poster—Visualizing

Visualizing

What pictures, smells, sounds, tastes, and touches come to my mind?

Balanced Literacy • Fourth Grade • Skidmore & Graber
Kagan Publishing • 1 (800) 933-2667 • www.KaganOnline.com

Student Bookmark

Metacognitive Awareness

- Clarifying
- Connecting
- Deciding What Is Important
- Evaluating
- Inferring
- Monitoring
- Predicting
- Prior Knowledge
- Purpose Setting
- Questioning
- Responding Emotionally
- Retelling or Summarizing
- Visualizing

Balanced Literacy • Fourth Grade • Skidmore & Graber
Kagan Publishing • 1 (800) 933-2667 • www.KaganOnline.com

27

Metacognitive Awareness Student Tally Sheet

	Clarifying
	Connecting
	Deciding What Is Important
	Evaluating
	Inferring
	Monitoring
	Predicting
	Prior Knowledge
	Purpose Setting
	Questioning
	Responding Emotionally
	Retelling or Summarizing
	Visualizing

Metacognitive Awareness Student Page Response

p. _____ p. _____ p. _____	**Clarifying**
p. _____ p. _____ p. _____	**Connecting**
p. _____ p. _____ p. _____	**Deciding What Is Important**
p. _____ p. _____ p. _____	**Evaluating**
p. _____ p. _____ p. _____	**Inferring**
p. _____ p. _____ p. _____	**Monitoring**
p. _____ p. _____ p. _____	**Predicting**
p. _____ p. _____ p. _____	**Prior Knowledge**
p. _____ p. _____ p. _____	**Purpose Setting**
p. _____ p. _____ p. _____	**Questioning**
p. _____ p. _____ p. _____	**Responding Emotionally**
p. _____ p. _____ p. _____	**Retelling or Summarizing**
p. _____ p. _____ p. _____	**Visualizing**

Student Clarification Checklist

Page #	Word/Phrases

I used these strategies to help me:
- say the word
- understand the word
- understand the idea

❏ I looked for word parts.

❏ I asked where I had seen the word before.

❏ I reread.

❏ I used picture clues.

❏ I used context clues and punctuation.

❏ I used text features.

❏ I used the glossary or dictionary.

❏ other _____

# Metacognitive Awareness Student Rubric

Readers are actively thinking about their reading as they read.

	1	2	3	4
Metacognitive Awareness ❏ Clarifying ❏ Connecting ❏ Deciding What Is Important ❏ Evaluating ❏ Inferring ❏ Monitoring ❏ Predicting ❏ Prior Knowledge ❏ Purpose Setting ❏ Questioning ❏ Responding Emotionally ❏ Retelling or Summarizing ❏ Visualizing	• I wrote the strategy that I used while reading.	• I wrote the strategy that I used while reading. • My example of how I used the strategy was not clearly connected to the text.	• I wrote the strategy that I used while reading. • I gave at least one specific example from the text of when I used the strategy. • I explained how the strategy helped me as I read.	• I wrote several strategies that I used while reading. • I gave text support with explicit details of how I used the strategies. • I explained how the strategies helped me as I read.

Metacognitive Awareness Student Response

(Step 1): Name the strategy or strategies that you used while reading.

(Step 2): Text support: What were you reading about when you used the strategy or strategies?

(Step 3): How did the strategy or strategies help you as you read?

Comprehension Lesson

Metacognitive Awareness Lesson Planning Form
Shared Read Aloud

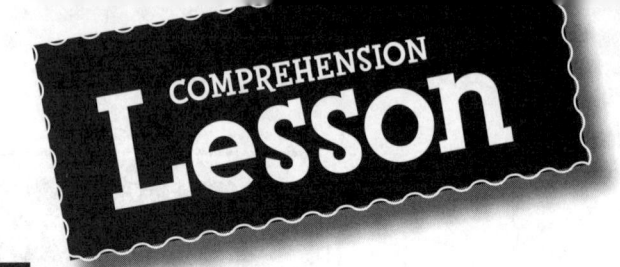

The teacher thinks aloud as she reads to the students. Overhead transparencies of specific pages from the book are used several times. Students participate by reading from the transparencies and then discussing the use of metacognitive strategies in teams.

Directions: Use this page to plan your lesson.

_____
by: _____

Page	Reading Materials	Metacognitive Strategies (Teacher Think Aloud)

Metacognitive Awareness Shared Read Alouds

Comprehension Book List

Book Title	Author
America's Champion Swimmer	Adler, David A.
Lou Gehrig, The Luckiest Man	Adler, David A.
The Quiltmaker's Gift	Brumbeau, Jeff
Dandelions	Bunting, Eve
So Far From the Sea	Bunting, Eve
Train to Somewhere	Bunting, Eve
Home Run	Burleigh, Robert
The Great Kapok Tree	Cherry, Lynne
The Bat Boy and His Violin	Curtis, Gavin
Because of Winn Dixie	DiCamillo, Kate
My Brother Martin: A Sister Remembers Growing Up With the Rev. Dr. Martin Luther King Jr.	Farris, Christine King
Teammates	Golenbock, Peter
Sweet Clara and the Freedom Quilt	Hopkinson, Deborah
The Log Cabin Quilt	Howard, Ellen
Harvesting Hope: The Story of Cesar Chavez	Krull, Kathleen
Wilma Unlimited	Krull, Kathleen
She's Wearing a Dead Bird on Her Head	Lasky, Kathryn
The Rag Coat	Mills, Lauren
Uncle Jed's Barbershop	Mitchell, Margaree King
Baseball Saved Us	Mochizuki, Ken
The Drinking Gourd: A Story of the Underground Railroad	Monjo, F. N.
Almost to Freedom	Nelson, Vaunda Micheaux
The Keeping Quilt	Polacco, Patricia
Mrs. Katz and Tush	Polacco, Patricia
My Rotten Red-Headed Older Brother	Polacco, Patricia
Pink and Say	Polacco, Patricia
Thank You, Mr. Falker	Polacco, Patricia
Tar Beach	Ringgold, Faith
When Marian Sang	Ryan, Pam Munoz
Grandfather's Journey	Say, Allen

COMPREHENSION Book List

Metacognitive Awareness Shared Read Alouds (continued)

Book Title	Author
Amazing Animal Disguises	Sowler, Sandie
Faithful Elephants	Tsuchiya, Yukio
Follow the Drinking Gourd	Winter, Jeanette
Sixteen Years in Sixteen Seconds: The Sammy Lee Story	Yoo, Paula

Text Types and Text Structures Resource Descriptions

Awareness of text types and text structures benefits readers' comprehension.

Text Types	Purpose
Narrative	to entertain
Expository	to inform
Technical	to tell how to…
Persuasive	to persuade

Text Structures
Sequence
Problem and Solution
Compare and Contrast
Description
Cause and Effect

There are four general reasons why authors write. These are identified as text types. Identifying the text type of a passage lets the reader know what the author's goal was for writing the text. This knowledge allows the reader to set a purpose for reading.

Text structures are the organizational patterns found within the text types, which alert the reader to the arrangement of the text. Being aware of these structures and being able to identify them makes the text easier to understand. An author often chooses one main text structure for a piece, but may incorporate several of the structures throughout the writing.

The following text type and text structure resources are for teacher and student use as instruction is scaffolded. The cooperative learning structures, Showdown and Quiz-Quiz-Trade, located in this section of the book provide practice in identifying definitions, graphic organizers, and specific text examples for text types and text structures.

Text Types and Text Structures
Resource Comprehension (continued)

Four Text Types (p. 37)
These two pages, listing general characteristics of the four text types and examples of each, are resources for the teacher and students. The teacher and the students may want to collect authentic examples for each of these four categories as they are introduced.

Text Structures (p. 39)
Signal words are frequently used by authors, which give hints about the text structure used in the writing. This chart lists some of those words, as well as a brief description of the text structures.

Four Text Types and Five Text Structures (p. 40)
This chart was designed as a resource, allowing students to visualize both basic text type and text structure information. As students learn to identify the text structure(s) used in a text, a graphic organizer matching the organizational structure becomes a tool for increasing comprehension. The graphic organizers included here are basic examples; students should be encouraged to experiment with the use of additional graphic organizers.

Four Text Types

Text Type Resource Page

Text Type	Characteristics	Examples	
Narrative	• Entertains the reader • Tells a story • Contains character(s) and a setting • Contains events • Has a problem/resolution • Contains theme that explains meaning of story • May be written in first, second, or third person • Makes sense when read from beginning to end	• Biographies • Drama • Diaries • Fables • Fantasies • Folk tales • Historical fiction • Legends • Mysteries	• Myths • Novels • Personal narratives • Plays • Poetry • Science fiction • Short stories • Tall tales
Expository	• Informs the reader • Contains facts and information • Explains, describes, discusses • May compare and contrast or present problem and solution • Includes text features such as headings, subheadings, bolded words, charts, graphs, diagrams, captions, indexes, glossaries, table of contents, etc.	• ABC books • Autobiographies • Biographies • Book reports • Brochures • Catalogs • Definitions • Essays • Interviews	• Invitations • Journals • Lists • Magazine articles • Newspaper articles • Recounts of an event • Research papers • Speeches

Four Text Types

Text Types Resource Page (continued)

Text Type	Characteristics	Examples	
Technical	• Nonfiction text • Gives information used to perform a task • May include explicit steps or graphics to show steps • Shortened or fragmented sentences • Numbered or bulleted lists • Organized in logical, orderly way • Focused on identified topic • Uses specific vocabulary terms • Balance of white space and text	• Brochures • Classified ads • Consumer information • Directions • Floor plans • Forms • Graphs and charts • How-to guides • Instructions • Job preparation manuals	• Maps • Menus • Questionnaires • Recipes • Regulations • Schedules • School forms • Syllabi • Transcripts • Warranties
Persuasive	• Nonfiction • Author intends to convince reader to take a particular opinion or perform a certain action • Attempts to solve problem through change • Uses appeal to reason, emotional appeal, or endorsement by an influential figure (bandwagon approach, glittering gerentalities, testimonials, citing authority, statistics)	• Advertisements • Book reviews • Brochures • Business letters • Charitable campaign appeals • Commercials • Debates (written) • Editorials • Essays • Letters to the editor • Movie critiques • Political campaign literature • Position papers • Posters • Speeches	

Text Structures

Text Structures Resource Page

Text Type	Tells...	Signal Words
Sequence	series or steps	• first • second • third • next • finally • then • before • after • now • during • while • not long after
Description	attributes, facts, and details about something	• some characteristics are • for instance • in fact • in addition • for example • has a • about • is • does
Compare and Contrast	similarities and differences	• different from • like • same as • similar to • resembles • both • also • too • more than • however
Cause and Effect	reasons why something happens or exists	• so that • because of • as a result of • since • so • for this reason • in order to • therefore • if...then
Problem and Solution	problem, attempted solutions, and results	• problem is • solution is • have solved this problem by • possible answer

Balanced Literacy • Fourth Grade • Skidmore & Graber
Kagan Publishing • 1 (800) 933-2667 • www.KaganOnline.com

Four Text Types

Text Type & Text Structures Resource Page

The four text types describe four general types of writing. Identifying the text type of a passage helps the reader set the purpose for reading and alerts the reader to the organization of the piece.

Narrative	Expository	Technical	Persuasive
• Entertains • Tells a story • Character(s), setting, problem, resolution	• Facts/information • Text features (headings, bold words, charts, graphs, captions)	• Information to perform a task • Steps	• Author tries to convince reader to take a certain opinion or perform a certain action

Five Text Structures

Text structures are organizational patterns found within the text types. An author often chooses one main text structure for a piece but may incorporate several of the text structures throughout the piece.

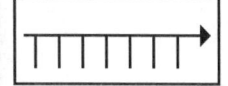

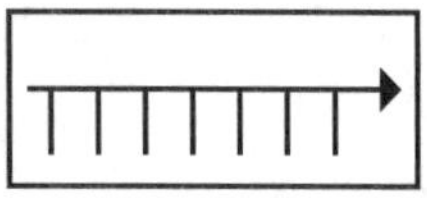

Sequence	Problem and Solution	Compare and Contrast	Description	Cause and Effect
• Steps • Specific order 1. 2. 3. 4. 5.	• Problem, which is solved Problem Event Event Event Solution	• Comparing how things are the same/different	• Details	• Something causes something else to happen

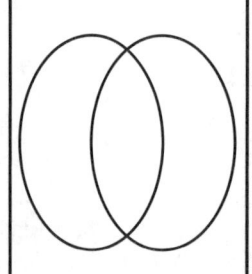

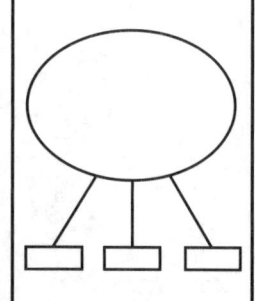

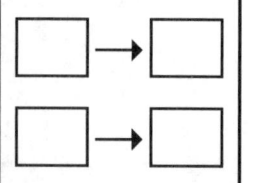

Figurative Language Resource Descriptions

Figurative language uses words in ways different from their literal meanings to add interest and appeal to the senses. Figurative language is a tool that authors use to help readers visualize what is happening. The following resources can be used to help students identify various types of figurative language in their reading and attach a label to them. As students become familiar with the various types of figurative language, why the author chose to use it, and the affect it has on the reader, they will gain more confidence in their writing abilities and use of alliteration, hyperboles, idioms, metaphors, onomatopoeia, and similes.

Figurative Language Definitions (p. 42)
Six different figurative language techniques are identified and defined on this chart. In addition, an example of each is provided. This chart is designed to be used as a teacher and student resource.

Figurative Language Student Record Sheet (p. 43)
This resource is used by students as they read independently, with partners, or in guided reading groups. Students record the figurative language (alliteration, hyperbole, idiom, metaphor, onomatopoeia, simile) they identify in their reading under the appropriate heading. Recording the page number provides opportunities to revisit the location of figurative language in the text. This page may be used for one text selection, or they may be used to keep ongoing records of identified figurative language over a period of time.

Figurative Language Definitions

Figurative Language Term	Definition	Example
Alliteration	The repetition of the same letter at the beginning of two or more words	Nine new nickels are needed now.
Hyperbole	An exaggeration	I'm so hungry, I could eat a bear.
Idiom	A familiar phrase that means something other than what it literally says	It's raining cats and dogs.
Metaphor	States that one thing is something else; is a comparison, but does not use the word *like* or *as*	My hands are icicles.
Onomatopoeia (on-o-mat-o-PEE-a)	A word that sounds like what it is describing; a sound effect	Murmur, creak, drip, pop, zip, wheeze
Simile	A comparison using the word *like* or *as*	The milk was as white as snow.

Figurative Language Student Record Sheet
(Alliteration, Idiom, Onomatopoeia, Hyperbole, Metaphor, Simile)

Your Name: _____

Title of Text: _____

Page	Example of Figurative Language	Page	Example of Figurative Language
Alliteration		**Hyperbole**	
Idiom		**Metaphor**	
Onomatopoeia		**Simile**	

Comprehension Activities and Lessons

Comprehension Lesson

Metacognitive Awareness Shared Read Aloud

Lou Gehrig, The Luckiest Man
by David A. Adler

The teacher thinks aloud as he or she reads to the students. Overhead transparencies of specific pages from the book are used several times. Students participate by reading from the transparencies and then discussing the use of metacognitive strategies in teams.

Text Page	Reading Materials	Metacognitive Strategies Teacher Think Aloud
2	Read Aloud	**Connection: Text to World** Read. *The text says that Henry Ford sold his first automobile, and I can see from the picture that horses and wagons were still being used. It also says that the Wright Brothers successfully flew their first airplane. So 1903, when this story took place, was a time very different from today.*
1–2	Hold up book to let students see pictures.	**Questioning:** *Using what I already know and the pictures, what else was different in 1903 compared with today?* **Timed Pair Share** The teacher leads a discussion about the time period using Timed Pair Share to engage students.
3	Read Aloud	Read.
6	Read Aloud	**Understanding Character's Feelings:** Read. *The text says that Lou's mother was furious. Lou must have really wanted to play baseball. He knew that his mother thought that games and sports were a waste of time. She dreamed that he would attend college and become an accountant or engineer.*

Balanced Literacy • Fourth Grade • Skidmore & Graber
Kagan Publishing • 1 (800) 933-2667 • www.KaganOnline.com

Comprehension Lesson

Metacognitive Awareness
Shared Read Aloud (continued)

Lou Gehrig, The Luckiest Man

Text Page	Reading Materials	Metacognitive Strategies Teacher Think Aloud
8	Shared Reading *overhead transparency page*	**Clarifying:** Teacher reads aloud, as students follow with their eyes. *I'm wondering what the word, consecutive, means. I need to reread the sentence before and after to get clues to help me understand the word. (Teacher rereads.)* *It gives the number of games Lou played, and it says that he never missed a game, so the word, consecutive, might mean games in a row.* *Let me reread to make sure it makes sense. It would make sense if I said, Lou Gehrig played 2,130 games in a row.*
9–10	Read Aloud	Read. **Timed Pair Share** Students discuss why they think Lou Gehrig was selected Most Valuable Player (MVP). (Reliable, athletic, dedicated, Iron Horse, etc.)
11	Read Aloud	**Questioning:** *I wonder why Lou Gehrig is having problems hitting the ball. The text says that he exercised, took extra batting practice, and watched his diet, but his playing continued to get worse. I'm going to think about this question, as I continue to read.*

Comprehension Lesson

Metacognitive Awareness Shared Read Aloud (continued)

Lou Gehrig, The Luckiest Man

Page	Reading Materials	Metacognitive Strategies Teacher Think Aloud
14	**Shared Reading** *overhead transparency page*	**Clarifying:** Uncover and read only the first paragraph, as the class follows along. *The text says that Lou Gehrig wasn't selfish.* **Timed Pair Share** Pairs share reasons why Lou Gehrig wasn't selfish. (He took himself out of the game, because he wasn't hitting well. He wanted what was best for the team, even if it didn't include him.) Read the rest of the page, as the class follows along. **Clarifying:** The teacher should explain that the disease Lou Gehrig has affects the ability to control muscles.
15	Read Aloud	**Understanding Character's Feelings:** Read. *This page tells me that the team members and fans loved and respected Lou Gehrig because of the way they treated him.*
17	**Shared Reading** *overhead transparency of text*	**Clarifying:** Partners read together. **Timed Pair Share** Students discuss the meaning of the word *prototype*. (*The sentence talks about Lou Gehrig being a good sportsman and citizen. I think synonyms might be,* example *or* role model.)
20	Read Aloud	**Understanding Character's Feelings:** *Lou Gehrig has a very hard road ahead, battling this disease. Yet, he says that he is lucky. He has a very positive outlook and continues to think about all the good things that he has.*

COMPREHENSION LESSON

Metacognitive Awareness Shared Read Aloud (continued)

Lou Gehrig, The Luckiest Man

Text Page	Reading Materials	Metacognitive Strategies Teacher Think Aloud
21	Read Aloud	**Understanding Character's Feelings:** Read. **Timed Pair Share** Pairs discuss some possible reasons why Lou Gehrig said, "I'll remember this day for a long time."
24–25	Read Aloud	Read.
29	Read Aloud	Read. **RoundTable** Teams write words to describe Lou Gehrig. (Courageous, modest, sportsman, athlete, positive, reliable, thankful, hero, determined, sick, etc.) The teacher uses a spinner to select a member from each team to give one of their describing words. The student must also give a reason why that word was chosen to describe Lou Gehrig. The teacher writes the words on a poster or overhead. The teacher uses a spinner to continue to choose team members to share until everyone's list is shared. *Variation:* **Team Stand-N-Share** **Evaluating:** **Timed Pair Share** Pairs share what personal lessons they can learn from Lou Gehrig's story and apply to their own life.

Activity
Comprehension Showdown

Teams play Showdown to master metacognitive terms, text types, text structure definitions, and label text structure paragraphs.

Activity Steps

1. Each team receives a Team Set of cards and every student receives a Student Set of cards.
2. The Team Set is placed facedown in the middle of the team. Students hold their Student Set in their hands.
3. The teacher selects one student to be the Showdown Captain for the first round.
4. The Showdown Captain selects the top card from the middle and reads it aloud.
5. Working alone, students individually identify an answer from their card set.
6. When finished, teammates signal they are ready.
7. The Showdown Captain calls, "Showdown!"
8. Teammates show their answers at the same time.
9. The Showdown Captain leads checking.
10. If correct, the team celebrates. If not, the teammates coach, then celebrate.
11. The person to the left of the Showdown Captain becomes the Showdown Captain for the next round.

STRUCTURE
Showdown

Blacklines

- Metacognitive Terms and Definitions (Team and Student Set) 51–54
- Text Types—Author's Purpose (Team and Student Set) 55–57
- Text Structures—Definitions, Signal Words, Graphic Organizers
  (Team and Student Set) 58–64
- Text Structures and Paragraphs (Team Set, Student Set, and Answer Key)...65–68
- Text Structures—Signal Words (Team and Student Set)..............................69–75
- Fact or Opinion (Team and Student Set)...76–82

Metacognitive Terms & Definitions
Showdown (Team Set)

Instructions: Copy one set of cards for each team. Cut apart.

Metacognitive Terms & Definitions (Team Set)

When I think about how the text reminds me of another text that I read, I am using _____.

Metacognitive Terms & Definitions (Team Set)

When I decide what is most important to remember, I am using _____.

Metacognitive Terms & Definitions (Team Set)

When I think about how I can use the information from the text in my life, I am using _____.

Metacognitive Terms & Definitions (Team Set)

When I think about how the characters must feel, I am using _____.

Metacognitive Terms & Definitions (Team Set)

When I ask myself questions about what I am reading, I am using _____.

Metacognitive Terms & Definitions (Team Set)

When I put clues together from what I already knew before I read, and the new information I just read, I am using _____.

Metacognitive Terms & Definitions
Showdown (Team Set)

Instructions: Copy one set of cards for each team. Cut apart.

Metacognitive Terms & Definitions (Team Set)

When I think about what might happen next, I am using _____.

Metacognitive Terms & Definitions (Team Set)

When I think about the reasons why I am reading the text, I am using _____.

Metacognitive Terms & Definitions (Team Set)

When I think about what happened in the text or what it was about, I am using _____.

Metacognitive Terms & Definitions (Team Set)

When I figure out words or ideas which I don't understand, I am using _____.

Metacognitive Terms & Definitions (Team Set)

When I realize that I did not understand what I read and decide what fix-up strategies to use, I am using _____.

Metacognitive Terms & Definitions (Team Set)

When I use my senses to think about what the author wrote, I am using _____.

Metacognitive Terms & Definitions
Showdown (Team Set)

Instructions: Copy one set of cards for each team. Cut apart.

Metacognitive Terms & Definitions (Team Set)

When I think about how the text reminds me of something that happened to me, I am using _____.

Metacognitive Terms & Definitions (Team Set)

When I ask myself what I already know about the topic, I am using _____.

Metacognitive Terms & Definitions (Team Set)

When I think about the reasons for something happening and how that will affect something else, I am using _____.

Metacognitive Terms & Definitions (Team Set)

When I picture in my mind what happened in the text, I am using _____.

Metacognitive Terms & Definitions (Team Set)

When I wonder about something and ask questions that I hope I will find out about, I am using _____.

Metacognitive Terms & Definitions (Team Set)

When I think about something that happened in the world and it reminds me of the text, I am using _____.

Metacognitive Terms & Definitions
Showdown (Student Set)

Instructions: Copy one set of cards for each student. Cut apart.

Terms & Definitions (Student Set)	Terms & Definitions (Student Set)
Monitoring	Summarizing and Retelling
Inferring	Responding Emotionally
Evaluating	Questioning
Deciding What Is Important	Purpose Setting
Connecting	Prior Knowledge
Clarifying	Predicting
Visualizing	

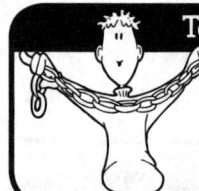

54 Balanced Literacy • Fourth Grade • Skidmore & Graber
Kagan Publishing • 1 (800) 933-2667 • www.KaganOnline.com

Text Types–Author's Purpose
Showdown (Team Set)

Instructions: Copy one set of cards for each team. Cut apart.

Text Types–Author's Purpose (Team Set)

Which text type's purpose is to entertain?

Text Types–Author's Purpose (Team Set)

Which text type's purpose is to persuade the reader?

Text Types–Author's Purpose (Team Set)

Which text type's purpose is to explain how to do something?

Text Types–Author's Purpose (Team Set)

Which text type's purpose is to give information?

Text Types–Author's Purpose (Team Set)

Which text type's purpose is to let the reader know the author's opinion?

Text Types–Author's Purpose (Team Set)

Which text type's purpose is for enjoyment?

Text Types–Author's Purpose
Showdown (Team Set)

Instructions: Copy one set of cards for each team. Cut apart.

Text Types–Author's Purpose (Team Set)

Which text type's purpose is to help you perform a task?

Text Types–Author's Purpose (Team Set)

Which text type's purpose is to get you to change your thinking?

Text Types–Author's Purpose (Team Set)

Which text type's purpose is to tell you a story?

Text Types–Author's Purpose (Team Set)

Which text type's purpose is to give you true facts about a topic?

Text Types–Author's Purpose (Team Set)

Which text type's purpose is to give you reasons to do something or believe something?

Text Types–Author's Purpose (Team Set)

Which text type's purpose is to help you fix something or put something together?

Text Types–Author's Purpose
Showdown (Student Set)

Instructions: Copy one set of cards for each student. Cut apart.

Narrative

Expository

Technical

Persuasive

Text Structures—Definitions, Signal Words, and Graphic Organizers
Showdown (Team Set)

Instructions: Copy one set of cards for each team. Cut apart.

Text Structures—Definitions, Signal Words, and Graphic Organizers (Team Set)

_____ has steps.

Text Structures—Definitions, Signal Words, and Graphic Organizers (Team Set)

_____ has a problem, which is solved.

Text Structures—Definitions, Signal Words, and Graphic Organizers (Team Set)

_____ explains how things are the same or different.

Text Structures—Definitions, Signal Words, and Graphic Organizers (Team Set)

_____ has details.

Text Structures—Definitions, Signal Words, and Graphic Organizers (Team Set)

_____ tells how something makes something else happen.

Text Structures—Definitions, Signal Words, and Graphic Organizers (Team Set)

_____ is written in a specific time order.

Text Structures—Definitions, Signal Words, and Graphic Organizers
Showdown (Team Set)

Instructions: Copy one set of cards for each team. Cut apart.

Text Structures—Definitions, Signal Words, and Graphic Organizers (Team Set)

_____ has events, which lead to figuring out the problem at the end.

Text Structures—Definitions, Signal Words, and Graphic Organizers (Team Set)

_____ compares similarities and differences.

Text Structures—Definitions, Signal Words, and Graphic Organizers (Team Set)

_____ tells more about someone, something, or someplace.

Text Structures—Definitions, Signal Words, and Graphic Organizers (Team Set)

_____ explains how something occurred because of something else.

Text Structures—Definitions, Signal Words, and Graphic Organizers (Team Set)

_____ might use this graphic organizer.

[arrow of sequential boxes]

Text Structures—Definitions, Signal Words, and Graphic Organizers (Team Set)

_____ might use this graphic organizer.

| Problem |
| Event |
| Event |
| Event |
| Solution |

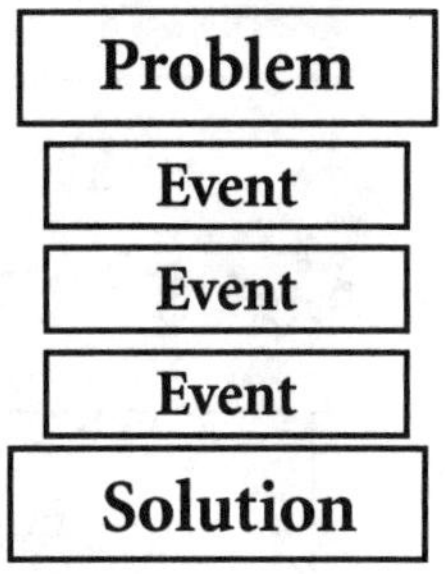

Text Structures—Definitions, Signal Words, and Graphic Organizers
Showdown (Team Set)

Instructions: Copy one set of cards for each team. Cut apart.

Text Structures—Definitions, Signal Words, and Graphic Organizers (Team Set)

_____ might use this graphic organizer.

(Topic web graphic organizer)

Text Structures—Definitions, Signal Words, and Graphic Organizers (Team Set)

_____ might use these signal words.

first…   second…
third…   fourth…

Text Structures—Definitions, Signal Words, and Graphic Organizers (Team Set)

_____ might use this graphic organizer.

If…	Then…	Because…

Text Structures—Definitions, Signal Words, and Graphic Organizers (Team Set)

_____ might use these signal words.

The problem is…
The solution is…

Text Structures—Definitions, Signal Words, and Graphic Organizers (Team Set)

_____ might use these signal words.

For example…

Text Structures—Definitions, Signal Words, and Graphic Organizers (Team Set)

_____ might use these signal words.

same as…

Text Structures—Definitions, Signal Words, and Graphic Organizers
Showdown (Team Set)

Instructions: Copy one set of cards for each team. Cut apart.

Text Structures—Definitions, Signal Words, and Graphic Organizers (Team Set)

_____ might use this graphic organizer.

1.
2.
3.
4.
5.

Text Structures—Definitions, Signal Words, and Graphic Organizers (Team Set)

_____ might use these signal words.

Some characteristics are…

Text Structures—Definitions, Signal Words, and Graphic Organizers (Team Set)

_____ might use this signal word.

Then…

Text Structures—Definitions, Signal Words, and Graphic Organizers (Team Set)

_____ might use these signal words.

For instance…

Text Structures—Definitions, Signal Words, and Graphic Organizers (Team Set)

_____ might use these signal words.

Because of…

Text Structures—Definitions, Signal Words, and Graphic Organizers (Team Set)

_____ might use these signal words.

Finally…

Text Structures—Definitions, Signal Words, and Graphic Organizers
Showdown (Team Set)

Instructions: Copy one set of cards for each team. Cut apart.

Text Structures—Definitions, Signal Words, and Graphic Organizers (Team Set)

_____ might use these signal words.

different than…

Text Structures—Definitions, Signal Words, and Graphic Organizers (Team Set)

_____ might use these signal words.

If…, then

Text Structures—Definitions, Signal Words, and Graphic Organizers (Team Set)

_____ might use this signal word.

Next…

Text Structures—Definitions, Signal Words, and Graphic Organizers (Team Set)

_____ might use these signal words.

As a result of…

Text Structures—Definitions, Signal Words, and Graphic Organizers (Team Set)

_____ might use these signal words.

solved by…

Text Structures—Definitions, Signal Words, and Graphic Organizers (Team Set)

_____ might use these signal words.

To begin with…

Balanced Literacy • Fourth Grade • Skidmore & Graber
Kagan Publishing • 1 (800) 933-2667 • www.KaganOnline.com

Text Structures—Definitions, Signal Words, and Graphic Organizers
Showdown (Team Set)

Instructions: Copy one set of cards for each team. Cut apart.

Text Structures—Definitions, Signal Words, and Graphic Organizers (Team Set)

_____ might use this graphic organizer.

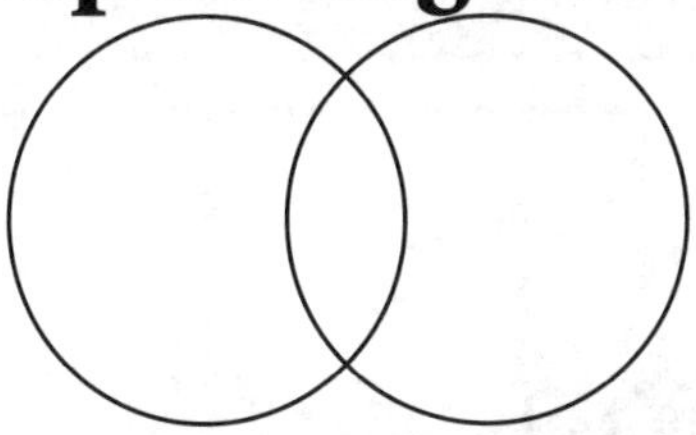

Text Structures—Definitions, Signal Words, and Graphic Organizers (Team Set)

_____ might use this graphic organizer.

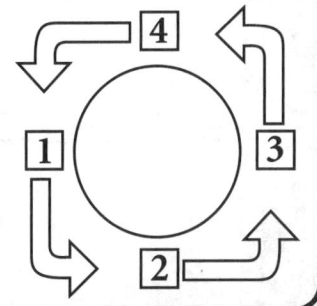

Text Structures—Definitions, Signal Words, and Graphic Organizers (Team Set)

_____ might use this graphic organizer.

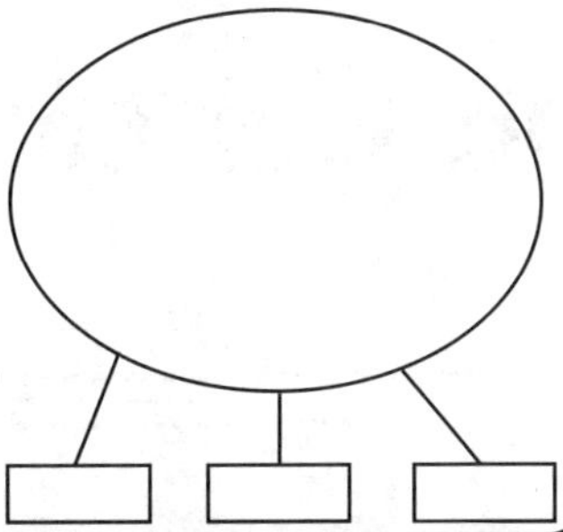

Text Structures—Definitions, Signal Words, and Graphic Organizers (Team Set)

_____ might use this graphic organizer.

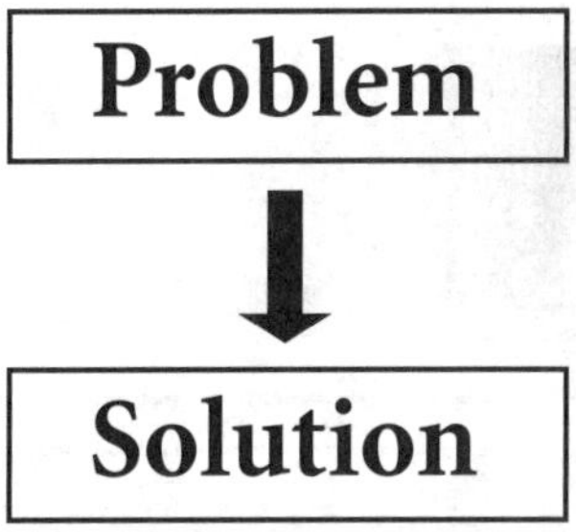

Problem → Solution

Text Structures—Definitions, Signal Words, and Graphic Organizers (Team Set)

_____ might use this graphic organizer.

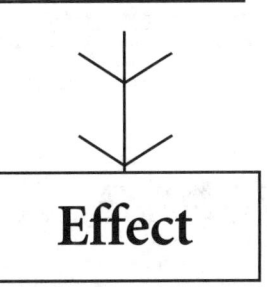

Effect

Text Structures—Definitions, Signal Words, and Graphic Organizers (Team Set)

_____ might use this graphic organizer.

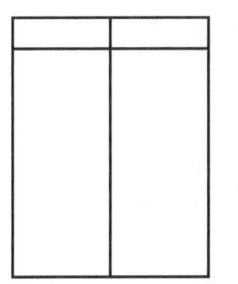

Text Structures—Definitions, Signal Words, and Graphic Organizers
Showdown (Student Set)

Instructions: Copy one set of cards for each student. Cut apart.

Cause and Effect

Description

Compare and Contrast

Problem and Solution

Sequence

Text Structures and Paragraphs
Showdown (Team Set)

Instructions: Copy one set of cards for each team. Cut apart.

Text Structures and Paragraphs (Team Set)

Frank H. Rose had trouble smashing flies with a rolled up newspaper. He figured out that the fly could sense the air pressure of a solid object coming toward it and would fly away. Mr. Rose solved this by inventing a flyswatter from a yardstick and a wire screen that allowed air to pass through. He was able to surprise flies with his new invention.

Text Structures and Paragraphs (Team Set)

When Frank H. Rose was bothered by a fly, he rolled up a newspaper and tried to swat it. The fly could sense the air pressure of a solid object coming toward it. As a result, the fly would take off before Mr. Rose could hit it.

Text Structures and Paragraphs (Team Set)

In 1905, Frank H. Rose invented a fly-smashing device called a "fly bat." He attached a 5 x 5 inch square wire screen to the end of a yardstick. The holes in the wire were big enough to let air pass through and the fly could not sense air movement coming toward it. Mr. Rose changed the name from "fly-bat" to "flyswatter."

Text Structures and Paragraphs
Showdown (Team Set)

Instructions: Copy one set of cards for each team. Cut apart.

Text Structures and Paragraphs (Team Set)

In 1905, Frank H. Rose invented the flyswatter. First, he searched for wire screen with big enough holes that would allow air to pass through. Next, he cut the wire screen into a 5 x 5 inch square. Then, he attached the screen to a yardstick. Finally, he was ready to try out his new invention.

Text Structures and Paragraphs (Team Set)

Both a newspaper and a flyswatter can be used to kill flies. They are similar in the fact that they both serve as an arm extension and allow for the quick snap of the wrist. The fly's ability to sense air movement is what makes their effectiveness different. The newspaper is a solid object that pushes air forward, whereas, the flyswatter is made from a screen that lets air pass through. This difference is what makes the fly swatter a better choice for successfully swatting flies.

Text Structures and Paragraphs
Showdown (Student Set)

Instructions: Copy one set of cards for each student. Cut apart.

Cause and Effect

Description

Compare and Contrast

Problem and Solution

Sequence

Text Structures and Paragraphs Answer Key
Showdown (Student Set)

Problem and Solution
Frank H. Rose had trouble smashing flies with a rolled up newspaper. He figured out that the fly could sense the air pressure of a solid object coming toward it and would fly away. Mr. Rose solved this by inventing a flyswatter from a yardstick and a wire screen that allowed air to pass through. He was able to surprise flies with his new invention.

Cause and Effect
When Frank H. Rose was bothered by a fly, he rolled up a newspaper and tried to swat it. The fly could sense the air pressure of a solid object coming toward it. As a result, the fly would take off before Mr. Rose could hit it.

Description
In 1905, Frank H. Rose invented a fly-smashing device called a "fly-bat." He attached a 5 x 5 inch square wire screen to the end of a yardstick. The holes in the wire were big enough to let air pass through and the fly could not sense air movement coming toward it. Later, Mr. Rose changed the name from "fly-bat" to "flyswatter."

Sequence
In 1905, Frank H. Rose invented the flyswatter. First, he searched for wire screen with big enough holes that would allow air to pass through. Next, he cut the wire screen into a 5 x 5 inch square. Then, he attached the screen to a yardstick. Finally, he was ready to try out his new invention.

Compare and Contrast
Both a newspaper and a flyswatter can be used to kill flies. They are similar in the fact that they both serve as an arm extension and allow for a quick snap of the wrist. The fly's ability to sense air movement is what makes their effectiveness different. The newspaper is a solid object that pushes air forward, whereas, the flyswatter is made from a screen that lets air pass through. This difference is what makes the fly swatter a better choice for successfully swatting flies.

Text Structures—Signal Words
Showdown (Team Set)

Instructions: Copy one set of cards for each team. Cut apart.

Text Structures– Signal Words (Team Set)

_____ might use this signal word.

finally

Text Structures– Signal Words (Team Set)

_____ might use this signal word.

after

Text Structures– Signal Words (Team Set)

_____ might use this signal word.

later

Text Structures– Signal Words (Team Set)

_____ might use this signal word.

before

Text Structures– Signal Words (Team Set)

_____ might use this signal word.

like

Text Structures– Signal Words (Team Set)

_____ might use this signal word.

different

Text Structures– Signal Words (Team Set)

_____ might use this signal word.

unlike

Text Structures– Signal Words (Team Set)

_____ might use this signal word.

resembles

Text Structures– Signal Words (Team Set)

_____ might use this signal word.

both

Text Structures—Signal Words
Showdown (Team Set)

Instructions: Copy one set of cards for each team. Cut apart.

Text Structures–Signal Words (Team Set)

_____

might use this signal word.

similarly

Text Structures–Signal Words (Team Set)

_____

might use this signal word.

since

Text Structures–Signal Words (Team Set)

_____

might use this signal word.

thus

Text Structures–Signal Words (Team Set)

_____

might use this signal word.

therefore

Text Structures–Signal Words (Team Set)

_____

might use this signal word.

alternative

Text Structures–Signal Words (Team Set)

_____

might use this signal word.

following

Text Structures–Signal Words (Team Set)

_____

might use this signal word.

first

Text Structures–Signal Words (Team Set)

_____

might use this signal word.

second

Text Structures–Signal Words (Team Set)

_____

might use this signal word.

third

Text Structures — Signal Words
Showdown (Team Set)

Instructions: Copy one set of cards for each team. Cut apart.

Text Structures–Signal Words (Team Set)

_____ might use this signal word.

contain

Text Structures–Signal Words (Team Set)

_____ might use this signal word.

during

Text Structures–Signal Words (Team Set)

_____ might use this signal word.

difficulty

Text Structures–Signal Words (Team Set)

_____ might use this signal word.

then

Text Structures–Signal Words (Team Set)

_____ might use this signal word.

consequently

Text Structures–Signal Words (Team Set)

_____ might use these signal words.

to begin with

Text Structures–Signal Words (Team Set)

_____ might use these signal words.

for instance

Text Structures–Signal Words (Team Set)

_____ might use these signal words.

some characteristics are

Text Structures–Signal Words (Team Set)

_____ might use these signal words.

can be defined

Text Structures—Signal Words
Showdown (Team Set)

Instructions: Copy one set of cards for each team. Cut apart.

Text Structures–Signal Words (Team Set)

_____ might use these signal words.

on the other hand

Text Structures–Signal Words (Team Set)

_____ might use these signal words.

more than

Text Structures–Signal Words (Team Set)

_____ might use these signal words.

because of

Text Structures–Signal Words (Team Set)

_____ might use these signal words.

as a result of

Text Structures–Signal Words (Team Set)

_____ might use these signal words.

if...then

Text Structures–Signal Words (Team Set)

_____ might use these signal words.

problem is

Text Structures–Signal Words (Team Set)

_____ might use these signal words.

solution is

Text Structures–Signal Words (Team Set)

_____ might use these signal words.

so that

Text Structures–Signal Words (Team Set)

_____ might use these signal words.

a possible answer

Text Structures—Signal Words
Showdown (Team Set)

Instructions: Copy one set of cards for each team. Cut apart.

Text Structures—Signal Words (Team Set)

_____ might use these signal words.

solved by

Text Structures—Signal Words (Team Set)

_____ might use these signal words.

same as

Text Structures—Signal Words (Team Set)

_____ might use these signal words.

this led to

Text Structures—Signal Words (Team Set)

_____ might use these signal words.

is a

Text Structures—Signal Words (Team Set)

_____ might use these signal words.

in addition

Text Structures—Signal Words (Team Set)

_____ might use this signal word.

involves

Text Structures—Signal Words (Team Set)

_____ might use these signal words.

similar to

Text Structures—Signal Words (Team Set)

_____ might use this signal word.

soon

Text Structures—Signal Words (Team Set)

_____ might use these signal word.

has a

Text Structures—Signal Words
Showdown (Team Set)

Instructions: Copy one set of cards for each team. Cut apart.

Text Structures–Signal Words (Team Set)

_____

might use these signal words.

for example

Text Structures–Signal Words (Team Set)

_____

might use these signal words.

not long after

Text Structures–Signal Words (Team Set)

_____

might use these signal words.

because of

Text Structures–Signal Words (Team Set)

_____

might use these signal words.

then...so

Text Structures–Signal Words (Team Set)

_____

might use these signal words.

in contrast

Text Structures–Signal Words (Team Set)

_____

might use this signal words.

does

Text Structures–Signal Words (Team Set)

_____

might use these signal words.

next to

Text Structures–Signal Words (Team Set)

_____

might use these signal words.

for this reason

Text Structures–Signal Words (Team Set)

_____

might use these signal words.

in fact

Text Structures—Signal Words
Showdown (Student Set)

Instructions: Copy one set of cards for each student. Cut apart.

Cause and Effect

Description

Compare and Contrast

Problem and Solution

Sequence

Fact or Opinion
Showdown (Team Set)

Instructions: Copy one set of cards for each team. Cut apart.

Fact or Opinion (Team Set)

It was Jim's birthday, so he chose to go out to eat at a restaurant across town.

Fact or Opinion (Team Set)

Keith and Sharon sat in the front row at the movies last Saturday night.

Fact or Opinion (Team Set)

My brother, Todd, is the fastest player on the basketball team.

Fact or Opinion (Team Set)

The Missouri River is located in the United States.

Fact or Opinion (Team Set)

My mom looks best dressed in blue.

Fact or Opinion (Team Set)

Arielle got all the answers on her science test correct.

Fact or Opinion (Team Set)

Katrina makes reading look easy.

Fact or Opinion (Team Set)

Micah is wearing a red shirt, blue jeans, and white sneakers.

Fact or Opinion
Showdown (Team Set)

Instructions: Copy one set of cards for each team. Cut apart.

Fact or Opinion (Team Set)

Matt's team won a trophy in the debate tournament last weekend.

Fact or Opinion (Team Set)

Melinda was overjoyed to receive five letters in the mail on Tuesday.

Fact or Opinion (Team Set)

Chloe's parents unloaded their car after a long, exhausting trip to Kansas City.

Fact or Opinion (Team Set)

Hannah called her grandma to tell her about her concert.

Fact or Opinion (Team Set)

The tour group will stop in Paris overnight.

Fact or Opinion (Team Set)

Teenagers are older than toddlers.

Fact or Opinion (Team Set)

Coffee tastes best without sugar or cream.

Fact or Opinion (Team Set)

Nine times nine equals eighty-one.

Fact or Opinion
Showdown (Team Set)

Instructions: Copy one set of cards for each team. Cut apart.

Fact or Opinion (Team Set)

It is easy to learn how to use a computer.

Fact or Opinion (Team Set)

Valentine's Day is on February 14 every year.

Fact or Opinion (Team Set)

If you have a cold, you should stay home from work.

Fact or Opinion (Team Set)

Cardinals are prettier birds than blue jays.

Fact or Opinion (Team Set)

The streets in our city are dangerous.

Fact or Opinion (Team Set)

Ross was an energetic runner in the marathon.

Fact or Opinion (Team Set)

Ice cream will melt in hot weather.

Fact or Opinion (Team Set)

Houses may be built with bricks.

Fact or Opinion
Showdown (Team Set)

Instructions: Copy one set of cards for each team. Cut apart.

Fact or Opinion (Team Set)

South Ridge Elementary School has 400 students.

Fact or Opinion (Team Set)

Dogs sometimes chase cats up trees.

Fact or Opinion (Team Set)

That picture was painted by my uncle, who was a very expressive artist.

Fact or Opinion (Team Set)

Strawberry milk tastes better than chocolate milk.

Fact or Opinion (Team Set)

It is relaxing to sit in the sun and take a nap.

Fact or Opinion (Team Set)

The book, *Mystery of the Lost Key*, is filled with exciting suspense.

Fact or Opinion (Team Set)

Today is Saturday, January 14.

Fact or Opinion (Team Set)

I had a temperature this morning of 100 degrees.

Fact or Opinion
Showdown (Team Set)

Instructions: Copy one set of cards for each team. Cut apart.

Fact or Opinion (Team Set)

The most disappointing loss of the football season came last Friday night.

Fact or Opinion (Team Set)

For supper we ate pizza, salad, and fresh fruit.

Fact or Opinion (Team Set)

Amelia Earhart was the bravest woman to ever fly an airplane.

Fact or Opinion (Team Set)

Those cookies were too crumbly.

Fact or Opinion (Team Set)

Fall is the most spectacular season of the entire year.

Fact or Opinion (Team Set)

Many tourists visit Washington DC in the summer.

Fact or Opinion (Team Set)

The team is researching a cure for the disease.

Fact or Opinion (Team Set)

Mayfield Springs has the cutest shops to visit.

Fact or Opinion
Showdown (Team Set)

Instructions: Copy one set of cards for each team. Cut apart.

Fact or Opinion (Team Set)

Marco Polo was only 17 years old when he left Italy to explore China.

Fact or Opinion (Team Set)

Every year except leap year has 365 days.

Fact or Opinion (Team Set)

Kathy read the last sentence on the page to her partner.

Fact or Opinion (Team Set)

Julie counted three syllables in the word *dinosaur*.

Fact or Opinion (Team Set)

Marci decorated her newly painted room with beautiful cream colored accents.

Fact or Opinion (Team Set)

It is better to run early in the day when the air is cool and fresh.

Fact or Opinion (Team Set)

Toast is made from bread.

Fact or Opinion (Team Set)

A glass plate will probably break if dropped on a cement floor.

Fact or Opinion
Showdown (Student Set)

Instructions: Copy one set of cards for each student. Cut apart. (Note: This page contains cards for four students.)

Fact or Opinion (Student Set)	Fact or Opinion (Student Set)	Fact or Opinion (Student Set)	Fact or Opinion (Student Set)
Fact	Opinion	Fact	Opinion

Fact or Opinion (Student Set)	Fact or Opinion (Student Set)	Fact or Opinion (Student Set)	Fact or Opinion (Student Set)
Fact	Opinion	Fact	Opinion

QUIZ-QUIZ-TRADE Activity

Comprehension Quizzes

Class plays Quiz-Quiz-Trade for repeated practice on text types, text structures, cause and effect, text features, homophones, word meanings, possessive nouns, and present and past tense verbs.

Activity Steps

1. Each student receives a card with a question on the front and an answer on the back.
2. Students stand up, put a hand up, and pair up with another student.
3. Partner A quizzes Partner B using the card.
4. Partner B answers the question.
5. Partner A praises or coaches.
6. Partner B now quizzes Partner A, Partner A answers, and Partner B praises or coaches.
7. Partners trade cards and find a new partner to quiz. The activity continues for multiple rounds, allowing students to quiz and get quizzed multiple times.

STRUCTURE
Quiz-Quiz-Trade

Blacklines

- Text Types—Definitions 84–87
- Text Types—Author's Purpose 88–95
- Text Types—Examples 96–102
- Determining Author's Purpose and Text Types from Titles 103–110
- Text Structures—Definitions, Signal Words, and Graphic Organizers 112–118
- Text Structure Passages 119–123
- Cause and Effect 124–131
- Text Features 132–135
- Homophone Definitions 136–142
- Figurative Language 143–148
- Homophone Sentences 149–156
- Word Meanings 157–163
- Possessive Nouns 164–170
- Present and Past Tense Verbs 171–178

Text Types—Definitions
Quiz-Quiz-Trade

Instructions: Copy enough cards so each student has one card. Cut on dotted lines and fold in half.

Text Types—Definitions

Question

What text type **has a character(s), setting, problem, and solution?**

Text Types—Definitions

Answer

Narrative

Text Types—Definitions

Question

What text type **has text features** (headings, bold words, charts, graphs, captions, glossaries, etc.)?

Text Types—Definitions

Answer

Expository

Text Types—Definitions

Question

What text type **gives the steps** needed to do something or make something?

Text Types—Definitions

Answer

Technical

Text Types—Definitions

Question

What text type **gives reasons to** perform a certain action?

Text Types—Definitions

Answer

Persuasive

Text Types—Definitions
Quiz-Quiz-Trade

Instructions: Copy enough cards so each student has one card. Cut on dotted lines and fold in half.

Text Types—Definitions	Text Types—Definitions
Question What text type **tells a story**?	**Answer** **Narrative**
Question What text type **gives facts and information**?	**Answer** **Expository**
Question What text type **gives information needed to perform a task**?	**Answer** **Technical**
Question What text type **tries to convince the reader**?	**Answer** **Persuasive**

Text Types—Definitions
Quiz-Quiz-Trade

Instructions: Copy enough cards so each student has one card. Cut on dotted lines and fold in half.

Text Types—Definitions

Question

What text type has a beginning, middle, and end?

Text Types—Definitions

Answer

Narrative

Text Types—Definitions

Question

What text type gives information that is true and can be proven (nonfiction)?

Text Types—Definitions

Answer

Expository

Text Types—Definitions

Question

What text type often uses vocabulary specific to the topic and numbered/bulleted lists?

Text Types—Definitions

Answer

Technical

Text Types—Definitions

Question

In what text type does the author take an informed stand and gives reasons?

Text Types—Definitions

Answer

Persuasive

Text Types—Definitions
Quiz-Quiz-Trade

Instructions: Copy enough cards so each student has one card. Cut on dotted lines and fold in half.

Text Types—Definitions

Question

What text type **makes sense when read from beginning to end?**

Text Types—Definitions

Answer

Narrative

Text Types—Definitions

Question

What text type **explains, describes, and discusses information?**

Text Types—Definitions

Answer

Expository

Text Types—Definitions

Question

What text type **often uses graphics to show steps?**

Text Types—Definitions

Answer

Technical

Text Types—Definitions

Question

What text type **sometimes uses emotional appeal to persuade the reader?**

Text Types—Definitions

Answer

Persuasive

Text Types—Author's Purpose
Quiz-Quiz-Trade

Instructions: Copy enough cards so each student has one card. Cut on dotted lines and fold in half.

Text Types—Author's Purpose

Question What is the author's purpose and the text type for …?

a story about a frog and a toad, who are best friends

Text Types—Author's Purpose

Answer
a story about a frog and a toad, who are best friends

to entertain (Narrative)

Text Types—Author's Purpose

Question What is the author's purpose and the text type for …?

a book about kinds of flowers

Text Types—Author's Purpose

Answer
a book about kinds of flowers

to inform (Expository)

Text Types—Author's Purpose

Question What is the author's purpose and the text type for …?

directions on how to get from one city to another

Text Types—Author's Purpose

Answer
directions on how to get from one city to another

to tell how to do something (Technical)

Text Types—Author's Purpose

Question What is the author's purpose and the text type for …?

an article telling why students should wear uniforms to school

---

Text Types—Author's Purpose

Answer
an article telling why students should wear uniforms to school

to convince (Persuasive)

Text Types—Author's Purpose
Quiz-Quiz-Trade

Instructions: Copy enough cards so each student has one card. Cut on dotted lines and fold in half.

Text Types — Author's Purpose

Question What is the author's purpose and the text type for …?

a story about cousins, who were best friends

Text Types — Author's Purpose

Answer
a story about cousins, who were best friends

to entertain (Narrative)

Text Types — Author's Purpose

Question What is the author's purpose and the text type for …?

a letter to the editor of a newspaper listing reasons to attend a community event

---

Text Types — Author's Purpose

Answer
a letter to the editor of a newspaper listing reasons to attend a community event

to convince (Persuasive)

Text Types — Author's Purpose

Question What is the author's purpose and the text type for …?

a brochure listing reasons to attend a certain college

Text Types — Author's Purpose

Answer
a brochure listing reasons to attend a certain college

to convince (Persuasive)

Text Types — Author's Purpose

Question What is the author's purpose and the text type for …?

an article telling about the benefits of living in a certain city

---

Text Types — Author's Purpose

Answer
an article telling about the benefits of living in a certain city

to convince (Persuasive)

Text Types—Author's Purpose
Quiz-Quiz-Trade

Instructions: Copy enough cards so each student has one card. Cut on dotted lines and fold in half.

Text Types — Author's Purpose

Question What is the author's purpose and the text type for…?

a mystery story about a missing treasure

Text Types — Author's Purpose

Answer

a mystery story about a missing treasure

to entertain (Narrative)

Text Types — Author's Purpose

Question What is the author's purpose and the text type for…?

a story about two dogs who got into mischief

Text Types — Author's Purpose

Answer

a story about two dogs who got into mischief

to entertain (Narrative)

Text Types — Author's Purpose

Question What is the author's purpose and the text type for…?

a story about three little pigs who built houses

Text Types — Author's Purpose

Answer

a story about three little pigs who built houses

to entertain (Narrative)

Text Types — Author's Purpose

Question What is the author's purpose and the text type for…?

a story about a huge man who owned a blue ox

Text Types — Author's Purpose

Answer

a story about a huge man who owned a blue ox

to entertain (Narrative)

Text Types—Author's Purpose
Quiz-Quiz-Trade

Instructions: Copy enough cards so each student has one card. Cut on dotted lines and fold in half.

Text Types—Author's Purpose

Question What is the author's purpose and the text type for …?

a story about a girl, a fairy godmother, a prince, and a glass slipper

---

Text Types—Author's Purpose

Answer

a story about a girl, a fairy godmother, a prince, and a glass slipper

to entertain (Narrative)

Text Types—Author's Purpose

Question What is the author's purpose and the text type for …?

a story about a dragon who popped popcorn in a cornfield with his fiery breath

---

Text Types—Author's Purpose

Answer

a story about a dragon who popped popcorn in a cornfield with his fiery breath

to entertain (Narrative)

Text Types—Author's Purpose

Question What is the author's purpose and the text type for …?

a story about a cricket who talked to a boy

Text Types—Author's Purpose

Answer

a story about a cricket who talked to a boy

to entertain (Narrative)

Text Types—Author's Purpose

Question What is the author's purpose and the text type for …?

a story about a giant who shook the earth when he walked down the mountain

---

Text Types—Author's Purpose

Answer

a story about a giant who shook the earth when he walked down the mountain

to entertain (Narrative)

Balanced Literacy • Fourth Grade • Skidmore & Graber
Kagan Publishing • 1 (800) 933-2667 • www.KaganOnline.com

Text Types—Author's Purpose
Quiz-Quiz-Trade

Instructions: Copy enough cards so each student has one card. Cut on dotted lines and fold in half.

Text Types—Author's Purpose

Question What is the author's purpose and the text type for…?

a recipe for making a chocolate cake

Text Types—Author's Purpose

Answer
a recipe for making a chocolate cake

to tell how to do something
(Technical)

Text Types—Author's Purpose

Question What is the author's purpose and the text type for…?

directions on how to put together a lawn mower

Text Types—Author's Purpose

Answer
directions on how to put together a lawn mower

to tell how to do something
(Technical)

Text Types—Author's Purpose

Question What is the author's purpose and the text type for…?

a book about China

Text Types—Author's Purpose

Answer
a book about China

to inform
(Expository)

Text Types—Author's Purpose

Question What is the author's purpose and the text type for…?

a direction sheet that came with a craft kit

Text Types—Author's Purpose

Answer
a direction sheet that came with a craft kit

to tell how to do something
(Technical)

Text Types—Author's Purpose
Quiz-Quiz-Trade

Instructions: Copy enough cards so each student has one card. Cut on dotted lines and fold in half.

Text Types — Author's Purpose

Question What is the author's purpose and the text type for...?

a book with plans and steps to build a tree house

Text Types — Author's Purpose

Answer

a book with plans and steps to build a tree house

to tell how to do something (Technical)

Text Types — Author's Purpose

Question What is the author's purpose and the text type for...?

a page in a magazine telling how to make a Halloween mask

Text Types — Author's Purpose

Answer

a page in a magazine telling how to make a Halloween mask

to tell how to do something (Technical)

Text Types — Author's Purpose

Question What is the author's purpose and the text type for...?

a direction book that came with a new computer

Text Types — Author's Purpose

Answer

a direction book that came with a new computer

to tell how to do something (Technical)

Text Types — Author's Purpose

Question What is the author's purpose and the text type for...?

an article about the steps to planting and growing tomatoes

Text Types — Author's Purpose

Answer

an article about the steps to planting and growing tomatoes

to tell how to do something (Technical)

Text Types—Author's Purpose
Quiz-Quiz-Trade

Instructions: Copy enough cards so each student has one card. Cut on dotted lines and fold in half.

Text Types—Author's Purpose

Question What is the author's purpose and the text type for …?

a drawing with labels showing where to attach bolts on a swing set

---

Text Types—Author's Purpose

Answer
a drawing with labels showing where to attach bolts on a swing set

to tell how to do something
(Technical)

Text Types—Author's Purpose

Question What is the author's purpose and the text type for …?

a book about how to take care of a guinea pig

Text Types—Author's Purpose

Answer
a book about how to take care of a guinea pig

to tell how to do something
(Technical)

Text Types—Author's Purpose

Question What is the author's purpose and the text type for …?

a book about landforms such as mountains, mesas, and valleys

Text Types—Author's Purpose

Answer
a book about landforms such as mountains, mesas, and valleys

to inform
(Expository)

Text Types—Author's Purpose

Question What is the author's purpose and the text type for …?

a book about amazing natural wonders

Text Types—Author's Purpose

Answer
a book about amazing natural wonders

to inform
(Expository)

---

94 Balanced Literacy • Fourth Grade • Skidmore & Graber
Kagan Publishing • 1 (800) 933-2667 • www.KaganOnline.com

Text Types—Author's Purpose
Quiz-Quiz-Trade

Instructions: Copy enough cards so each student has one card. Cut on dotted lines and fold in half.

Text Types—Author's Purpose

Question What is the author's purpose and the text type for...?

a book about famous Kansans

Text Types—Author's Purpose

Answer
a book about famous Kansans

to inform (Expository)

Text Types—Author's Purpose

Question What is the author's purpose and the text type for...?

a book about endangered animals living in Africa

Text Types—Author's Purpose

Answer
a book about endangered animals living in Africa

to inform (Expository)

Text Types—Author's Purpose

Question What is the author's purpose and the text type for...?

a report about pelicans

Text Types—Author's Purpose

Answer
a report about pelicans

to inform (Expository)

Text Types—Author's Purpose

Question What is the author's purpose and the text type for...?

an article in *Ranger Rick* about hyenas

Text Types—Author's Purpose

Answer
an article in *Ranger Rick* about hyenas

to inform (Expository)

Text Types—Examples
Quiz-Quiz-Trade

Instructions: Copy enough cards so each student has one card. Cut on dotted lines and fold in half.

Text Types—Examples

Question

A <u>recipe</u> is an example of which text type?

- a) technical
- b) narrative
- c) persuasive

Text Types—Examples

Answer

a) Technical

Text Types—Examples

Question

A <u>mystery</u> is an example of which text type?

- a) expository
- b) narrative
- c) persuasive

Text Types—Examples

Answer

b) Narrative

Text Types—Examples

Question

A <u>newspaper article</u> is an example of which text type?

- a) narrative
- b) persuasive
- c) expository

Text Types—Examples

Answer

c) Expository

Text Types—Examples

Question

An <u>advertisement</u> is an example of which text type?

- a) persuasive
- b) narrative
- c) technical

Text Types—Examples

Answer

a) Persuasive

Text Types—Examples
Quiz-Quiz-Trade

Instructions: Copy enough cards so each student has one card. Cut on dotted lines and fold in half.

Text Types — Examples

Question
A <u>travel brochure</u> is an example of which text type?

- a) narrative
- b) technical
- c) persuasive

Text Types — Examples

Answer

c) Persuasive

Text Types — Examples

Question
An <u>interview</u> is an example of which text type?

- a) expository
- b) technical
- c) persuasive

Text Types — Examples

Answer

a) Expository

Text Types — Examples

Question
A <u>written debate</u> is an example of which text type?

- a) technical
- b) persuasive
- c) expository

Text Types — Examples

Answer

b) Persuasive

Text Types — Examples

Question
A <u>menu</u> is an example of which text type?

- a) persuasive
- b) narrative
- c) technical

Text Types — Examples

Answer

c) Technical

Text Types–Examples
Quiz-Quiz-Trade

Instructions: Copy enough cards so each student has one card. Cut on dotted lines and fold in half.

Text Types — Examples

Question
A <u>novel</u> is an example of which text type?
- a) narrative
- b) expository
- c) persuasive

Text Types — Examples

Answer

a) Narrative

Text Types — Examples

Question
A <u>floor plan</u> is an example of which text type?
- a) technical
- b) persuasive
- c) expository

Text Types — Examples

Answer

a) Technical

Text Types — Examples

Question
A <u>book review</u> is an example of which text type?
- a) narrative
- b) persuasive
- c) expository

Text Types — Examples

Answer

b) Persuasive

Text Types — Examples

Question
<u>Instructions</u> are an example of which text type?
- a) technical
- b) narrative
- c) expository

Text Types — Examples

Answer

a) Technical

Text Types–Examples
Quiz-Quiz-Trade

Instructions: Copy enough cards so each student has one card. Cut on dotted lines and fold in half.

Text Types — Examples

Question

A <u>book report</u> is an example of which text type?

- a) narrative
- b) technical
- c) expository

Text Types — Examples

Answer

c) Expository

Text Types — Examples

Question

A <u>play</u> is an example of which text type?

- a) narrative
- b) persuasive
- c) technical

Text Types — Examples

Answer

a) Narrative

Text Types — Examples

Question

A <u>recount of an event</u> is an example of which text type?

- a) narrative
- b) expository
- c) technical

Text Types — Examples

Answer

b) Expository

Text Types — Examples

Question

A <u>questionnaire</u> is an example of which text type?

- a) technical
- b) narrative
- c) persuasive

Text Types — Examples

Answer

a) Technical

Text Types–Examples
Quiz-Quiz-Trade

Instructions: Copy enough cards so each student has one card. Cut on dotted lines and fold in half.

Text Types — Examples

Question
A <u>map</u> is an example of which text type?
- a) persuasive
- b) technical
- c) expository

Text Types — Examples

Answer

b) Technical

Text Types — Examples

Question
<u>Historical fiction</u> is an example of which text type?
- a) technical
- b) persuasive
- c) narrative

Text Types — Examples

Answer

c) Narrative

Text Types — Examples

Question
A <u>warranty</u> is an example of which text type?
- a) expository
- b) narrative
- c) technical

Text Types — Examples

Answer

c) Technical

Text Types — Examples

Question
A <u>letter to the editor</u> is an example of which text type?
- a) technical
- b) persuasive
- c) expository

Text Types — Examples

Answer

b) Persuasive

Balanced Literacy • Fourth Grade • Skidmore & Graber
Kagan Publishing • 1 (800) 933-2667 • www.KaganOnline.com

Text Types–Examples
Quiz-Quiz-Trade

Instructions: Copy enough cards so each student has one card. Cut on dotted lines and fold in half.

Text Types — Examples

Question

A <u>short story</u> is an example of which text type?

- a) narrative
- b) technical
- c) expository

Text Types — Examples

Answer

a) Narrative

Text Types — Examples

Question

An <u>editorial</u> is an example of which text type?

- a) technical
- b) persuasive
- c) narrative

Text Types — Examples

Answer

b) Persuasive

Text Types — Examples

Question

A <u>tall tale</u> is an example of which text type?

- a) narrative
- b) persuasive
- c) technical

Text Types — Examples

Answer

a) Narrative

Text Types — Examples

Question

A <u>commercial</u> is an example of which text type?

- a) technical
- b) expository
- c) persuasive

Text Types — Examples

Answer

c) Persuasive

Text Types–Examples
Quiz-Quiz-Trade

Instructions: Copy enough cards so each student has one card. Cut on dotted lines and fold in half.

Text Types—Examples

Question
A <u>schedule</u> is an example of which text type?
- a) technical
- b) narrative
- c) expository

Text Types—Examples

Answer

a) Technical

Text Types—Examples

Question
A <u>recount of a personal experience</u> is an example of which text type?
- a) technical
- b) persuasive
- c) narrative

Text Types—Examples

Answer

c) Narrative

Text Types—Examples

Question
A <u>fantasy</u> is an example of which text type?
- a) expository
- b) persuasive
- c) narrative

Text Types—Examples

Answer

c) Narrative

Text Types—Examples

Question
A <u>research paper</u> is an example of which text type?
- a) technical
- b) expository
- c) persuasive

Text Types—Examples

Answer

b) Expository

Determining Author's Purpose and Text Types from Titles
Quiz-Quiz-Trade

Instructions: Copy enough cards so each student has one card. Cut on dotted lines and fold in half.

Determining Author's Purpose and Text Types

Question What is the author's purpose and the text type for …?

Kinds of Trees

Determining Author's Purpose and Text Types

Answer

Kinds of Trees

to inform
(Expository)

Determining Author's Purpose and Text Types

Question What is the author's purpose and the text type for …?

How to Make a Birdhouse

Determining Author's Purpose and Text Types

Answer

How to Make a Birdhouse

to tell how to do something
(Technical)

Determining Author's Purpose and Text Types

Question What is the author's purpose and the text type for …?

Cats Make the Best Pets

Determining Author's Purpose and Text Types

Answer

Cats Make the Best Pets

to convince
(Persuasive)

Determining Author's Purpose and Text Types

Question What is the author's purpose and the text type for …?

Japan Is the Best Country to Visit

Determining Author's Purpose and Text Types

Answer

Japan Is the Best Country to Visit

to convince
(Persuasive)

Balanced Literacy • Fourth Grade • Skidmore & Graber
Kagan Publishing • 1 (800) 933-2667 • www.KaganOnline.com

Determining Author's Purpose and Text Types from Titles
Quiz-Quiz-Trade

Instructions: Copy enough cards so each student has one card. Cut on dotted lines and fold in half.

Determining Author's Purpose and Text Types

Question What is the author's purpose and the text type for ...?

Frogs and Their Habitat

Determining Author's Purpose and Text Types

Answer

Frogs and Their Habitat

to inform (Expository)

Determining Author's Purpose and Text Types

Question What is the author's purpose and the text type for ...?

How to Train a Dog

Determining Author's Purpose and Text Types

Answer

How to Train a Dog

to tell how to do something (Technical)

Determining Author's Purpose and Text Types

Question What is the author's purpose and the text type for ...?

Indian Chiefs

Determining Author's Purpose and Text Types

Answer

Indian Chiefs

to inform (Expository)

Determining Author's Purpose and Text Types

Question What is the author's purpose and the text type for ...?

The Southwestern Region of the United States

Determining Author's Purpose and Text Types

Answer

The Southwestern Region of the United States

to inform (Expository)

Balanced Literacy • Fourth Grade • Skidmore & Graber
Kagan Publishing • 1 (800) 933-2667 • www.KaganOnline.com

Determining Author's Purpose and Text Types from Titles
Quiz-Quiz-Trade

Instructions: Copy enough cards so each student has one card. Cut on dotted lines and fold in half.

Determining Author's Purpose and Text Types

Question What is the author's purpose and the text type for …?

The Very Lonely Firefly

Determining Author's Purpose and Text Types

Answer

The Very Lonely Firefly

to entertain
(Narrative)

Determining Author's Purpose and Text Types

Question What is the author's purpose and the text type for …?

A Light in the Attic

Determining Author's Purpose and Text Types

Answer

A Light in the Attic

to entertain
(Narrative)

Determining Author's Purpose and Text Types

Question What is the author's purpose and the text type for …?

How to Draw Animals

Determining Author's Purpose and Text Types

Answer

How to Draw Animals

to tell how to do something
(Technical)

Determining Author's Purpose and Text Types

Question What is the author's purpose and the text type for …?

Should We Have Pets?

Determining Author's Purpose and Text Types

Answer

Should We Have Pets?

to convince
(Persuasive)

Balanced Literacy • Fourth Grade • Skidmore & Graber
Kagan Publishing • 1 (800) 933-2667 • www.KaganOnline.com

Determining Author's Purpose and Text Types from Titles
Quiz-Quiz-Trade

Instructions: Copy enough cards so each student has one card. Cut on dotted lines and fold in half.

Determining Author's Purpose and Text Types

Question What is the author's purpose and the text type for …?

Amelia Earhart's Life

Determining Author's Purpose and Text Types

Answer

Amelia Earhart's Life

to inform
(Expository)

Determining Author's Purpose and Text Types

Question What is the author's purpose and the text type for …?

The Adventures of Daring Dusty

Determining Author's Purpose and Text Types

Answer

The Adventures of Daring Dusty

to entertain
(Narrative)

Determining Author's Purpose and Text Types

Question What is the author's purpose and the text type for …?

Saint George and the Dragon

Determining Author's Purpose and Text Types

Answer

Saint George and the Dragon

to entertain
(Narrative)

Determining Author's Purpose and Text Types

Question What is the author's purpose and the text type for …?

Cinderella

Determining Author's Purpose and Text Types

Answer

Cinderella

to entertain
(Narrative)

# Determining Author's Purpose and Text Types from Titles
Quiz-Quiz-Trade

Instructions: Copy enough cards so each student has one card. Cut on dotted lines and fold in half.

Determining Author's Purpose and Text Types

Question What is the author's purpose and the text type for …?

Cuddly Dudley

Determining Author's Purpose and Text Types

Answer

Cuddly Dudley

to entertain
(Narrative)

Determining Author's Purpose and Text Types

Question What is the author's purpose and the text type for …?

How to Dry Fruit

Determining Author's Purpose and Text Types

Answer

How to Dry Fruit

to tell how to do something
(Technical)

Determining Author's Purpose and Text Types

Question What is the author's purpose and the text type for …?

Preparing for Mountain Climbing

Determining Author's Purpose and Text Types

Answer

Preparing for Mountain Climbing

to tell how to do something
(Technical)

Determining Author's Purpose and Text Types

Question What is the author's purpose and the text type for …?

Making Candles

Determining Author's Purpose and Text Types

Answer

Making Candles

to tell how to do something
(Technical)

Balanced Literacy • Fourth Grade • Skidmore & Graber
Kagan Publishing • 1 (800) 933-2667 • www.KaganOnline.com

Determining Author's Purpose and Text Types from Titles
Quiz-Quiz-Trade

Instructions: Copy enough cards so each student has one card. Cut on dotted lines and fold in half.

Determining Author's Purpose and Text Types

Question What is the author's purpose and the text type for...?

Seasons

Determining Author's Purpose and Text Types

Answer

Seasons

to inform
(Expository)

Determining Author's Purpose and Text Types

Question What is the author's purpose and the text type for...?

Winter Is the Best Season

Determining Author's Purpose and Text Types

Answer

Winter Is the Best Season

to convince
(Persuasive)

Determining Author's Purpose and Text Types

Question What is the author's purpose and the text type for...?

The Little Dinosaur

Determining Author's Purpose and Text Types

Answer

The Little Dinosaur

to entertain
(Narrative)

Determining Author's Purpose and Text Types

Question What is the author's purpose and the text type for...?

Should Students Have Recess?

Determining Author's Purpose and Text Types

Answer

Should Students Have Recess?

to convince
(Persuasive)

Balanced Literacy • Fourth Grade • Skidmore & Graber
Kagan Publishing • 1 (800) 933-2667 • www.KaganOnline.com

Determining Author's Purpose and Text Types from Titles
Quiz-Quiz-Trade

Instructions: Copy enough cards so each student has one card. Cut on dotted lines and fold in half.

Determining Author's Purpose and Text Types

Question What is the author's purpose and the text type for...?

Kinds of Shoes

Determining Author's Purpose and Text Types

Answer

Kinds of Shoes

to inform
(Expository)

Determining Author's Purpose and Text Types

Question What is the author's purpose and the text type for...?

*How to Use
Sign Language*

Determining Author's Purpose and Text Types

Answer

*How to Use
Sign Language*

to tell how to do something
(Technical)

Determining Author's Purpose and Text Types

Question What is the author's purpose and the text type for...?

*The Basics of Using
Your New Computer*

Determining Author's Purpose and Text Types

Answer

*The Basics of Using
Your New Computer*

to tell how to do something
(Technical)

Determining Author's Purpose and Text Types

Question What is the author's purpose and the text type for...?

*The Differences Between
Crocodiles and Alligators*

Determining Author's Purpose and Text Types

Answer

*The Differences Between
Crocodiles and Alligators*

to inform
(Expository)

Determining Author's Purpose and Text Types from Titles
Quiz-Quiz-Trade

Instructions: Copy enough cards so each student has one card. Cut on dotted lines and fold in half.

Determining Author's Purpose and Text Types

Question What is the author's purpose and the text type for…?

How to Trim a Tree

Determining Author's Purpose and Text Types

Answer

How to Trim a Tree

to tell how to do something
(Technical)

Determining Author's Purpose and Text Types

Question What is the author's purpose and the text type for…?

Harry's Fishing Trip

Determining Author's Purpose and Text Types

Answer

Harry's Fishing Trip

to entertain
(Narrative)

Determining Author's Purpose and Text Types

Question What is the author's purpose and the text type for…?

Mouse and Cat Become Friends

Determining Author's Purpose and Text Types

Answer

Mouse and Cat Become Friends

to entertain
(Narrative)

Determining Author's Purpose and Text Types

Question What is the author's purpose and the text type for…?

Tips for Successful Mountain Biking

Determining Author's Purpose and Text Types

Answer

Tips for Successful Mountain Biking

to tell how to do something
(Technical)

Balanced Literacy • Fourth Grade • Skidmore & Graber
Kagan Publishing • 1 (800) 933-2667 • www.KaganOnline.com

Determining Author's Purpose and Text Types from Titles
Quiz-Quiz-Trade

Instructions: Copy enough cards so each student has one card. Cut on dotted lines and fold in half.

Determining Author's Purpose and Text Types

Question What is the author's purpose and the text type for...?

Our Amazing Sun

Determining Author's Purpose and Text Types

Answer

Our Amazing Sun

to inform
(Expository)

Determining Author's Purpose and Text Types

Question What is the author's purpose and the text type for...?

Curious Tiger's Balloon Adventure

Determining Author's Purpose and Text Types

Answer

Curious Tiger's Balloon Adventure

to entertain
(Narrative)

Determining Author's Purpose and Text Types

Question What is the author's purpose and the text type for...?

Decorating a Birthday Cake

Determining Author's Purpose and Text Types

Answer

Decorating a Birthday Cake

to tell how to do something
(Technical)

Determining Author's Purpose and Text Types

Question What is the author's purpose and the text type for...?

Students Should Wear Uniforms at School

Determining Author's Purpose and Text Types

Answer

Students Should Wear Uniforms at School

to convince
(Persuasive)

Text Structures—Definitions, Signal Words, and Graphic Organizers
Quiz-Quiz-Trade

Instructions: Copy enough cards so each student has one card. Cut on dotted lines and fold in half.

Text Structures–Definitions, Signal Words, and Graphic Organizers

Question
What text structure has **steps**?

Text Structures–Definitions, Signal Words, and Graphic Organizers

Answer
Sequence

Text Structures–Definitions, Signal Words, and Graphic Organizers

Question
What text structure has **a problem that is solved**?

Text Structures–Definitions, Signal Words, and Graphic Organizers

Answer
Problem and Solution

Text Structures–Definitions, Signal Words, and Graphic Organizers

Question
What text structure explains **how things are the same or different**?

Text Structures–Definitions, Signal Words, and Graphic Organizers

Answer
Compare and Contrast

Text Structures–Definitions, Signal Words, and Graphic Organizers

Question
What text structure has **details**?

Text Structures–Definitions, Signal Words, and Graphic Organizers

Answer
Description

Text Structures–Definitions, Signal Words, and Graphic Organizers

Question
What text structure tells how something makes something else happen?

Text Structures–Definitions, Signal Words, and Graphic Organizers

Answer
Cause and Effect

Text Structures—Definitions, Signal Words, and Graphic Organizers
Quiz-Quiz-Trade

Instructions: Copy enough cards so each student has one card. Cut on dotted lines and fold in half.

Text Structures–Definitions, Signal Words, and Graphic Organizers

Question
What text structure is **written in a specific time order**?

Text Structures–Definitions, Signal Words, and Graphic Organizers

Answer
Sequence

Text Structures–Definitions, Signal Words, and Graphic Organizers

Question
What text structure **has events that lead to figuring out the problem at the end**?

Text Structures–Definitions, Signal Words, and Graphic Organizers

Answer
Problem and Solution

Text Structures–Definitions, Signal Words, and Graphic Organizers

Question
What text structure **compares similarities and differences**?

Text Structures–Definitions, Signal Words, and Graphic Organizers

Answer
Compare and Contrast

Text Structures–Definitions, Signal Words, and Graphic Organizers

Question
What text structure **tells more about someone, something, or someplace**?

Text Structures–Definitions, Signal Words, and Graphic Organizers

Answer
Description

Text Structures–Definitions, Signal Words, and Graphic Organizers

Question
What text structure explains **how something occurred because of something else**?

Text Structures–Definitions, Signal Words, and Graphic Organizers

Answer
Cause and Effect

Text Structures—Definitions, Signal Words, and Graphic Organizers
Quiz-Quiz-Trade

Instructions: Copy enough cards so each student has one card. Cut on dotted lines and fold in half.

Text Structures–Definitions, Signal Words, and Graphic Organizers

Question
What text structure would use this graphic organizer?

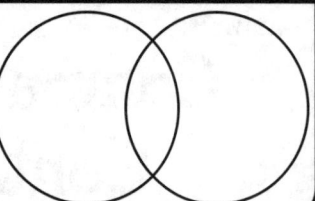

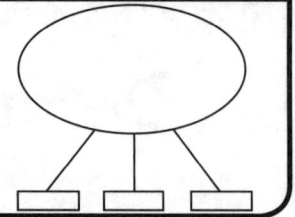

1.
2.
3.
4.
5.

Text Structures–Definitions, Signal Words, and Graphic Organizers

Answer

Sequence

Text Structures–Definitions, Signal Words, and Graphic Organizers

Question
What text structure would use this graphic organizer?

Problem
Event
Event
Event
Solution

Text Structures–Definitions, Signal Words, and Graphic Organizers

Answer

Problem and Solution

Text Structures–Definitions, Signal Words, and Graphic Organizers

Question
What text structure would use this graphic organizer?

(Venn diagram)

Text Structures–Definitions, Signal Words, and Graphic Organizers

Answer

Compare and Contrast

Text Structures–Definitions, Signal Words, and Graphic Organizers

Question
What text structure would use this graphic organizer?

(Oval with three boxes branching below)

Text Structures–Definitions, Signal Words, and Graphic Organizers

Answer

Description

Text Structures–Definitions, Signal Words, and Graphic Organizers

Question
What text structure would use this graphic organizer?

(Box → Box)

Text Structures–Definitions, Signal Words, and Graphic Organizers

Answer

Cause and Effect

Text Structures—Definitions, Signal Words, and Graphic Organizers
Quiz-Quiz-Trade

Instructions: Copy enough cards so each student has one card. Cut on dotted lines and fold in half.

Text Structures–Definitions, Signal Words, and Graphic Organizers

Question: What text structure would use this graphic organizer?

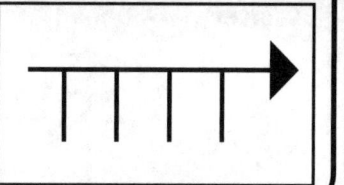

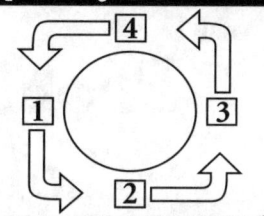

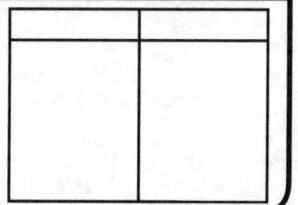

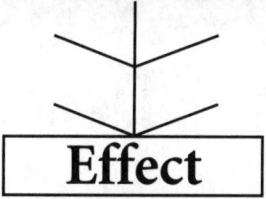

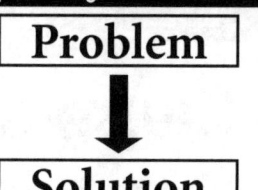

Text Structures–Definitions, Signal Words, and Graphic Organizers

Answer: **Sequence**

Text Structures–Definitions, Signal Words, and Graphic Organizers

Question: What text structure would use this graphic organizer?

Text Structures–Definitions, Signal Words, and Graphic Organizers

Answer: **Sequence**

Text Structures–Definitions, Signal Words, and Graphic Organizers

Question: What text structure would use this graphic organizer?

Text Structures–Definitions, Signal Words, and Graphic Organizers

Answer: **Compare and Contrast**

Text Structures–Definitions, Signal Words, and Graphic Organizers

Question: What text structure would use this graphic organizer? (Effect)

Text Structures–Definitions, Signal Words, and Graphic Organizers

Answer: **Cause and Effect**

Text Structures–Definitions, Signal Words, and Graphic Organizers

Question: What text structure would use this graphic organizer? (Problem → Solution)

Text Structures–Definitions, Signal Words, and Graphic Organizers

Answer: **Problem and Solution**

Text Structures—Definitions, Signal Words, and Graphic Organizers
Quiz-Quiz-Trade

Instructions: Copy enough cards so each student has one card. Cut on dotted lines and fold in half.

Text Structures–Definitions, Signal Words, and Graphic Organizers

Question

Which text structure sometimes uses these words?

> first   second
> third   fourth

Text Structures–Definitions, Signal Words, and Graphic Organizers

Answer

Sequence

Text Structures–Definitions, Signal Words, and Graphic Organizers

Question

Which text structure sometimes uses these words?

> The problem is...
> The solution is...

Text Structures–Definitions, Signal Words, and Graphic Organizers

Answer

Problem and Solution

Text Structures–Definitions, Signal Words, and Graphic Organizers

Question

Which text structure sometimes uses these words?

> different from
> same as

Text Structures–Definitions, Signal Words, and Graphic Organizers

Answer

Compare and Contrast

Text Structures–Definitions, Signal Words, and Graphic Organizers

Question

Which text structure sometimes uses these words?

> Some characteristics are...

Text Structures–Definitions, Signal Words, and Graphic Organizers

Answer

Description

Text Structures–Definitions, Signal Words, and Graphic Organizers

Question

Which text structure sometimes uses these words?

> because of

Text Structures–Definitions, Signal Words, and Graphic Organizers

Answer

Cause and Effect

Comprehension Blackline

Balanced Literacy • Fourth Grade • Skidmore & Graber
Kagan Publishing • 1 (800) 933-2667 • www.KaganOnline.com

Text Structures—Definitions, Signal Words, and Graphic Organizers
Quiz-Quiz-Trade

Instructions: Copy enough cards so each student has one card. Cut on dotted lines and fold in half.

Text Structures–Definitions, Signal Words, and Graphic Organizers

Question

Which text structure sometimes uses these words?

next
then

Text Structures–Definitions, Signal Words, and Graphic Organizers

Answer

Sequence

Text Structures–Definitions, Signal Words, and Graphic Organizers

Question

Which text structure sometimes uses these words?

have solved this problem by...

Text Structures–Definitions, Signal Words, and Graphic Organizers

Answer

Problem and Solution

Text Structures–Definitions, Signal Words, and Graphic Organizers

Question

Which text structure sometimes uses these words?

is like
resembles

Text Structures–Definitions, Signal Words, and Graphic Organizers

Answer

Compare and Contrast

Text Structures–Definitions, Signal Words, and Graphic Organizers

Question

Which text structure sometimes uses these words?

for example

Text Structures–Definitions, Signal Words, and Graphic Organizers

Answer

Description

Text Structures–Definitions, Signal Words, and Graphic Organizers

Question

Which text structure sometimes uses these words?

if...then

Text Structures–Definitions, Signal Words, and Graphic Organizers

Answer

Cause and Effect

Text Structures—Definitions, Signal Words, and Graphic Organizers
Quiz-Quiz-Trade

Instructions: Copy enough cards so each student has one card. Cut on dotted lines and fold in half.

Text Structures–Definitions, Signal Words, and Graphic Organizers

Question

Which text structure sometimes uses these words?

before
after

Text Structures–Definitions, Signal Words, and Graphic Organizers

Answer

Sequence

Text Structures–Definitions, Signal Words, and Graphic Organizers

Question

Which text structure sometimes uses these words?

alternative
possible answer

Text Structures–Definitions, Signal Words, and Graphic Organizers

Answer

Problem and Solution

Text Structures–Definitions, Signal Words, and Graphic Organizers

Question

Which text structure sometimes uses these words?

also
too

Text Structures–Definitions, Signal Words, and Graphic Organizers

Answer

Compare and Contrast

Text Structures–Definitions, Signal Words, and Graphic Organizers

Question

Which text structure sometimes uses these words?

for instance

Text Structures–Definitions, Signal Words, and Graphic Organizers

Answer

Description

Text Structures–Definitions, Signal Words, and Graphic Organizers

Question

Which text structure sometimes uses these words?

since
therefore

Text Structures–Definitions, Signal Words, and Graphic Organizers

Answer

Cause and Effect

Text Structure Passages
Quiz-Quiz-Trade

Instructions: Copy enough cards so each student has one card. Cut on dotted lines and fold in half.

Text Structure Passages

Question: What text structure would the author use?

The author writes an article that describes zebras, tells where they are found, and explains about the herds they live in.

Text Structure Passages

Answer

Description

Text Structure Passages

Question: What text structure would the author use?

The author tells about events that happened using time order, such as the events in the life of Amelia Earhart.

Text Structure Passages

Answer

Sequence

Text Structure Passages

Question: What text structure would the author use?

The author points out what's the same and what's different about monkeys and apes.

Text Structure Passages

Answer

Compare and Contrast

Text Structure Passages

Question: What text structure would the author use?

The author writes about the damage caused by a recent hurricane.

Text Structure Passages

Answer

Cause and Effect

Text Structure Passages

Question: What text structure would the author use?

The author writes an article about spilled oil from an ocean tanker and what people did to protect the animals.

Text Structure Passages

Answer

Problem and Solution

Text Structure Passages
Quiz-Quiz-Trade

Instructions: Copy enough cards so each student has one card. Cut on dotted lines and fold in half.

Text Structure Passages
Question: What text structure would the author use?

The author describes the steps in a process, such as how peanut butter is made.

Text Structure Passages
Answer

Sequence

Text Structure Passages
Question: What text structure would the author use?

The author points out differences between frogs and toads.

Text Structure Passages
Answer

Compare and Contrast

Text Structure Passages
Question: What text structure would the author use?

The author tells about the characteristics of cats.

Text Structure Passages
Answer

Description

Text Structure Passages
Question: What text structure would the author use?

The author describes the steps for making chocolate.

Text Structure Passages
Answer

Sequence

Text Structure Passages
Question: What text structure would the author use?

The author explains what workers did to make the Leaning Tower of Pisa straighter.

Text Structure Passages
Answer

Problem and Solution

---

120 Balanced Literacy • Fourth Grade • Skidmore & Graber
Kagan Publishing • 1 (800) 933-2667 • www.KaganOnline.com

Text Structure Passages
Quiz-Quiz-Trade

Instructions: Copy enough cards so each student has one card. Cut on dotted lines and fold in half.

Text Structure Passages

Question: What text structure would the author use?

The author explains what weather conditions cause hail to form.

Text Structure Passages

Answer

Cause and Effect

Text Structure Passages

Question: What text structure would the author use?

The author discusses what it was like to live in the US 100 years ago in relation to what it is like today.

Text Structure Passages

Answer

Compare and Contrast

Text Structure Passages

Question: What text structure would the author use?

The author explains the differences and similarities between a violin and a viola.

Text Structure Passages

Answer

Compare and Contrast

Text Structure Passages

Question: What text structure would the author use?

The author gives details of the countryside in Scotland.

Text Structure Passages

Answer

Description

Text Structure Passages

Question: What text structure would the author use?

The author explains the steps in using a street map to find a store location.

Text Structure Passages

Answer

Sequence

Text Structure Passages
Quiz-Quiz-Trade

Instructions: Copy enough cards so each student has one card. Cut on dotted lines and fold in half.

Text Structure Passages

Question: What text structure would the author use?

The author explains the differences and similarities between types of clouds, so the reader will be able to tell them apart when identifying them.

Text Structure Passages

Answer

Compare and Contrast

Text Structure Passages

Question: What text structure would the author use?

The author tells how the mountain climbers responded to the drastic change in weather conditions while they were on the face of the mountain.

Text Structure Passages

Answer

Problem and Solution

Text Structure Passages

Question: What text structure would the author use?

The author writes about the invention of the car and the changes it brought about.

Text Structure Passages

Answer

Cause and Effect

Text Structure Passages

Question: What text structure would the author use?

The author tells how the pioneers dealt with hardships and troubles they encountered on their westward journey.

Text Structure Passages

Answer

Problem and Solution

Text Structure Passages

Question: What text structure would the author use?

The author reports the years various sports were introduced in this country.

Text Structure Passages

Answer

Sequence

Text Structure Passages
Quiz-Quiz-Trade

Instructions: Copy enough cards so each student has one card. Cut on dotted lines and fold in half.

Text Structure Passages

Question: What text structure would the author use?

The author explains the similarities between baking brownies and cookies.

Text Structure Passages

Answer

Compare and Contrast

Text Structure Passages

Question: What text structure would the author use?

The author explained how the city solved the problem of unsafe water.

Text Structure Passages

Answer

Problem and Solution

Text Structure Passages

Question: What text structure would the author use?

The author compares the Senate and the House of Representatives in relation to the roles they play in our government.

Text Structure Passages

Answer

Compare and Contrast

Text Structure Passages

Question: What text structure would the author use?

The author relates his personal experience breaking a leg, while backpacking in the wilderness, and how medical personnel were able to reach him.

Text Structure Passages

Answer

Problem and Solution

Text Structure Passages

Question: What text structure would the author use?

The author shares her feelings during her first skydiving experience.

Text Structure Passages

Answer

Description

Cause-Effect
Quiz-Quiz-Trade

Instructions: Copy enough cards so each student has one card. Cut on dotted lines and fold in half.

Cause-Effect
Question: Which is the cause? Which is the effect?

It was possible to make portable radios.

Transistors were invented to replace heavy radio parts.

Cause-Effect
Answer

Cause: Transistors were invented to replace heavy radio parts.

Effect: It was possible to make portable radios.

Cause-Effect
Question: Which is the cause? Which is the effect?

I have two knee joints.

I am able to bend my legs backward.

Cause-Effect
Answer

Cause: I have two knee joints.

Effect: I am able to bend my legs backward.

Cause-Effect
Question: Which is the cause? Which is the effect?

Food could be kept cool and fresh for a longer period of time.

Refrigerators were invented.

Cause-Effect
Answer

Cause: Refrigerators were invented.

Effect: Food could be kept cool and fresh for a longer period of time.

Cause-Effect
Question: Which is the cause? Which is the effect?

Jenny had more time to study.

Jenny decided to work fewer hours at her job as a store clerk.

Cause-Effect
Answer

Cause: Jenny decided to work fewer hours at her job as a store clerk.

Effect: Jenny had more time to study.

Cause-Effect
Question: Which is the cause? Which is the effect?

John is good at working with numbers.

John chose to study accounting in school.

Cause-Effect
Answer

Cause: John is good at working with numbers.

Effect: John chose to study accounting in school.

Cause-Effect
Quiz-Quiz-Trade

Instructions: Copy enough cards so each student has one card. Cut on dotted lines and fold in half.

Cause-Effect
Question: Which is the cause? Which is the effect?

We lost our electricity for several days.

There was an ice storm last week.

Cause-Effect
Answer

Cause: There was an ice storm last week.

Effect: We lost our electricity for several days.

Cause-Effect
Question: Which is the cause? Which is the effect?

The goldfish were hungry.

The goldfish quickly ate the food I threw into the pond.

Cause-Effect
Answer

Cause: The goldfish were hungry.

Effect: The goldfish quickly ate the food I threw into the pond.

Cause-Effect
Question: Which is the cause? Which is the effect?

The spaghetti sauce cooking on the burner ran all over the stovetop.

I was preoccupied talking on the phone to a friend.

Cause-Effect
Answer

Cause: I was preoccupied talking on the phone to a friend.

Effect: The spaghetti sauce cooking on the burner ran all over the stovetop.

Cause-Effect
Question: Which is the cause? Which is the effect?

Alex forgot to wind the clock with a special key.

The antique clock stopped running.

Cause-Effect
Answer

Cause: Alex forgot to wind the clock with a special key.

Effect: The antique clock stopped running.

Cause-Effect
Question: Which is the cause? Which is the effect?

Katie's back hurt.

Katie carried a humongous box of heavy books to her car.

Cause-Effect
Answer

Cause: Katie carried a humongous box of heavy books to her car.

Effect: Katie's back hurt.

Cause-Effect
Quiz-Quiz-Trade

Instructions: Copy enough cards so each student has one card. Cut on dotted lines and fold in half.

Cause-Effect

Question: Which is the cause? Which is the effect?

Jen's friend lost her new mailing address.

Jen waited patiently for three weeks for a letter from her friend.

Cause-Effect

Answer

Cause: Jen's friend lost her new mailing address.

Effect: Jen waited patiently for three weeks for a letter from her friend.

Cause-Effect

Question: Which is the cause? Which is the effect?

For the rest of the day, Chris' socks and shoes were soggy and uncomfortable.

While walking through the parking lot this morning, Chris accidentally stepped in the middle of a deep puddle.

Cause-Effect

Answer

Cause: While walking through the parking lot this morning, Chris accidentally stepped in the middle of a deep puddle.

Effect: For the rest of the day, Chris' socks and shoes were soggy and uncomfortable.

Cause-Effect

Question: Which is the cause? Which is the effect?

Both Carrie and Polly felt dizzy.

Carrie and Polly played on the merry-go-round all afternoon at the park.

Cause-Effect

Answer

Cause: Carrie and Polly played on the merry-go-round all afternoon at the park.

Effect: Both Carrie and Polly felt dizzy.

Cause-Effect

Question: Which is the cause? Which is the effect?

A spider spun an orb web in the corner of the old barn.

A fly was caught in the sticky spider web.

Cause-Effect

Answer

Cause: A spider spun an orb web in the corner of the old barn.

Effect: A fly was caught in the sticky spider web.

Cause-Effect

Question: Which is the cause? Which is the effect?

Erin folded all the clothes, which were in the dryer.

The basketful of folded clothes was ready to be put into drawers.

Cause-Effect

Answer

Cause: Erin folded all the clothes, which were in the dryer.

Effect: The basketful of folded clothes was ready to be put into drawers.

Cause-Effect

Quiz-Quiz-Trade

Instructions: Copy enough cards so each student has one card. Cut on dotted lines and fold in half.

Cause-Effect

Question: Which is the cause? Which is the effect?

Cindy's earache continued to worsen.

Cindy made a doctor's appointment.

Cause-Effect

Answer

Cause: Cindy's earache continued to worsen.

Effect: Cindy made a doctor's appointment.

Cause-Effect

Question: Which is the cause? Which is the effect?

The wood was as smooth as a mirror.

Molly spent most of the day sanding the top of the new table she made.

Cause-Effect

Answer

Cause: Molly spent most of the day sanding the top of the new table she made.

Effect: The wood was as smooth as a mirror.

Cause-Effect

Question: Which is the cause? Which is the effect?

Corey practiced running on the track after school everyday for one month.

Corey was the winner of the race at the track meet yesterday.

Cause-Effect

Answer

Cause: Corey practiced running on the track after school everyday for one month.

Effect: Corey was the winner of the race at the track meet yesterday.

Cause-Effect

Question: Which is the cause? Which is the effect?

I ran out of paper.

The story, which I wrote for class, was much longer than I had planned.

Cause-Effect

Answer

Cause: The story, which I wrote for class, was much longer than I had planned.

Effect: I ran out of paper.

Cause-Effect

Question: Which is the cause? Which is the effect?

We finished all of our chores and jobs around the house without wasting time.

We had time to play a board game before bedtime.

Cause-Effect

Answer

Cause: We finished all of our chores and jobs around the house without wasting time.

Effect: We had time to play a board game before bedtime.

Cause-Effect
Quiz-Quiz-Trade

Instructions: Copy enough cards so each student has one card. Cut on dotted lines and fold in half.

Cause-Effect
Question: Which is the cause? Which is the effect?

Snow began to fall from the clouds.

The water drops froze.

Cause-Effect
Answer

Cause: The water drops froze.

Effect: Snow began to fall from the clouds.

Cause-Effect
Question: Which is the cause? Which is the effect?

The radishes began to push their way through the ground.

The sun shone down on the little garden we planted in the backyard.

Cause-Effect
Answer

Cause: The sun shone down on the little garden we planted in the backyard.

Effect: The radishes began to push their way through the ground.

Cause-Effect
Question: Which is the cause? Which is the effect?

Jim was a hermit, who lived on an island by himself.

Sometimes several years went by when Jim did not see another person.

Cause-Effect
Answer

Cause: Jim was a hermit, who lived on an island by himself.

Effect: Sometimes several years went by when Jim did not see another person.

Cause-Effect
Question: Which is the cause? Which is the effect?

The music hurt our ears when we turned on the stereo.

The baby played with the knobs on the stereo.

Cause-Effect
Answer

Cause: The baby played with the knobs to the stereo.

Effect: The music hurt our ears when we turned on the stereo.

Cause-Effect
Question: Which is the cause? Which is the effect?

A tsunami was formed.

There was an earthquake under the sea.

Cause-Effect
Answer

Cause: There was an earthquake under the sea.

Effect: A tsunami was formed.

Cause-Effect
Quiz-Quiz-Trade

Instructions: Copy enough cards so each student has one card. Cut on dotted lines and fold in half.

Cause-Effect
Question: Which is the cause? Which is the effect?

The message was found on a nearby island.

A message in a bottle was thrown overboard from a ship off Australia.

Cause-Effect
Answer

Cause: A message in a bottle was thrown overboard from a ship off Australia.

Effect: The message was found on a nearby island.

Cause-Effect
Question: Which is the cause? Which is the effect?

My arms and neck are red and sunburned.

It was sunny and warm outside yesterday, so I planted my vegetable garden.

Cause-Effect
Answer

Cause: It was sunny and warm outside yesterday, so I planted my vegetable garden.

Effect: My arms and neck are red and sunburned.

Cause-Effect
Question: Which is the cause? Which is the effect?

The new dam blocked the river.

Hydroelectric power was generated for the people living in the valley.

Cause-Effect
Answer

Cause: The new dam blocked the river.

Effect: Hydroelectric power was generated for the people living in the valley.

Cause-Effect
Question: Which is the cause? Which is the effect?

The instruments all played the first note at the same time.

The conductor signaled to the orchestra when to start the concerto.

Cause-Effect
Answer

Cause: The conductor signaled to the orchestra when to start the concerto.

Effect: The instruments all played the first note at the same time.

Cause-Effect
Question: Which is the cause? Which is the effect?

A person passing by heard an echo.

The sound waves bounced off the surface beneath the bridge.

Cause-Effect
Answer

Cause: The sound waves bounced off the surface beneath the bridge.

Effect: A person passing by heard an echo.

Balanced Literacy • Fourth Grade • Skidmore & Graber
Kagan Publishing • 1 (800) 933-2667 • www.KaganOnline.com

Cause-Effect
Quiz-Quiz-Trade

Instructions: Copy enough cards so each student has one card. Cut on dotted lines and fold in half.

Cause-Effect

Question: Which is the cause? Which is the effect?

The river overflowed its banks.

Rain poured from the sky for 24 hours.

Cause-Effect

Answer

Cause: Rain poured from the sky for 24 hours.

Effect: The river overflowed its banks.

Cause-Effect

Question: Which is the cause? Which is the effect?

In 1955, an African American woman named Rosa Parks refused to give up her bus seat to a white man.

Rosa Parks was arrested and put in jail.

Cause-Effect

Answer

Cause: In 1955, an African American woman named Rosa Parks refused to give up her bus seat to a white man.

Effect: Rosa Parks was arrested and put in jail.

Cause-Effect

Question: Which is the cause? Which is the effect?

Martin Luther King Jr. had a dream that all Americans should be treated equally.

As a child, Martin Luther King Jr. learned that there were laws that treated African Americans unfairly.

Cause-Effect

Answer

Cause: As a child, Martin Luther King Jr. learned that there were laws that treated African Americans unfairly.

Effect: Martin Luther King Jr. had a dream that all Americans should be treated equally.

Cause-Effect

Question: Which is the cause? Which is the effect?

A cloud of swirling gases hides the planet of Jupiter.

The actual surface of Jupiter cannot be seen.

Cause-Effect

Answer

Cause: A cloud of swirling gases hides the planet of Jupiter.

Effect: The actual surface of Jupiter cannot be seen.

Cause-Effect

Question: Which is the cause? Which is the effect?

Pocahontas begged her father to spare John Smith's life.

There was an old Indian custom that said a woman could save a prisoner's life.

Cause-Effect

Answer

Cause: There was an old Indian custom that said a woman could save a prisoner's life.

Effect: Pocahontas begged her father to spare John Smith's life.

Cause-Effect
Quiz-Quiz-Trade

Instructions: Copy enough cards so each student has one card. Cut on dotted lines and fold in half.

Cause-Effect
Question: Which is the cause? Which is the effect?

Jan took a different route to work this morning.

The street sign said, "Closed."

Cause-Effect
Answer

Cause: The street sign said, "Closed."

Effect: Jan took a different route to work this morning.

Cause-Effect
Question: Which is the cause? Which is the effect?

Jupiter is 483 million miles from the sun.

It takes Jupiter 12 years to complete an orbit around the sun.

Cause-Effect
Answer

Cause: Jupiter is 483 million miles from the sun.

Effect: It takes Jupiter 12 years to complete an orbit around the sun.

Cause-Effect
Question: Which is the cause? Which is the effect?

The cookies were burnt.

I didn't hear the oven timer go off.

Cause-Effect
Answer

Cause: I didn't hear the oven timer go off.

Effect: The cookies were burnt.

Cause-Effect
Question: Which is the cause? Which is the effect?

Jeff practiced free throws for 30 minutes every evening.

Jeff made seven out of eight free throws during the basketball game.

Cause-Effect
Answer

Cause: Jeff practiced free throws for 30 minutes every evening.

Effect: Jeff made seven out of eight free throws during the basketball game.

Cause-Effect
Question: Which is the cause? Which is the effect?

I couldn't finish typing my report on the computer.

Suddenly, the electricity went off.

Cause-Effect
Answer

Cause: Suddenly, the electricity went off.

Effect: I couldn't finish typing my report on the computer.

Text Features
Quiz-Quiz-Trade

Instructions: Copy enough cards so each student has one card. Cut on dotted lines and fold in half.

Text Features

Question: What text feature is this example?
- Tyrannosaurus
- Apatosuarus
- Stegosaurus
- Triceratops

Text Features

Answer

Bullets

Text Features

Question: What text feature is this example?

Animals that don't like meat are **herbivorous.**
↑

Text Features

Answer

Bolded Word

Text Features

Question: What text feature is this example?

Text Features

Answer

Map

Text Features

Question: What text feature is this example?

1700   1725   1750   1775

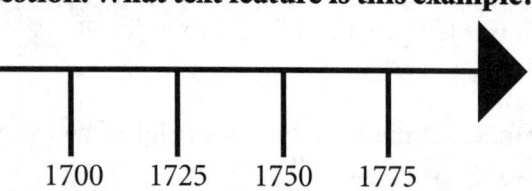

Text Features

Answer

Timeline

Text Features

Question: What text feature is this example?

Many rainforest plants are used to make drugs to fight disease and illness.

Text Features

Answer

Boxed Item

---

132 Balanced Literacy • Fourth Grade • Skidmore & Graber
Kagan Publishing • 1 (800) 933-2667 • www.KaganOnline.com

Text Features
Quiz-Quiz-Trade

Instructions: Copy enough cards so each student has one card. Cut on dotted lines and fold in half.

Text Features

Question: What text feature is this example?

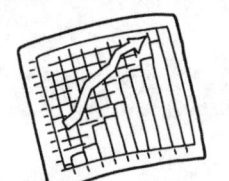

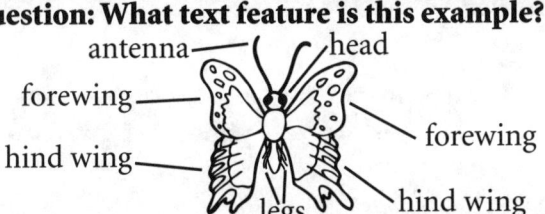

Books Read

	1st Grade	2nd Grade	3rd Grade	4th Grade
Feb.	153	95	83	56
Mar.	189	111	118	77

Text Features

Answer

Chart

Text Features

Question: What text feature is this example?

Text Features

Answer

Graph

Text Features

Question: What text feature is this example?

(butterfly labeled with: antenna, head, forewing, forewing, hind wing, hind wing, legs)

Text Features

Answer

Diagram

Text Features

Question: What text feature is this example?

water,   20, 80, 105
water clock,   17, 62
waterfalls,   10
water vapor,   51, 55, 60
waterwheels,   86

Text Features

Answer

Index

Text Features

Question: What text feature is this example?

This polar bear is walking on the snow without falling in because of his big, flat paws.

Text Features

Answer

Caption

Balanced Literacy • Fourth Grade • Skidmore & Graber
Kagan Publishing • 1 (800) 933-2667 • www.KaganOnline.com

Text Features
Quiz-Quiz-Trade

Instructions: Copy enough cards so each student has one card. Cut on dotted lines and fold in half.

Text Features

Question: What text feature is this example?

The fastest watercraft has underwater wings and is called a *hydrofoil*.
↑

Text Features

Answer

Italicized Word

Text Features

Question: What text feature is this example?

Fun Fact
There are approximately 20,000 different butterflies in the world.
←
Page 189

Text Features

Answer

Sidebar

Text Features

Question: What text feature is this example?

Text Features

Answer

Photograph

Text Features

Question: What text feature is this example?

The beam of light shining through a **prism** is broken up into the colors of a rainbow. ↑

Text Features

Answer

Bolded Word

Text Features

Question: What text feature is this example?

↓
Mt. Everest, the highest mountain in the world, is located in the Himalayas in Asia.

Text Features

Answer

Stylized Word

Text Features
Quiz-Quiz-Trade

Instructions: Copy enough cards so each student has one card. Cut on dotted lines and fold in half.

Text Features

Question: What text feature is this example?

Moving About	2
Protection	4
Food	7
Living Together	11

Text Features

Answer

Table of Contents

Text Features

Question: What text feature is this example?

Power from Steam

Text Features

Answer

Heading

Text Features

Question: What text feature is this example?

download—transferring data from another computer
Email—message sent from one computer to another via computer
login—connection to a computer system by giving a username and password

---

Text Features

Answer

Glossary

Text Features

Question: What text feature is this example?

petal, anther, filament, leaf, stem

Text Features

Answer

Labels

Text Features

Question: What text feature is this example?

Electricity ←

by Mary Hanes

Text Features

Answer

Title

Homophone Definitions
Quiz-Quiz-Trade

Instructions: Copy enough cards so each student has one card. Cut on dotted lines and fold in half.

Homophone Definitions

Question

peek

a) to glance quickly
b) the pointed summit of a mountain

Homophone Definitions

Answer

peek

a) to glance quickly

Homophone Definitions

Question

peak

a) to glance quickly
b) the pointed summit of a mountain

Homophone Definitions

Answer

peak

b) the pointed summit of a mountain

Homophone Definitions

Question

guest

a) predicted without information
b) a visitor

Homophone Definitions

Answer

guest

b) a visitor

Homophone Definitions

Question

guessed

a) predicted without information
b) a visitor

Homophone Definitions

Answer

guessed

a) predicted without information

Homophone Definitions
Quiz-Quiz-Trade

Instructions: Copy enough cards so each student has one card. Cut on dotted lines and fold in half.

Homophone Definitions

Question

war

a) a period of conflict or fighting
b) covered with clothing

Homophone Definitions

Answer

war

a) a period of conflict or fighting

Homophone Definitions

Question

wore

a) a period of conflict or fighting
b) covered with clothing

Homophone Definitions

Answer

wore

b) covered with clothing

Homophone Definitions

Question

chilly

a) cool enough to cause shivering
b) hot, spicy soup

Homophone Definitions

Answer

chilly

a) cool enough to cause shivering

Homophone Definitions

Question

chili

a) cool enough to cause shivering
b) hot, spicy soup

Homophone Definitions

Answer

chili

b) hot, spicy soup

# Homophone Definitions
Quiz-Quiz-Trade

Instructions: Copy enough cards so each student has one card. Cut on dotted lines and fold in half.

Homophone Definitions

Question

weave

a) a contraction for *we have*
b) to make cloth by interlacing threads

Homophone Definitions

Answer

weave

b) to make cloth by interlacing threads

Homophone Definitions

Question

we've

a) a contraction for *we have*
b) to make cloth by interlacing threads

Homophone Definitions

Answer

we've

a) a contraction for *we have*

Homophone Definitions

Question

sweet

a) having the taste of sugar
b) a series of connected rooms

Homophone Definitions

Answer

sweet

a) having the taste of sugar

Homophone Definitions

Question

suite

a) having the taste of sugar
b) a series of connected rooms

Homophone Definitions

Answer

suite

b) a series of connected rooms

Balanced Literacy • Fourth Grade • Skidmore & Graber
Kagan Publishing • 1 (800) 933-2667 • www.KaganOnline.com

Homophone Definitions
Quiz-Quiz-Trade

Instructions: Copy enough cards so each student has one card. Cut on dotted lines and fold in half.

Homophone Definitions
Question

principal

a) head of a school
b) basic truth

Homophone Definitions
Answer

principal

a) head of a school

Homophone Definitions
Question

principle

a) head of a school
b) basic truth

Homophone Definitions
Answer

principle

b) basic truth

Homophone Definitions
Question

quartz

a) a very hard mineral
b) liquid measure equal to four cups

Homophone Definitions
Answer

quartz

a) a very hard mineral

Homophone Definitions
Question

quarts

a) a very hard mineral
b) liquid measurement

Homophone Definitions
Answer

quarts

b) liquid measurement

COMPREHENSION Blackline

Homophone Definitions
Quiz-Quiz-Trade

Instructions: Copy enough cards so each student has one card. Cut on dotted lines and fold in half.

Homophone Definitions
Question

tide

a) change of the ocean's water level
b) fastened or secured

Homophone Definitions
Answer

tide

a) change of the ocean's water level

Homophone Definitions
Question

tied

a) change of the ocean's water level
b) fastened or secured

Homophone Definitions
Answer

tied

b) fastened or secured

Homophone Definitions
Question

seen

a) noticed with the eye
b) place where action occurs

Homophone Definitions
Answer

seen

a) noticed with the eye

Homophone Definitions
Question

scene

a) noticed with the eye
b) place where action occurs

Homophone Definitions
Answer

scene

b) place where action occurs

Balanced Literacy • Fourth Grade • Skidmore & Graber
Kagan Publishing • 1 (800) 933-2667 • www.KaganOnline.com

Homophone Definitions
Quiz-Quiz-Trade

Instructions: Copy enough cards so each student has one card. Cut on dotted lines and fold in half.

Homophone Definitions

Question

tax

a) money paid to the government
b) short nails with sharp points and flat heads

Homophone Definitions

Answer

tax

a) money paid to the government

Homophone Definitions

Question

tacks

a) money paid to the government
b) short nails with sharp points and flat heads

Homophone Definitions

Answer

tacks

b) short nails with sharp points and flat heads

Homophone Definitions

Question

overdo

a) unpaid when owed
b) to stress too far; to wear out

Homophone Definitions

Answer

overdo

b) to stress too far; to wear out

Homophone Definitions

Question

overdue

a) unpaid when owed
b) to stress too far; to wear out

Homophone Definitions

Answer

overdue

a) unpaid when owed

Homophone Definitions
Quiz-Quiz-Trade

Instructions: Copy enough cards so each student has one card. Cut on dotted lines and fold in half.

Homophone Definitions
Question

chord

a) combination of three or more notes
b) rope-like strands for tying or connecting

Homophone Definitions
Answer

chord

a) combination of three or more notes

Homophone Definitions
Question

cord

a) combination of three or more notes
b) rope-like strands for tying or connecting

Homophone Definitions
Answer

cord

b) rope-like strands for tying or connecting

Homophone Definitions
Question

doe

a) a female deer
b) soft, thick mixture used to make bread

Homophone Definitions
Answer

doe

a) a female deer

Homophone Definitions
Question

dough

a) a female deer
b) soft, thick mixture used to make bread

Homophone Definitions
Answer

dough

b) soft, thick mixture used to make bread

Figurative Language
Quiz-Quiz-Trade

Instructions: Copy enough cards so each student has one card. Cut on dotted lines and fold in half.

Figurative Language
Question

The snake hissed at the intruder.

This is an example of:
  a) alliteration
  b) onomatopoeia

Figurative Language
Answer

The snake hissed at the intruder.

b) onomatopoeia

Figurative Language
Question

We observed the lightning flash across the night sky.

This is an example of:
  a) alliteration
  b) onomatopoeia

Figurative Language
Answer

We observed the lightning flash across the night sky.

b) onomatopoeia

Figurative Language
Question

Six sad sailors sailed out to sea on Saturday.

This is an example of:
  a) alliteration
  b) onomatopoeia

Figurative Language
Answer

Six sad sailors sailed out to sea on Saturday.

a) alliteration

Figurative Language
Question

Ten tired turtles lounged on a log.

This is an example of:
  a) alliteration
  b) onomatopoeia

Figurative Language
Answer

Ten tired turtles lounged on a log.

a) alliteration

Figurative Language
Quiz-Quiz-Trade

Instructions: Copy enough cards so each student has one card. Cut on dotted lines and fold in half.

Figurative Language
Question

A sizzling fire crackled in the fireplace.

This is an example of:
 a) alliteration
 b) onomatopoeia

Figurative Language
Answer

A sizzling fire crackled in the fireplace.

b) onomatopoeia

Figurative Language
Question

Water slowly trickled from the gurgling hose.

This is an example of:
 a) alliteration
 b) onomatopoeia

Figurative Language
Answer

Water slowly trickled from the gurgling hose.

b) onomatopoeia

Figurative Language
Question

Gary grabbed a group of green grapes.

This is an example of:
 a) alliteration
 b) onomatopoeia

Figurative Language
Answer

Gary grabbed a group of green grapes.

a) alliteration

Figurative Language
Question

Eddie eluded eleven elderly elephants.

This is an example of:
 a) alliteration
 b) onomatopoeia

Figurative Language
Answer

Eddie eluded eleven elderly elephants.

a) alliteration

Figurative Language
Quiz-Quiz-Trade

Instructions: Copy enough cards so each student has one card. Cut on dotted lines and fold in half.

Figurative Language
Question

I have told you a million times to clean your room.

This is an example of:
 a) idiom
 b) hyperbole

Figurative Language
Answer

I have told you a million times to clean your room.

b) hyperbole

Figurative Language
Question

It was so cold even the polar bears were wearing jackets.

This is an example of:
 a) idiom
 b) hyperbole

Figurative Language
Answer

It was so cold even the polar bears were wearing jackets.

b) hyperbole

Figurative Language
Question

That cool glass of juice hit the spot.

This is an example of:
 a) idiom
 b) hyperbole

Figurative Language
Answer

That cool glass of juice hit the spot.

a) idiom

Figurative Language
Question

If Dad finds out, he'll hit the roof.

This is an example of:
 a) idiom
 b) hyperbole

Figurative Language
Answer

If Dad finds out, he'll hit the roof.

a) idiom

Balanced Literacy • Fourth Grade • Skidmore & Graber
Kagan Publishing • 1 (800) 933-2667 • www.KaganOnline.com

Figurative Language
Quiz-Quiz-Trade

Instructions: Copy enough cards so each student has one card. Cut on dotted lines and fold in half.

Figurative Language
Question

I'm so hungry, I could eat a horse.

This is an example of:
- a) idiom
- b) hyperbole

Figurative Language
Answer

I'm so hungry, I could eat a horse.

b) hyperbole

Figurative Language
Question

That music is so loud it can be heard across the ocean.

This is an example of:
- a) idiom
- b) hyperbole

Figurative Language
Answer

That music is so loud it can be heard across the ocean.

b) hyperbole

Figurative Language
Question

She was pulling my leg.

This is an example of:
- a) idiom
- b) hyperbole

Figurative Language
Answer

She was pulling my leg.

a) idiom

Figurative Language
Question

That assignment is a piece of cake.

This is an example of:
- a) idiom
- b) hyperbole

Figurative Language
Answer

That assignment is a piece of cake.

a) idiom

Figurative Language
Quiz-Quiz-Trade

Instructions: Copy enough cards so each student has one card. Cut on dotted lines and fold in half.

Figurative Language

Question

Books are a dream.

This is an example of:
 a) simile
 b) metaphor

Figurative Language

Answer

Books are a dream.

b) metaphor

Figurative Language

Question

My hands are cold ice.

This is an example of:
 a) simile
 b) metaphor

Figurative Language

Answer

My hands are cold ice.

b) metaphor

Figurative Language

Question

She ran like the wind.

This is an example of:
 a) simile
 b) metaphor

Figurative Language

Answer

She ran like the wind.

a) simile

Figurative Language

Question

The jewel twinkled like a star.

This is an example of:
 a) simile
 b) metaphor

Figurative Language

Answer

The jewel twinkled like a star.

a) simile

Figurative Language
Quiz-Quiz-Trade

Instructions: Copy enough cards so each student has one card. Cut on dotted lines and fold in half.

Figurative Language

Question

Her eyes were emeralds.

This is an example of:
  a) simile
  b) metaphor

Figurative Language

Answer

Her eyes were emeralds.

b) metaphor

Figurative Language

Question

The snow was a blanket covering the brown earth.

This is an example of:
  a) simile
  b) metaphor

Figurative Language

Answer

The snow was a blanket covering the brown earth.

b) metaphor

Figurative Language

Question

Dancing is like twirling on ice.

This is an example of:
  a) simile
  b) metaphor

Figurative Language

Answer

Dancing is like twirling on ice.

a) simile

Figurative Language

Question

Sue's been working like a dog.

This is an example of:
  a) simile
  b) metaphor

Figurative Language

Answer

Sue's been working like a dog.

a) simile

Homophone Sentences
Quiz-Quiz-Trade

Instructions: Copy enough cards so each student has one card. Cut on dotted lines and fold in half.

Homophone Sentences
Question
Do not _____ at the surprise.

a) peak
b) peek

Homophone Sentences
Answer
Do not **peek** at the surprise.

b) peek

Homophone Sentences
Question
The mountain climber reached the _____ after two days.

a) peak
b) peek

Homophone Sentences
Answer
The mountain climber reached the **peak** after two days.

a) peak

Homophone Sentences
Question
After collecting several clues, we _____ the mystery.

a) guessed
b) guest

Homophone Sentences
Answer
After collecting several clues, we **guessed** the mystery.

a) guessed

Homophone Sentences
Question
We entertained our _____ during lunch.

a) guessed
b) guest

Homophone Sentences
Answer
We entertained our **guest** during lunch.

b) guest

Homophone Sentences
Quiz-Quiz-Trade

Instructions: Copy enough cards so each student has one card. Cut on dotted lines and fold in half.

Homophone Sentences
Question

The countries worked out their differences before going to _____.

a) war
b) wore

Homophone Sentences
Answer

The countries worked out their differences before going to <u>war</u>.

a) war

Homophone Sentences
Question

Sally _____ her new shoes to school.

a) war
b) wore

Homophone Sentences
Answer

Sally <u>wore</u> her new shoes to school.

b) wore

Homophone Sentences
Question

We cooked a pot of _____ for the party.

a) chilly
b) chili

Homophone Sentences
Answer

We cooked a pot of <u>chili</u> for the party.

b) chili

Homophone Sentences
Question

The cold, blowing wind made us _____.

a) chilly
b) chili

Homophone Sentences
Answer

The cold, blowing wind made us <u>chilly</u>.

a) chilly

Homophone Sentences
Quiz-Quiz-Trade

Instructions: Copy enough cards so each student has one card. Cut on dotted lines and fold in half.

Homophone Sentences

Question

Yarn can be used to _____ a rug.

  a) we've
  b) weave

Homophone Sentences

Answer

Yarn can be used to <u>weave</u> a rug.

  b) weave

Homophone Sentences

Question

_____ read all the books on the shelf.

  a) We've
  b) Weave

Homophone Sentences

Answer

<u>We've</u> read all the books on the shelf.

  a) We've

Homophone Sentences

Question

John had _____ the lawn yesterday.

  a) mown
  b) moan

Homophone Sentences

Answer

John had <u>mown</u> the lawn yesterday.

  a) mown

Homophone Sentences

Question

Kate let out a _____ after running into the wall.

  a) mown
  b) moan

Homophone Sentences

Answer

Kate let out a <u>moan</u> after running into the wall.

  b) moan

Balanced Literacy • Fourth Grade • Skidmore & Graber
Kagan Publishing • 1 (800) 933-2667 • www.KaganOnline.com

Homophone Sentences
Quiz-Quiz-Trade

Instructions: Copy enough cards so each student has one card. Cut on dotted lines and fold in half.

Homophone Sentences

Question

The forecast predicted a change in the _____.

a) whether
b) weather

Homophone Sentences

Answer

The forecast predicted a change in the <u>weather</u>.

b) weather

Homophone Sentences

Question

Our decision depends on _____ it rains or snows.

a) whether
b) weather

Homophone Sentences

Answer

Our decision depends on <u>whether</u> it rains or snows.

a) whether

Homophone Sentences

Question

How many _____ will you be on vacation?

a) daze
b) days

Homophone Sentences

Answer

How many <u>days</u> will you be on vacation?

b) days

Homophone Sentences

Question

After falling down the hill, Marty was in a _____.

a) daze
b) days

Homophone Sentences

Answer

After falling down the hill, Marty was in a <u>daze</u>.

a) daze

Homophone Sentences

Quiz-Quiz-Trade

Instructions: Copy enough cards so each student has one card. Cut on dotted lines and fold in half.

Homophone Sentences
Question

The freshly baked cookies tasted _____.

a) sweet
b) suite

Homophone Sentences
Answer

The freshly baked cookies tasted <u>sweet</u>.

a) sweet

Homophone Sentences
Question

We will stay in the luxury _____ at the hotel.

a) sweet
b) suite

Homophone Sentences
Answer

We will stay in the luxury <u>suite</u> at the hotel.

b) suite

Homophone Sentences
Question

The _____ welcomed the students to their first day of school.

a) principal
b) principle

Homophone Sentences
Answer

The <u>principal</u> welcomed the students to their first day of school.

a) principal

Homophone Sentences
Question

James based his decision on the _____ stated in the company's handbook.

a) principal
b) principle

Homophone Sentences
Answer

James based his decision on the <u>principle</u> stated in the company's handbook.

b) principle

Balanced Literacy • Fourth Grade • Skidmore & Graber
Kagan Publishing • 1 (800) 933-2667 • www.KaganOnline.com

Homophone Sentences
Quiz-Quiz-Trade

Instructions: Copy enough cards so each student has one card. Cut on dotted lines and fold in half.

Homophone Sentences

Question

We paid a ____ when we purchased our new car.

a) tax
b) tacks

Homophone Sentences

Answer

We paid a <u>tax</u> when we purchased our new car.

a) tax

Homophone Sentences

Question

Four _____ were needed to hold the poster on the wall.

a) tax
b) tacks

Homophone Sentences

Answer

Four <u>tacks</u> were needed to hold the poster on the wall.

b) tacks

Homophone Sentences

Question

While we were swimming at the ocean, the _____ became strong.

a) tide
b) tied

Homophone Sentences

Answer

While we were swimming at the ocean, the <u>tide</u> became strong.

a) tide

Homophone Sentences

Question

A heavy cord was _____ around the package.

a) tide
b) tied

Homophone Sentences

Answer

A heavy cord was <u>tied</u> around the package.

b) tied

Homophone Sentences
Quiz-Quiz-Trade

Instructions: Copy enough cards so each student has one card. Cut on dotted lines and fold in half.

Homophone Sentences
Question

The miners dug _____ from the rock quarry.

a) quartz
b) quarts

Homophone Sentences
Answer

The miners dug <u>quartz</u> from the rock quarry.

a) quartz

Homophone Sentences
Question

The recipe called for two _____ of boiling water.

a) quartz
b) quarts

Homophone Sentences
Answer

The recipe called for two <u>quarts</u> of boiling water.

b) quarts

Homophone Sentences
Question

_____ going to find a special surprise in this box.

a) Your
b) You're

Homophone Sentences
Answer

<u>You're</u> going to find a special surprise in this box.

b) You're

Homophone Sentences
Question

_____ sister is waiting to talk to you on the telephone.

a) Your
b) You're

Homophone Sentences
Answer

<u>Your</u> sister is waiting to talk to you on the telephone.

a) Your

Homophone Sentences
Quiz-Quiz-Trade

Instructions: Copy enough cards so each student has one card. Cut on dotted lines and fold in half.

Homophone Sentences
Question

The evidence placed him at the ___ of the crime.

a) seen
b) scene

Homophone Sentences
Answer

The evidence placed him at the <u>scene</u> of the crime.

b) scene

Homophone Sentences
Question

Kerry was _____ leaving the store at noon.

a) seen
b) scene

Homophone Sentences
Answer

Kerry was <u>seen</u> leaving the store at noon.

a) seen

Homophone Sentences
Question

_____ book is on the table by the door?

a) Whose
b) Who's

Homophone Sentences
Answer

<u>Whose</u> book is on the table by the door?

a) Whose

Homophone Sentences
Question

_____ leaving on the train in the morning?

a) Whose
b) Who's

Homophone Sentences
Answer

<u>Who's</u> leaving on the train in the morning?

b) Who's

Word Meanings
Quiz-Quiz-Trade

Instructions: Copy enough cards so each student has one card. Cut on dotted lines and fold in half.

Word Meanings
Question

Choose the sentence in which the underlined word has the same meaning as in the original sentence.

Wear your warm **coat** in the winter.

1. We will paint the chair with a **coat** of white paint.
2. John left his **coat** on the hook in the hallway.

Word Meanings
Answer

Wear your warm **coat** in the winter.

2. John left his **coat** on the hook in the hallway.

Word Meanings
Question

Choose the sentence in which the underlined word has the same meaning as in the original sentence.

That cat is my **pet**.

1. I like to **pet** my dog.
2. Jake has a **pet** hamster.

Word Meanings
Answer

That cat is my **pet**.

2. Jake has a **pet** hamster.

Word Meanings
Question

Choose the sentence in which the underlined word has the same meaning as in the original sentence.

The floor tile was one **foot** long.

1. A ruler is one **foot** in length.
2. I have a sore on my **foot**.

Word Meanings
Answer

The floor tile was one **foot** long.

1. A ruler is one **foot** in length.

Word Meanings
Question

Choose the sentence in which the underlined word has the same meaning as in the original sentence.

My cat had a **litter** of kittens.

1. Kim's dog had a **litter** of five puppies.
2. We picked up **litter** beside the street.

Word Meanings
Answer

My cat had a **litter** of kittens.

1. Kim's dog had a **litter** of five puppies.

Word Meanings
Quiz-Quiz-Trade

Instructions: Copy enough cards so each student has one card. Cut on dotted lines and fold in half.

Word Meanings
Question

Choose the sentence in which the underlined word has the same meaning as in the original sentence.

The trees lose their leaves in the **fall**.

1. In the **fall** the weather is cooler.
2. Pick up the toys, so no one will **fall** over them.

Word Meanings
Answer

The trees lose their leaves in the **fall**.

1. In the **fall** the weather is cooler.

Word Meanings
Question

Choose the sentence in which the underlined word has the same meaning as in the original sentence.

The children will **dress** for school.

1. Peg wore her new **dress**.
2. Please **dress** for cold weather.

Word Meanings
Answer

The children will **dress** for school.

2. Please **dress** for cold weather.

Word Meanings
Question

Choose the sentence in which the underlined word has the same meaning as in the original sentence.

My dad read a **story** to me.

1. Beth lives in a two-**story** house.
2. I wrote a **story** about my trip.

Word Meanings
Answer

My dad read a **story** to me.

2. I wrote a **story** about my trip.

Word Meanings
Question

Choose the sentence in which the underlined word has the same meaning as in the original sentence.

Fred has a different **kind** of pencil.

1. Opening the door for Ted was very **kind** of you.
2. What **kind** of animal is that?

Word Meanings
Answer

Fred has a different **kind** of pencil.

2. What **kind** of animal is that?

Word Meanings
Quiz-Quiz-Trade

Instructions: Copy enough cards so each student has one card. Cut on dotted lines and fold in half.

Word Meanings
Question

Choose the sentence in which the underlined word has the same meaning as in the original sentence.

My dog will **bark** if a stranger arrives.

1. Dip the pretzel in almond **bark**.
2. Cats don't **bark**.

Word Meanings
Answer

My dog will **bark** if a stranger arrives.

2. Cats don't **bark**.

Word Meanings
Question

Choose the sentence in which the underlined word has the same meaning as in the original sentence.

We planned a **trip** for the summer.

1. Be careful not to **trip** over the curb.
2. Our **trip** to Florida lasted one week.

Word Meanings
Answer

We planned a **trip** for the summer.

2. Our **trip** to Florida lasted one week.

Word Meanings
Question

Choose the sentence that the underlined word has the same meaning as in the original sentence.

Our house is two **stories** tall.

1. Kris read several funny **stories**.
2. The elevator took us up five **stories** to the top of the building.

Word Meanings
Answer

Our house is two **stories** tall.

2. The elevator took us up five **stories** to the top of the building.

Word Meanings
Question

Choose the sentence that the underlined word has the same meaning as in the original sentence.

The **mouse** emerged from his tiny hole in the wall.

1. We caught a **mouse** in the trap.
2. The **mouse** was connected to the computer.

Word Meanings
Answer

The **mouse** emerged from his tiny hole in the wall.

1. We caught a **mouse** in the trap.

Word Meanings
Quiz-Quiz-Trade

Instructions: Copy enough cards so each student has one card. Cut on dotted lines and fold in half.

Word Meanings
Question

Choose the sentence in which the underlined word has the same meaning as in the original sentence.

The house felt **cool** in the morning.

1. A chilly breeze made the air **cool**.
2. He remained **cool** during the heated discussion.

Word Meanings
Answer

The house felt **cool** in the morning.

1. A chilly breeze made the air **cool**.

Word Meanings
Question

Choose the sentence in which the underlined word has the same meaning as in the original sentence.

Lick your ice-cream cone before it melts.

1. Pete used his tongue to **lick** the lollipop.
2. He did not get a **lick** of work done over the weekend.

Word Meanings
Answer

Lick your ice-cream cone before it melts.

1. Pete used his tongue to **lick** the lollipop.

Word Meanings
Question

Choose the sentence in which the underlined word has the same meaning as in the original sentence.

We had a **general** idea of where to look for the lost kitten.

1. The article reported **general** information.
2. The **general** ordered his troops to retreat.

Word Meanings
Answer

We had a **general** idea of where to look for the lost kitten.

1. The article reported **general** information.

Word Meanings
Question

Choose the sentence in which the underlined word has the same meaning as in the original sentence.

The ship was so heavy it started to **sink**.

1. Wash your hands in the **sink**.
2. The penny will **sink** to the bottom of the wishing well.

Word Meanings
Answer

The ship was so heavy it started to **sink**.

2. The penny will **sink** to the bottom of the wishing well.

Word Meanings

Quiz-Quiz-Trade

Instructions: Copy enough cards so each student has one card. Cut on dotted lines and fold in half.

Word Meanings
Question

Choose the sentence in which the underlined word has the same meaning as in the original sentence.

They will **ship** the package overnight.

1. The cruise **ship** sailed into the harbor.
2. It took two weeks to **ship** our order.

Word Meanings
Answer

They will **ship** the package overnight.

2. It took two weeks to **ship** our order.

Word Meanings
Question

Choose the sentence in which the underlined word has the same meaning as in the original sentence.

The **saw** was used to cut down the dead tree.

1. We **saw** a forest of trees on vacation.
2. The **saw** needed to be sharpened before it could be used.

Word Meanings
Answer

The **saw** was used to cut down the dead tree.

2. The **saw** needed to be sharpened before it could be used.

Word Meanings
Question

Choose the sentence in which the underlined word has the same meaning as in the original sentence.

Remember not to **skip** a step in the directions.

1. I like to **skip** down the sidewalk.
2. Alex tried not to **skip** any of the questions on the test.

Word Meanings
Answer

Remember not to **skip** a step in the directions.

2. Alex tried not to **skip** any of the questions on the test.

Word Meanings
Question

Choose the sentence in which the underlined word has the same meaning as in the original sentence.

Will you **show** me how to bake a cake?

1. I want to **show** you my new game.
2. I went to the **show** with my friend.

Word Meanings
Answer

Will you **show** me how to bake a cake?

1. I want to **show** you my new game.

Word Meanings
Quiz-Quiz-Trade

Instructions: Copy enough cards so each student has one card. Cut on dotted lines and fold in half.

Word Meanings
Question

Choose the sentence in which the underlined word has the same meaning as in the original sentence.

The baby shook his **rattle**.

1. The crowd's cheering may **rattle** her before her speech.
2. The noise created by the **rattle** woke the sleeping child.

Word Meanings
Answer

The baby shook his **rattle**.

2. **The noise created by the rattle woke the sleeping child.**

Word Meanings
Question

Choose the sentence in which the underlined word has the same meaning as in the original sentence.

The goat may **upset** the basket of vegetables.

1. Do not **upset** the cart of leaves.
2. Mom was **upset** because the chores were not completed.

Word Meanings
Answer

The goat may **upset** the basket of vegetables.

1. **Do not upset the cart of leaves.**

Word Meanings
Question

Choose the sentence in which the underlined word has the same meaning as in the original sentence.

If you **rock** the canoe, it may tip.

1. We discovered a rare **rock** on our hike.
2. **Rock** the hammock gently.

Word Meanings
Answer

If you **rock** the canoe, it may tip.

2. **Rock the hammock gently.**

Word Meanings
Question

Choose the sentence in which the underlined word has the same meaning as in the original sentence.

I will **meet** you after school.

1. Let's talk about our plan when we **meet** next week.
2. The next track **meet** will be in two weeks.

Word Meanings
Answer

I will **meet** you after school.

1. **Let's talk about our plan when we meet next week.**

Word Meanings
Quiz-Quiz-Trade

Instructions: Copy enough cards so each student has one card. Cut on dotted lines and fold in half.

Word Meanings
Question

Choose the sentence in which the underlined word has the same meaning as in the original sentence.

The guard's job was to **block** the opponent.

1. Stack the last **block** on the top of the tower.
2. The barricade will **block** traffic.

Word Meanings
Answer

The guard's job was to **block** the opponent.

2. The barricade will **block** traffic.

Word Meanings
Question

Choose the sentence in which the underlined word has the same meaning as in the original sentence.

We needed a large **bolt** to secure the gate.

1. The **bolt** fell from the cart and was lost in the dirt.
2. Thunder may cause the horse to **bolt**.

Word Meanings
Answer

We needed a large **bolt** to secure the gate.

1. The **bolt** fell from the cart and was lost in the dirt.

Word Meanings
Question

Choose the sentence in which the underlined word has the same meaning as in the original sentence.

Tempers may **flare** during the argument.

1. The survivors sent off a bright **flare** into the sky.
2. Sometimes her emotions appear to **flare** for no apparent reason.

Word Meanings
Answer

Tempers may **flare** during the argument.

2. Sometimes her emotions appear to **flare** for no apparent reason.

Word Meanings
Question

Choose the sentence in which the underlined word has the same meaning as in the original sentence.

The farmer planted a new **crop** of corn.

1. We enjoyed an abundant **crop** of green beans this summer.
2. **Crop** the photograph before you print it.

Word Meanings
Answer

The farmer planted a new **crop** of corn.

1. We enjoyed an abundant **crop** of green beans this summer.

Possessive Nouns
Quiz-Quiz-Trade

Instructions: Copy enough cards so each student has one card. Cut on dotted lines and fold in half.

Possessive Nouns

Question: Which possessive noun completes the sentence?

The _____ face was covered with cereal.

a) baby's
b) babies'

Possessive Nouns

Answer

The <u>baby's</u> face was covered with cereal.

a) baby's

Possessive Nouns

Question: Which possessive noun completes the sentence?

We searched in the trees for the _____ nests.

a) bird's
b) birds'

Possessive Nouns

Answer

We searched in the trees for the <u>birds'</u> nests.

b) birds'

Possessive Nouns

Question: Which possessive noun completes the sentence?

The blue suitcase was _____.

a) Sandys'
b) Sandy's

Possessive Nouns

Answer

The blue suitcase was <u>Sandy's</u>.

b) Sandy's

Possessive Nouns

Question: Which possessive noun completes the sentence?

The only luggage that was lost was the _____.

a) managers'
b) manager's

Possessive Nouns

Answer

The only luggage that was lost was the <u>manager's</u>.

b) manager's

Possessive Nouns
Quiz-Quiz-Trade

Instructions: Copy enough cards so each student has one card. Cut on dotted lines and fold in half.

Possessive Nouns

Question: Which possessive noun completes the sentence?

The _____ boots were lined up in the entry.

a) children's
b) childrens'

Possessive Nouns

Answer

The <u>children's</u> boots were lined up in the entry.

a) children's

Possessive Nouns

Question: Which possessive noun completes the sentence?

One _____ room was filled with cleaning supplies.

a) custodian's
b) custodians'

Possessive Nouns

Answer

One <u>custodian's</u> room was filled with cleaning supplies.

a) custodian's

Possessive Nouns

Question: Which possessive noun completes the sentence?

The _____ noses twitched when the dog ran past.

a) rabbit's
b) rabbits'

Possessive Nouns

Answer

The <u>rabbits'</u> noses twitched when the dog ran past

b) rabbits'

Possessive Nouns

Question: Which possessive noun completes the sentence?

The _____ necks reached to the bottom of the pond.

a) duck's
b) ducks'

Possessive Nouns

Answer

The <u>ducks'</u> necks reached to the bottom of the pond.

b) ducks'

Possessive Nouns
Quiz-Quiz-Trade

Instructions: Copy enough cards so each student has one card. Cut on dotted lines and fold in half.

Possessive Nouns

Question: Which possessive noun completes the sentence?

The _____ soccer team won the championship game.

a) womens'
b) women's

Possessive Nouns

Answer

The <u>women's</u> soccer team won the championship game.

b) women's

Possessive Nouns

Question: Which possessive noun completes the sentence?

The _____ classrooms were filled with shelves of books.

a) teachers'
b) teacher's

Possessive Nouns

Answer

The <u>teachers'</u> classrooms were filled with shelves of books.

a) teachers'

Possessive Nouns

Question: Which possessive noun completes the sentence?

The _____ floor was slippery after the water spilled.

a) room's
b) rooms'

Possessive Nouns

Answer

The <u>room's</u> floor was slippery after the water spilled.

a) room's

Possessive Nouns

Question: Which possessive noun completes the sentence?

The _____ lily pad floated on the clear water.

a) frog's
b) frogs'

Possessive Nouns

Answer

The <u>frog's</u> lily pad floated on the clear water.

a) frog's

Possessive Nouns
Quiz-Quiz-Trade

Instructions: Copy enough cards so each student has one card. Cut on dotted lines and fold in half.

Possessive Nouns

Question: Which possessive noun completes the sentence?

The alarm _____ buzzers went off at the same time.

   a) clocks'
   b) clock's

Possessive Nouns

Answer

The alarm <u>clocks'</u> buzzers went off at the same time.

   a) clocks'

Possessive Nouns

Question: Which possessive noun completes the sentence?

All the _____ lawns needed mowing.

   a) neighbors'
   b) neighbor's

Possessive Nouns

Answer

All the <u>neighbors'</u> lawns needed mowing.

   a) neighbors'

Possessive Nouns

Question: Which possessive noun completes the sentence?

My pet _____ fur is long and silky.

   a) cats'
   b) cat's

Possessive Nouns

Answer

My pet <u>cat's</u> fur is long and silky.

   b) cat's

Possessive Nouns

Question: Which possessive noun completes the sentence?

The _____ uniforms were black and red.

   a) player's
   b) players'

Possessive Nouns

Answer

The <u>players'</u> uniforms were black and red.

   b) players'

Possessive Nouns
Quiz-Quiz-Trade

Instructions: Copy enough cards so each student has one card. Cut on dotted lines and fold in half.

Possessive Nouns

Question: Which possessive noun completes the sentence?

_____ tail wags when we come home from school.

a) Spots'
b) Spot's

Possessive Nouns

Answer

Spot's tail wags when we come home from school.

b) Spot's

Possessive Nouns

Question: Which possessive noun completes the sentence?

_____ flames brightened the room.

a) Candles'
b) Candle's

Possessive Nouns

Answer

Candles' flames brightened the room.

a) Candles'

Possessive Nouns

Question: Which possessive noun completes the sentence?

One _____ leaves wilted and turned brown without water.

a) plant's
b) plants'

Possessive Nouns

Answer

One plant's leaves wilted and turned brown without water.

a) plant's

Possessive Nouns

Question: Which possessive noun completes the sentence?

One _____ toy was missing.

a) childs'
b) child's

Possessive Nouns

Answer

One child's toy was missing.

b) child's

Possessive Nouns
Quiz-Quiz-Trade

Instructions: Copy enough cards so each student has one card. Cut on dotted lines and fold in half.

Possessive Nouns

Question: Which possessive noun completes the sentence?

_____ hives were full of sweet, sticky honey.

a) Honeybee's
b) Honeybees'

Possessive Nouns

Answer

Honeybees' hives were full of sweet, sticky honey.

b) Honeybees'

Possessive Nouns

Question: Which possessive noun completes the sentence?

_____ manes blew in the breeze as they galloped.

a) Horses'
b) Horse's

Possessive Nouns

Answer

Horses' manes blew in the breeze as they galloped.

a) Horses'

Possessive Nouns

Question: Which possessive noun completes the sentence?

The _____ trunk swayed from side to side.

a) elephant's
b) elephants'

Possessive Nouns

Answer

The elephant's trunk swayed from side to side.

a) elephant's

Possessive Nouns

Question: Which possessive noun completes the sentence?

The blanket covered the _____ shivering shoulders.

a) mans'
b) man's

Possessive Nouns

Answer

The blanket covered the man's shivering shoulders.

b) man's

Possessive Nouns
Quiz-Quiz-Trade

Instructions: Copy enough cards so each student has one card. Cut on dotted lines and fold in half.

Possessive Nouns

Question: Which possessive noun completes the sentence?

Potted plants lined the _____ sidewalk.

a) street's
b) streets'

Possessive Nouns

Answer

Potted plants lined the **street's** sidewalk.

a) street's

Possessive Nouns

Question: Which possessive noun completes the sentence?

Many _____ parents attended the band concert.

a) student's
b) students'

Possessive Nouns

Answer

Many **students'** parents attended the band concert.

b) students'

Possessive Nouns

Question: Which possessive noun completes the sentence?

The _____ waves crashed against the rocks.

a) ocean's
b) oceans'

Possessive Nouns

Answer

The **ocean's** waves crashed against the rocks.

a) ocean's

Possessive Nouns

Question: Which possessive noun completes the sentence?

_____ attention was held by the unfamiliar song.

a) Peoples'
b) People's

Possessive Nouns

Answer

People's attention was held by the unfamiliar song.

b) People's

Present-Past Tense Verbs
Quiz-Quiz-Trade

Instructions: Copy enough cards so each student has one card. Cut on dotted lines and fold in half.

Present-Past Tense Verbs

Question: Complete the sentence with the past tense of *wear*.

They all _____ matching shirts yesterday.

Present-Past Tense Verbs

Answer

wore

They all <u>wore</u> matching shirts yesterday.

Present-Past Tense Verbs

Question: Complete the sentence with the past tense of *sleep*.

The boy _____ in the tent last night.

Present-Past Tense Verbs

Answer

slept

The boy <u>slept</u> in the tent last night.

Present-Past Tense Verbs

Question: Complete the sentence with the past tense of *feed*.

John _____ his pets before school.

Present-Past Tense Verbs

Answer

fed

John <u>fed</u> his pets before school.

Present-Past Tense Verbs

Question: Complete the sentence with the past tense of *wake*.

The alarm clock _____ me at six o'clock this morning.

Present-Past Tense Verbs

Answer

woke

The alarm clock <u>woke</u> me at six o'clock this morning.

Balanced Literacy • Fourth Grade • Skidmore & Graber
Kagan Publishing • 1 (800) 933-2667 • www.KaganOnline.com

Present-Past Tense Verbs
Quiz-Quiz-Trade

Instructions: Copy enough cards so each student has one card. Cut on dotted lines and fold in half.

Present-Past Tense Verbs

Question: Complete the sentence with the past tense of *weave*.

The girl _____ a colorful rug with the yarn.

Present-Past Tense Verbs

Answer

wove

The girl <u>wove</u> a colorful rug with the yarn.

Present-Past Tense Verbs

Question: Complete the sentence with the past tense of *wind*.

Kurt _____ the string around the yoyo.

Present-Past Tense Verbs

Answer

wound

Kurt <u>wound</u> the string around the yoyo.

Present-Past Tense Verbs

Question: Complete the sentence with the past tense of *take*.

We _____ the short way home after school.

Present-Past Tense Verbs

Answer

took

We <u>took</u> the short way home after school.

Present-Past Tense Verbs

Question: Complete the sentence with the past tense of *feel*.

After running two miles Maggie _____ exhausted.

Present-Past Tense Verbs

Answer

felt

After running two miles Maggie <u>felt</u> exhausted.

Present-Past Tense Verbs
Quiz-Quiz-Trade

Instructions: Copy enough cards so each student has one card. Cut on dotted lines and fold in half.

Present-Past Tense Verbs

Question: Complete the sentence with the past tense of *throw*.

The pitcher _____ the baseball to first base.

Present-Past Tense Verbs

Answer

threw

The pitcher <u>threw</u> the baseball to first base.

Present-Past Tense Verbs

Question: Complete the sentence with the past tense of *ride*.

The cowgirl _____ the horse in the parade.

Present-Past Tense Verbs

Answer

rode

The cowgirl <u>rode</u> the horse in the parade.

Present-Past Tense Verbs

Question: Complete the sentence with the past tense of *tear*.

Chad _____ the page from the notebook.

Present-Past Tense Verbs

Answer

tore

Chad <u>tore</u> the page from the notebook.

Present-Past Tense Verbs

Question: Complete the sentence with the past tense of *leave*.

When the meeting was over, we _____ the room.

Present-Past Tense Verbs

Answer

left

When the meeting was over, we <u>left</u> the room.

Balanced Literacy • Fourth Grade • Skidmore & Graber
Kagan Publishing • 1 (800) 933-2667 • www.KaganOnline.com

Present-Past Tense Verbs
Quiz-Quiz-Trade

Instructions: Copy enough cards so each student has one card. Cut on dotted lines and fold in half.

Present-Past Tense Verbs

Question: Complete the sentence with the past tense of *go*.

Chuck and Bill _____ to the ballgame at the park.

Present-Past Tense Verbs

Answer

went

Chuck and Bill <u>went</u> to the ballgame at the park.

Present-Past Tense Verbs

Question: Complete the sentence with the past tense of *eat*.

The children _____ lunch in the cafeteria.

Present-Past Tense Verbs

Answer

ate

The children <u>ate</u> lunch in the cafeteria.

Present-Past Tense Verbs

Question: Complete the sentence with the past tense of *bite*.

We _____ into the juicy burger.

Present-Past Tense Verbs

Answer

bit

We <u>bit</u> into the juicy burger.

Present-Past Tense Verbs

Question: Complete the sentence with the past tense of *drink*.

After our long hike, we _____ a glass of cool, refreshing water.

Present-Past Tense Verbs

Answer

drank

After our long hike, we <u>drank</u> a glass of cool, refreshing water.

Present-Past Tense Verbs
Quiz-Quiz-Trade

Instructions: Copy enough cards so each student has one card. Cut on dotted lines and fold in half.

Present-Past Tense Verbs

Question: Complete the sentence with the past tense of *catch*.

They _____ a butterfly in the net.

Present-Past Tense Verbs

Answer

caught

They <u>caught</u> a butterfly in the net.

Present-Past Tense Verbs

Question: Complete the sentence with the past tense of *build*.

The carpenters _____ a new house for my family.

Present-Past Tense Verbs

Answer

built

The carpenters <u>built</u> a new house for my family.

Present-Past Tense Verbs

Question: Complete the sentence with the past tense of *meet*.

We _____ by the swings at recess.

Present-Past Tense Verbs

Answer

met

We <u>met</u> by the swings at recess.

Present-Past Tense Verbs

Question: Complete the sentence with the past tense of *see*.

The mountains we _____ on vacation were snow-covered.

Present-Past Tense Verbs

Answer

saw

The mountains we <u>saw</u> on vacation were snow-covered.

Balanced Literacy • Fourth Grade • Skidmore & Graber
Kagan Publishing • 1 (800) 933-2667 • www.KaganOnline.com

Present-Past Tense Verbs
Quiz-Quiz-Trade

Instructions: Copy enough cards so each student has one card. Cut on dotted lines and fold in half.

Present-Past Tense Verbs

Question: Complete the sentence with the past tense of *bring*.

Sid _____ me a sample of his famous cake.

Present-Past Tense Verbs

Answer

brought

Sid brought me a sample of his famous cake.

Present-Past Tense Verbs

Question: Complete the sentence with the past tense of *cling*.

The baby monkey _____ to his mother while she climbed the tree.

Present-Past Tense Verbs

Answer

clung

The baby monkey clung to his mother while she climbed the tree.

Present-Past Tense Verbs

Question: Complete the sentence with the past tense of *fly*.

A flock of ten birds _____ over the playground.

Present-Past Tense Verbs

Answer

flew

A flock of ten birds flew over the playground.

Present-Past Tense Verbs

Question: Complete the sentence with the past tense of *shine*.

The sun _____ down on the children splashing in the pond.

Present-Past Tense Verbs

Answer

shone

The sun shone down on the children splashing in the pond.

Present-Past Tense Verbs
Quiz-Quiz-Trade

Instructions: Copy enough cards so each student has one card. Cut on dotted lines and fold in half.

Present-Past Tense Verbs

Question: Complete the sentence with the past tense of *spin*.

A garden spider _____ a web between the plants.

Present-Past Tense Verbs

Answer

spun

A garden spider spun a web between the plants.

Present-Past Tense Verbs

Question: Complete the sentence with the past tense of *fling*.

Greg _____ the basketball toward the goal.

Present-Past Tense Verbs

Answer

flung

Greg flung the basketball toward the goal.

Present-Past Tense Verbs

Question: Complete the sentence with the past tense of *weep*.

The movie was so sad that we _____ all the way through it.

Present-Past Tense Verbs

Answer

wept

The movie was so sad that we wept all the way through it.

Present-Past Tense Verbs

Question: Complete the sentence with the past tense of *teach*.

Grandma _____ us how to make gingerbread cookies.

Present-Past Tense Verbs

Answer

taught

Grandma taught us how to make gingerbread cookies.

Present-Past Tense Verbs
Quiz-Quiz-Trade

Instructions: Copy enough cards so each student has one card. Cut on dotted lines and fold in half.

Present-Past Tense Verbs

Question: Complete the sentence with the past tense of *swim*.

Paul _____ five laps in the pool before lunch.

Present-Past Tense Verbs

Answer

swam

Paul <u>swam</u> five laps in the pool before lunch.

Present-Past Tense Verbs

Question: Complete the sentence with the past tense of *write*.

Tammy _____ two letters to her mom and dad yesterday.

Present-Past Tense Verbs

Answer

wrote

Tammy <u>wrote</u> two letters to her mom and dad yesterday.

Present-Past Tense Verbs

Question: Complete the sentence with the past tense of *draw*.

The picture you _____ for the art show was very creative.

Present-Past Tense Verbs

Answer

drew

The picture you <u>drew</u> for the art show was very creative.

Present-Past Tense Verbs

Question: Complete the sentence with the past tense of *buy*.

Friday we _____ food for the neighborhood party.

Present-Past Tense Verbs

Answer

bought

Friday we <u>bought</u> food for the neighborhood party.

NUMBERED HEADS TOGETHER

Activity

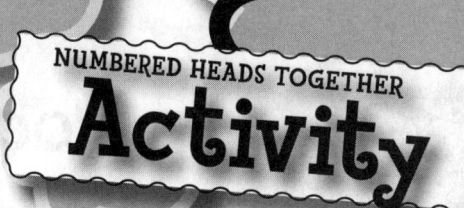

Which Definition?

After individually choosing a definition, teammates put their "heads together" to ensure all members can answer. The teacher then calls a number and students with that number share their answers simultaneously.

Activity Steps

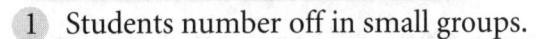

1. Students number off in small groups.
2. Students read the paragraph together from the overhead screen. *(Display the paragraph during the entire activity.)*
3. The teacher places one word with definition choices on the overhead screen and gives Think Time.
4. Students privately write the letter of the word definition corresponding to the word's use in the paragraph.
5. The teacher says, "Heads Together!" and students lift up from their chairs to put their heads together, show their answers, and discuss until they can come up with one definition for the word. Everyone sits down when they agree. Clear boards.
6. The teacher calls out a number. All students with that number write the letter of the agreed definition.
7. The students with the called number hold up their boards and orally call out the answer simultaneously.
8. The teacher leads the class in a discussion.
9. Teammates celebrate or correct answers on boards.
10. Repeat for a new vocabulary word.

STRUCTURE
Numbered Heads Together

Blacklines

- Vocabulary Definitions..180–181

Vocabulary Definitions
Numbered Heads Together

Instructions: Display the following text on an overhead screen. Read through it together. Individuals—and then teams—will determine the meaning of each of the underlined words (one at a time), as the corresponding word with possible definitions is displayed along with the text. Responses will be indicated with A, B, or C on markerboards.

In 1930, Ruth Wakefield was making chocolate cookies at the Toll House Inn in Whitman, Massachusetts. Unfortunately, she <u>ran out</u> of baking chocolate. Therefore, Ruth used her creativity and <u>broke</u> a <u>bar</u> of semi-sweet chocolate into little pieces. She added each <u>piece</u> to the <u>dough</u>. When the cookies were placed on a <u>sheet</u> and baked, the chocolate did not melt. Instead, there were little chips of chocolate throughout the cookies. Chocolate chip cookies had been invented through a mistake.

Vocabulary Definitions

1. ran out

A left the area

B no longer had something; the supply was gone

C to move away rapidly using legs

Vocabulary Definitions

2. broke

A shattered; made into pieces

B without any money

C feeling defeated

Vocabulary Definitions
Numbered Heads Together

Instructions: Individuals—and then teams—will determine the meaning of each word.

Vocabulary Definitions

3. bar

A to stop or prevent

B a solid block of something

C a vertical line on a musical staff

Vocabulary Definitions

4. piece

A a small part

B to fix by adding a portion

C an artistic or musical work

Vocabulary Definitions

5. dough

A money; cash

B a thick mixture of flour and other ingredients

C unbaked bread

Vocabulary Definitions

6. sheet

A a rectangular piece of cloth

B a thin rectangular pan

C a layer

FAN-N-PICK Activity

Pick a Card, Any Card

Using a Fan-N-Pick Mat and question cards, students play Fan-N-Pick to identify text features, answer story elements questions, and preview nonfiction.

Activity Steps

1. Each team receives the Fan-N-Pick Mat, an identical text for each student on the team, and a set of cards.
2. The Fan-N-Pick Mat is placed in the center of the team table, with each corner pointing to a student.
3. Student #1 (Fan) holds question cards in a fan and says, "Pick a card, any card!"
4. Student #2 (Pick and Read) picks a card, reads the question aloud, and allows think time.
5. Student #3 (Answer) responds orally and/or shows the answer.
6. Student #4 (Check and Praise) responds to the answer by tutoring or praising.
7. The Fan-N-Pick Mat is rotated one person clockwise for each new round, indicating each student's new role.

STRUCTURE
Fan-N-Pick

Blacklines

- Fan-N-Pick Mat (used for all activities) 183
- Metacognitive Awareness Strategies 184–185
- Text Features 186–188
- Story Elements (Fiction) 189–193
- Previewing Before Reading (Nonfiction) 194–195

COMPREHENSION BlackLine

Fan-N-Pick Mat

Instructions: Cut out this mat and place it in the center of the team. Each corner points to a student, indicating his or her role for that round of Fan-N-Pick. For each new round, rotate the mat clockwise one position, indicating each student's new role for that round.

- Fan
- Pick and Read
- Check and Praise
- Answer

Fan-N-Pick Mat

Balanced Literacy • Fourth Grade • Skidmore & Graber
Kagan Publishing • 1 (800) 933-2667 • www.KaganOnline.com

Metacognitive Awareness Strategies
Fan-N-Pick

Instructions: Copy one set of cards for each team. Cut apart. Use with Fan-N-Pick Mat.

Metacognitive Awareness Strategies

Show a place in the text where you <u>clarified</u> a word or idea that you didn't understand. Explain.

Metacognitive Awareness Strategies

Show a place in the text where you made a personal <u>connection</u>. Tell about your connection.

Metacognitive Awareness Strategies

Show a place in the text where you needed to <u>monitor</u> your reading. What fix-up strategy did you use?

Metacognitive Awareness Strategies

Show a place in the text where you <u>visualized</u>. Explain.

Metacognitive Awareness Strategies

Show a place in the text where <u>you responded emotionally</u> to how a character was feeling. Explain.

Metacognitive Awareness Strategies

Show a place in the text where you <u>predicted</u>. What did you predict?

Metacognitive Awareness Strategies

Fan-N-Pick

Instructions: Copy one set of cards for each team. Cut apart. Use with Fan-N-Pick Mat.

Metacognitive Awareness Strategies

Show a place in the text where you <u>inferred</u> about what something meant or about what was going to happen. Explain.

Metacognitive Awareness Strategies

Show a place in the text where you used <u>questioning</u>. Tell what the question was.

Metacognitive Awareness Strategies

Show something that you <u>decided was important</u> to remember. Why did you decide it was important?

Metacognitive Awareness Strategies

Show a place where you stopped to <u>retell</u> or <u>summarize</u> to yourself what you had already read. How did it help you?

Metacognitive Awareness Strategies

Show a place in the text where you stopped to think about your reason for reading the text (<u>purpose setting</u>).

Metacognitive Awareness Strategies

Show a place where your <u>prior knowledge</u> helped you understand what you were reading.

Text Features
Fan-N-Pick

Instructions: Copy one set of cards for each team. Cut apart. Use with Fan-N-Pick Mat.

Text Features	Text Features	Text Features
Find or locate a: **Bullet**	Find or locate a: **Bold Word**	Find or locate a: **Map**
Find or locate a: **Timeline**	Find or locate a: **Boxed Item**	Find or locate a: **Chart**

Text Features
Fan-N-Pick

Instructions: Copy one set of cards for each team. Cut apart. Use with Fan-N-Pick Mat.

Text Features	Text Features	Text Features
Find or locate a: Graph	**Find or locate a:** Diagram	**Find or locate an:** Index
Find or locate a: Caption	**Find or locate an:** Italicized Word	**Find or locate a:** Sidebar

Text Features
Fan-N-Pick

Instructions: Copy one set of cards for each team. Cut apart. Use with Fan-N-Pick Mat.

Text Features	Text Features	Text Features
Find or locate a: **Photograph**	Find or locate a: **Colored Word**	Find or locate a: **Stylized Word**
Find or locate a: **Table of Contents**	Find or locate a: **Heading**	Find or locate a: **Glossary**

Story Elements (Fiction)
Fan-N-Pick

Instructions: Copy one set of cards for each team. Cut apart. Use with Fan-N-Pick Mat.

Story Elements (Fiction)

Describe the main character.

Story Elements (Fiction)

What was the problem?

Story Elements (Fiction)

How did the character deal with the problem?

Story Elements (Fiction)

Tell about one event that happened in the story.

Story Elements (Fiction)

Should the character have done something differently?

What?

Why?

Story Elements (Fiction)

What was your favorite part of the story?

Why?

Story Elements (Fiction)
Fan-N-Pick

Instructions: Copy one set of cards for each team. Cut apart. Use with Fan-N-Pick Mat.

Story Elements (Fiction)

Have you ever read another story similar to this?

How were they the same?

How were they different?

Story Elements (Fiction)

How would you change the main character?

Story Elements (Fiction)

How are you like the main character?

How are you different?

Story Elements (Fiction)

What could be another name for this story?

Story Elements (Fiction)

Where did this story take place?

Story Elements (Fiction)

What is another way the story could have ended?

Story Elements (Fiction)
Fan-N-Pick

Instructions: Copy one set of cards for each team. Cut apart. Use with Fan-N-Pick Mat.

Story Elements (Fiction)

Is there a lesson to learn in this story?

What is it?

Story Elements (Fiction)

What was the main character's problem?

Story Elements (Fiction)

What did the main character do about his or her problem?

Story Elements (Fiction)

How did the story end?

Story Elements (Fiction)

Do you think the main character made the right decision concerning his or her problem?

Explain.

Story Elements (Fiction)

How was the problem solved?

Story Elements (Fiction)
Fan-N-Pick

Instructions: Copy one set of cards for each team. Cut apart. Use with Fan-N-Pick Mat.

Story Elements (Fiction)

What would you have done about the problem if you were the main character?

Story Elements (Fiction)

What was this story about?

Story Elements (Fiction)

What did the main character want?

Story Elements (Fiction)

How would you like the story to be different?

Story Elements (Fiction)

Did this story really happen?

How do you know?

Could this story really have happened?

Why?

Story Elements (Fiction)

What did you learn by reading this story?

Story Elements (Fiction)
Fan-N-Pick

Instructions: Copy one set of cards for each team. Cut apart. Use with Fan-N-Pick Mat.

Story Elements (Fiction)

What did you think was most interesting about this story?

Why?

Story Elements (Fiction)

What questions do you have after reading this story?

Story Elements (Fiction)

When did this story happen?

(time in history, time of day, season, etc.)

Story Elements (Fiction)

What does this story remind you of?

Story Elements (Fiction)

What is the setting for this story?

Story Elements (Fiction)

Briefly tell the three <u>most important</u> events from the story.

Previewing Before Reading (Nonfiction)
Fan-N-Pick

Instructions: Copy one set of cards for each team. Cut apart. Use with Fan-N-Pick Mat.

Previewing Before Reading (Nonfiction)

Show a text feature in your text and name it.

Previewing Before Reading (Nonfiction)

Show the text feature that you think will be most helpful to you when you read, and tell why.

Previewing Before Reading (Nonfiction)

Choose one type of text feature used, and count the number of times it is used.

Previewing Before Reading (Nonfiction)

Which table of contents item looks the most interesting? Why?

Previewing Before Reading (Nonfiction)

Find a word that is new to you. Tell some strategies that you could use to help learn about the word.

Previewing Before Reading (Nonfiction)

Why do you think the author wrote this text?

Previewing Before Reading (Nonfiction)
Fan-N-Pick

Instructions: Copy one set of cards for each team. Cut apart. Use with Fan-N-Pick Mat.

Previewing Before Reading (Nonfiction)

What would you like to learn from this text?

Previewing Before Reading (Nonfiction)

What do you think this text is mainly about?

Previewing Before Reading (Nonfiction)

How many <u>different</u> text features did the author use?

Previewing Before Reading (Nonfiction)

Tell what you already know about the topic of the text.

Previewing Before Reading (Nonfiction)

Ask a question you would like the text to answer. Start your question with Why...?

Previewing Before Reading (Nonfiction)

Which text feature will you spend the most time studying? Why?

TALKING CHIPS Activity

Comprehension Cubes

Teammates roll a comprehension cube to ask and answer questions relating to a selected text. Students may respond in any order, but they must place their Talking Chip in the center of the team table to indicate they've participated.

Activity Steps

1. Each team receives one cube and a text selection. Each teammate receives one Talking Chip (any chip or token will work).
2. Student #1 rolls the comprehension cube and reads the question or formulates a question.
3. All students take turns responding to the question, placing their chip in the center when talking.
4. When all chips are used, teammates each collect their chips.
5. Student #2 rolls the cube and repeats from Step 2.

STRUCTURES
Talking Chips

Blacklines

- Nonfiction Comprehension Question Cube (Before Reading) 197
- Nonfiction Comprehension Question Cube (After Reading).........................198
- Fiction Comprehension Question Cube (Reflection) 199
- Questioning Cube..200
- Metacognitive Cube (After Reading)..201
- Literature Circle Discussion Cube #1 (After Reading) 202
- Literature Circle Discussion Cube #2 (After Reading) 203

Nonfiction Comprehension Question Cube (Before Reading)
Talking Chips

Instructions: Copy the cube pattern on cardstock. Cut out, fold, and tape together to form a cube.

What text type do you think this selection is written in? What makes you think that?

What text structure(s) do you think the author has used?

What do you think the author's purpose is for writing this?

What might be some specific vocabulary words you will read?

What is one text feature you think will be helpful? Why?

What do you already know about this topic?

Nonfiction Comprehension Question Cube (Reflection)
Talking Chips

Instructions: Copy the cube pattern on cardstock. Cut out, fold, and tape together to form a cube.

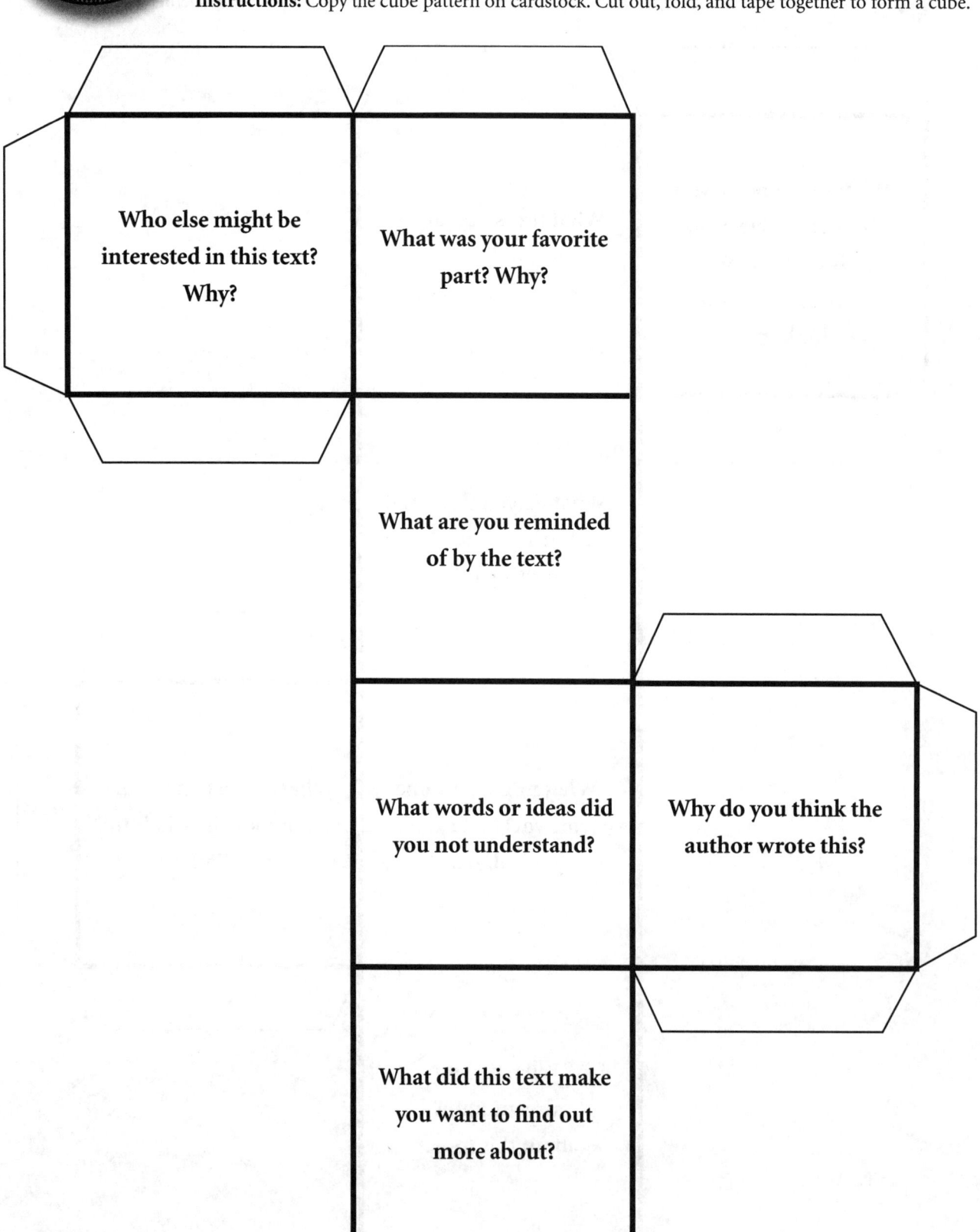

Who else might be interested in this text? Why?

What was your favorite part? Why?

What are you reminded of by the text?

What words or ideas did you not understand?

Why do you think the author wrote this?

What did this text make you want to find out more about?

Fiction Comprehension Question Cube (Reflection)
Talking Chips

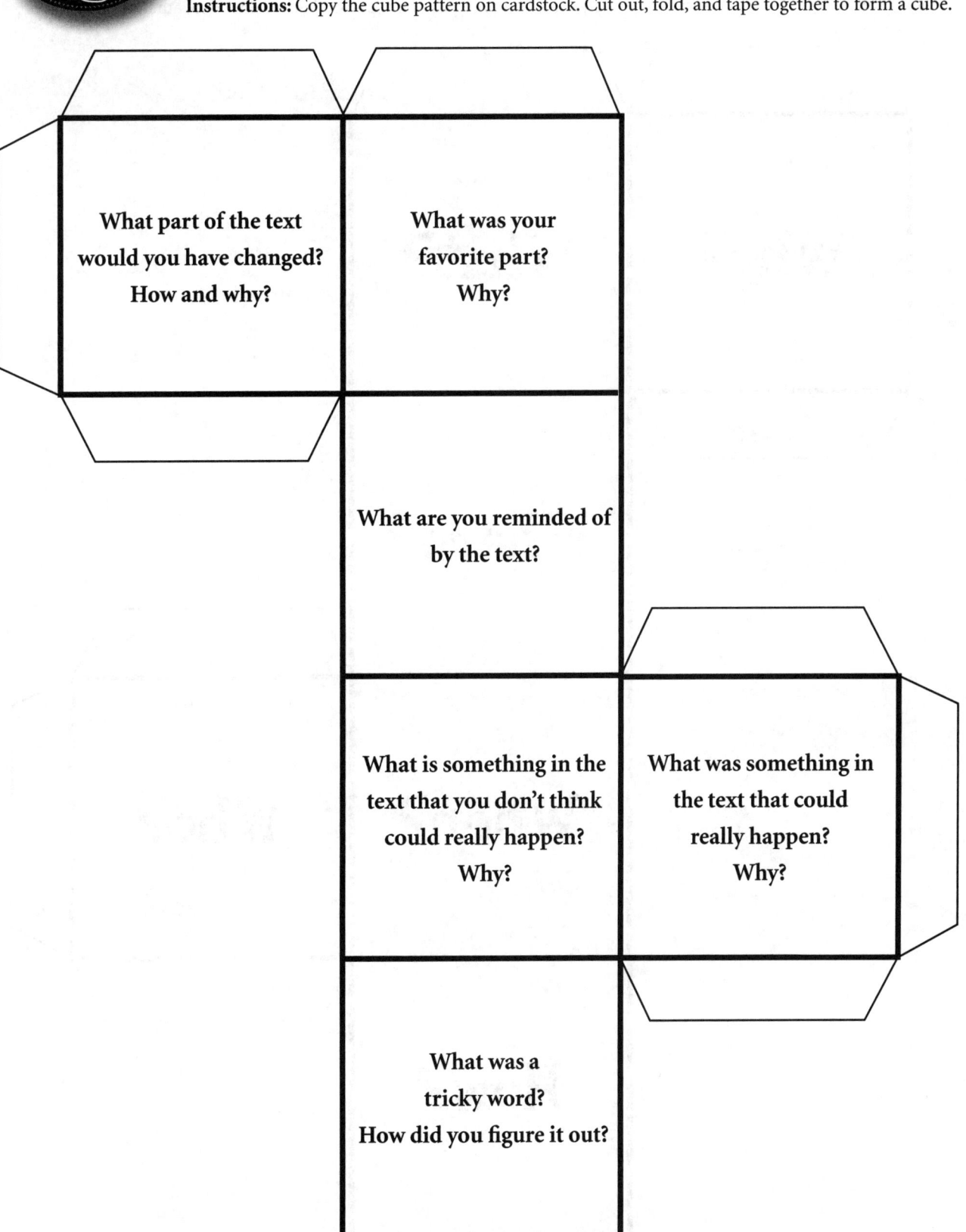

Instructions: Copy the cube pattern on cardstock. Cut out, fold, and tape together to form a cube.

What part of the text would you have changed? How and why?

What was your favorite part? Why?

What are you reminded of by the text?

What is something in the text that you don't think could really happen? Why?

What was something in the text that could really happen? Why?

What was a tricky word? How did you figure it out?

Balanced Literacy • Fourth Grade • Skidmore & Graber
Kagan Publishing • 1 (800) 933-2667 • www.KaganOnline.com

Questioning Cube
Talking Chips

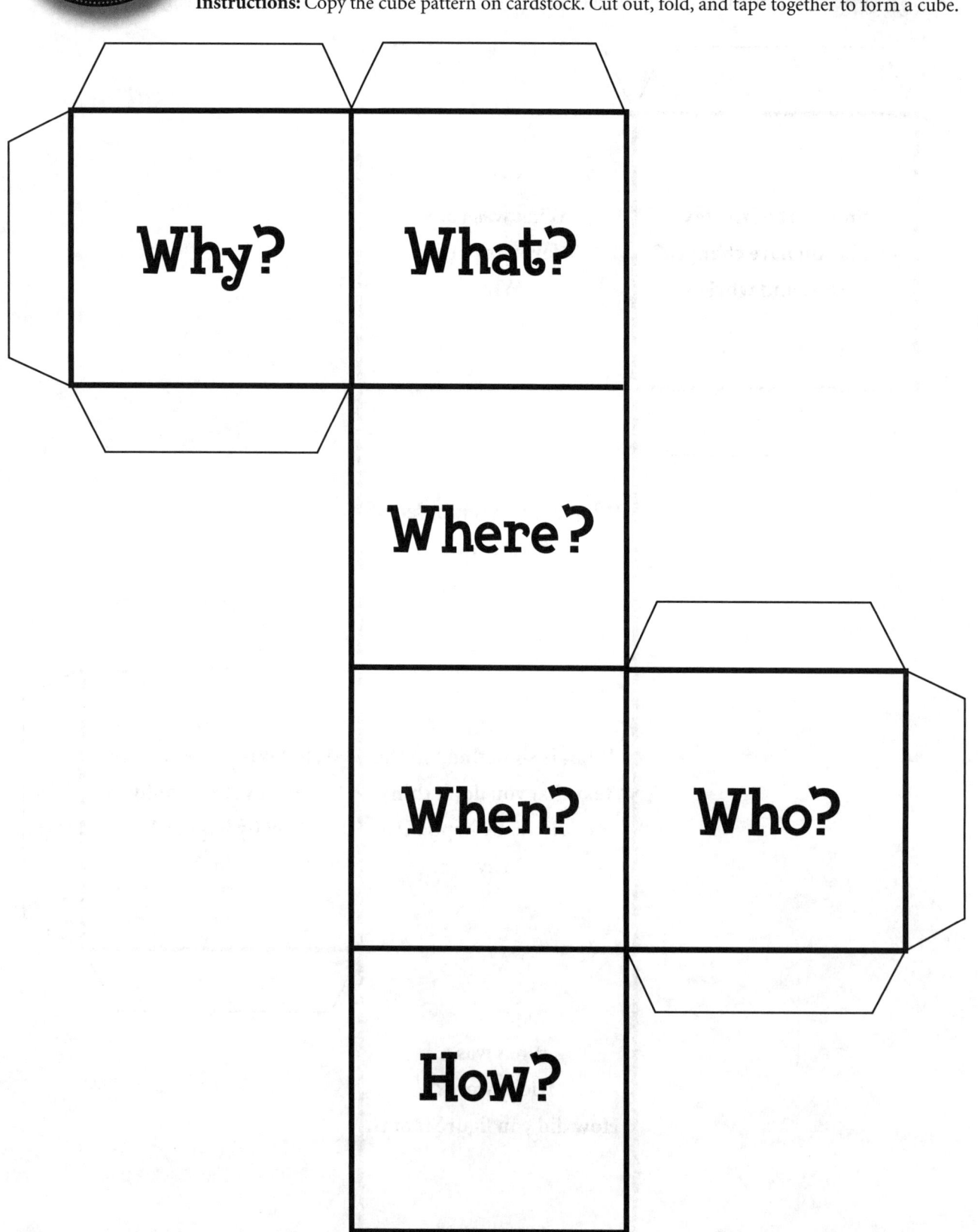

Instructions: Copy the cube pattern on cardstock. Cut out, fold, and tape together to form a cube.

Why?

What?

Where?

When?

Who?

How?

Balanced Literacy • Fourth Grade • Skidmore & Graber
Kagan Publishing • 1 (800) 933-2667 • www.KaganOnline.com

Metacognitive Cube
(After Reading)
Talking Chips

Instructions: Copy the cube pattern on cardstock. Cut out, fold, and tape together to form a cube.

What word/idea did you need to **clarify**?

(What clarification strategy helped you?)

Give an example of a **connection** you made in this text.

- Text to self
- Text to text
- Text to world

Where in the text did you **visualize**?

Evaluating

How will this information be useful to you?

Deciding What Is Important

What is one important fact/idea to remember? Why?

A **question** that I asked myself while reading was _____.

COMPREHENSION Blackline

Literature Circle Discussion Cube #1
(After Reading)
Talking Chips

Instructions: Copy the cube pattern on cardstock. Cut out, fold, and tape together to form a cube.

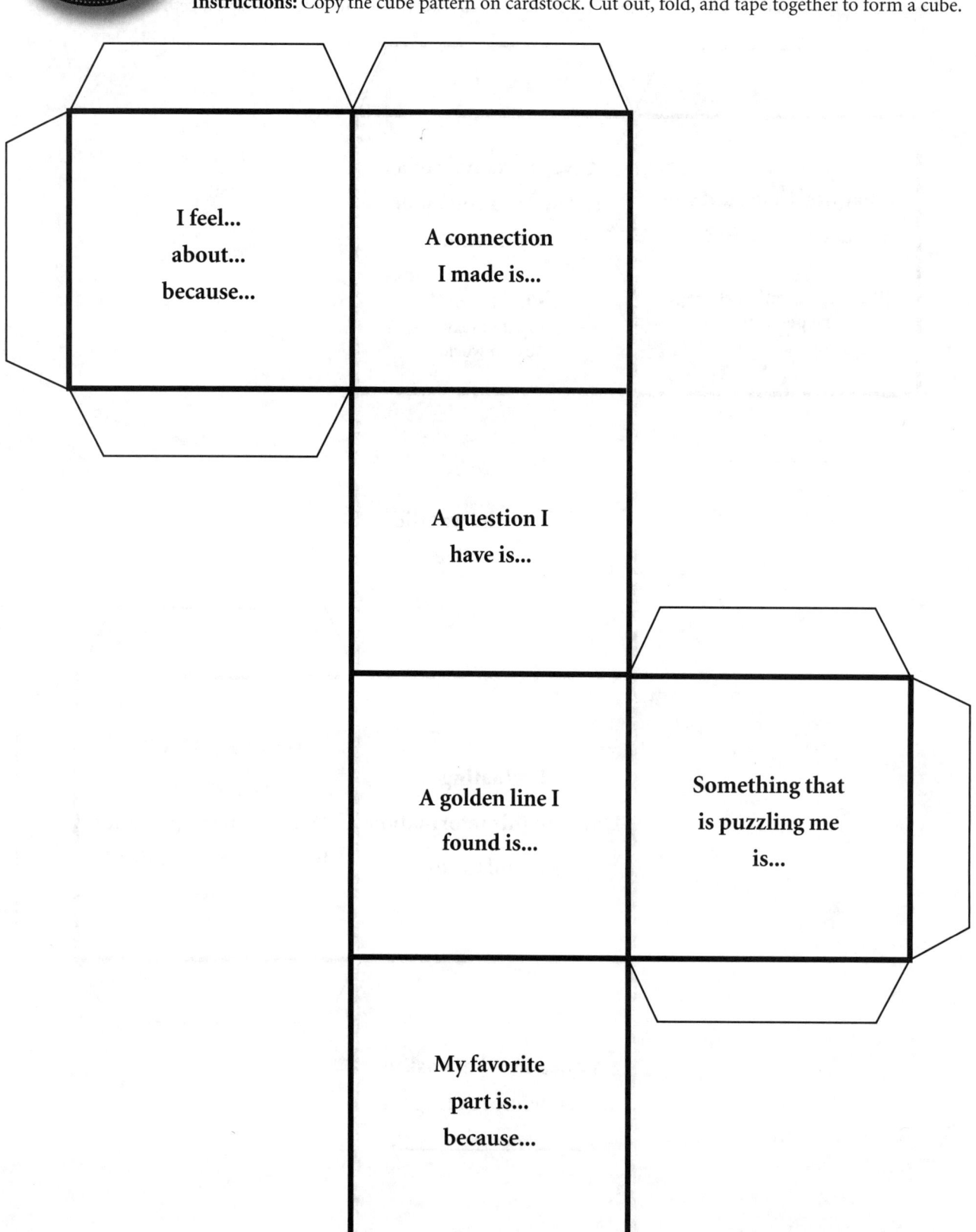

I feel... about... because...

A connection I made is...

A question I have is...

A golden line I found is...

Something that is puzzling me is...

My favorite part is... because...

Literature Circle Discussion Cube #2
Talking Chips

Instructions: Copy the cube pattern on cardstock. Cut out, fold, and tape together to form a cube.

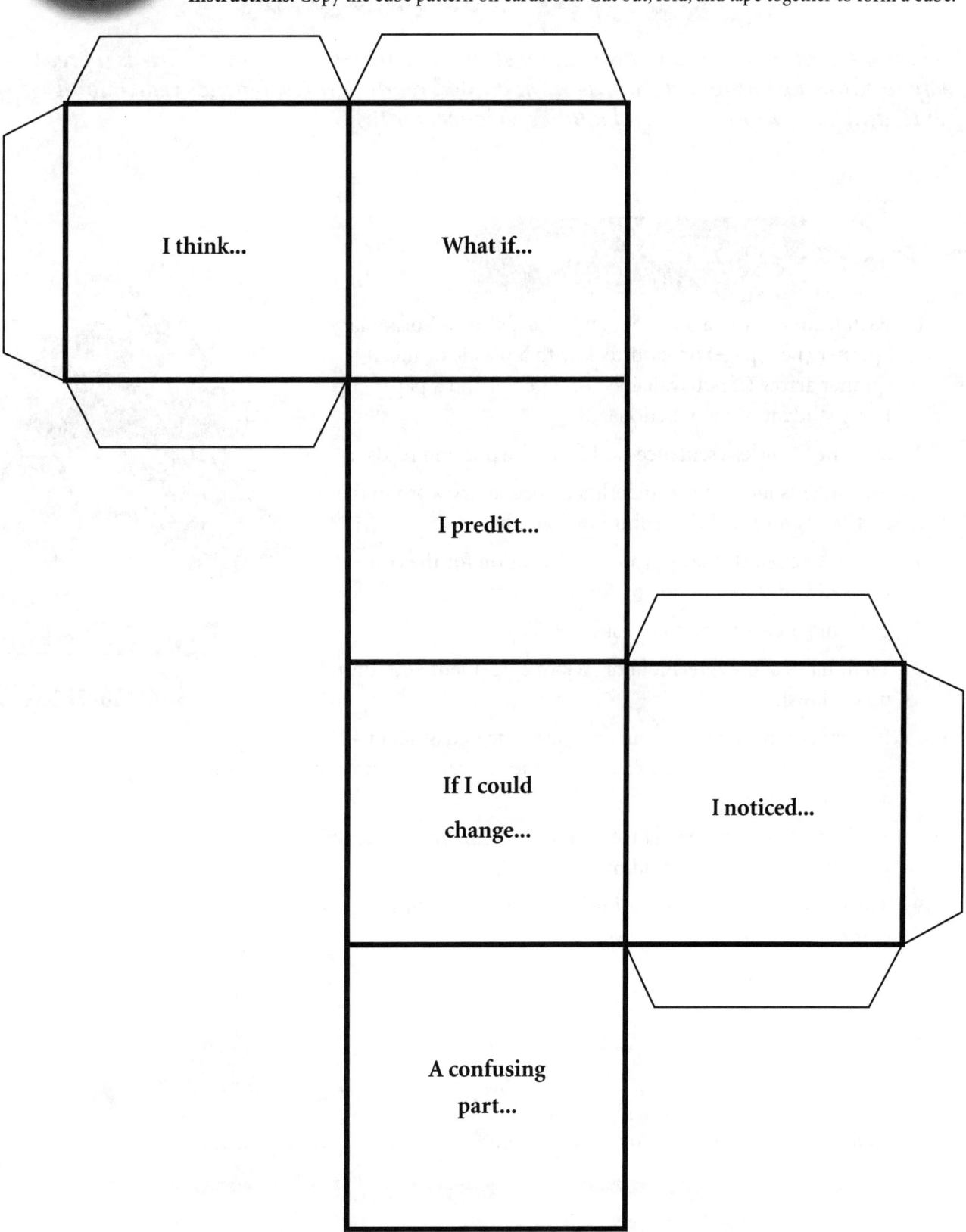

- I think...
- What if...
- I predict...
- If I could change...
- I noticed...
- A confusing part...

ROUNDTABLE CONSENSUS Activity

Spinning Vocabulary

Teammates use vocabulary cards and a spinner to learn vocabulary. This is a great way to examine vocabulary words from guided reading texts, teacher read-aloud texts, and content areas (social studies, science, math).

Activity Steps

1. Each team receives a set of Sentence Cards and a Vocabulary Spinner (next page) on cardstock with a plastic or metal spinner arrow (if not available, use a pencil and a paper clip). Every student needs a dictionary.
2. Student #1 picks a sentence card from the pile and reads it.
3. All students look up the underlined vocabulary word in the dictionary and read the definitions silently.
4. Student #2 selects the appropriate definition for the context, reads it, and states the reason for the choice.
5. Student #2 checks for consensus.
6. Teammates show agreement or lack of agreement with thumbs up or down.
7. If there is agreement, the students celebrate and Student #2 spins the spinner. Student #3 responds to the spinner's prompt and checks for consensus.
8. Student #4 begins the next rotation by picking up a Sentence Card from the pile and reading it.
9. The process continues until time's up or the team has completed their vocabulary words.

STRUCTURE
RoundTable Consensus

Blacklines

- Vocabulary Spinner 205
- Sentence Cards for Vocabulary Spinner 206
- Blank Sentence Cards for Vocabulary Spinner 207

Comprehension Blackline

Vocabulary Spinner
RoundTable Consensus

Instructions: Copy a spinner on cardstock for each team. Add a plastic/metal spinner in the middle or use a spinner made from a paper clip and a pencil. (To make a paper clip spinner: Place a paper clip over the center of the spinner. Place the pencil point on the center point of the spinner, through the paper clip. Using the other hand, spin the paper clip around the pencil point.) Students take turns spinning the spinner and following the directions.

What is another word that means about the same as your word? (synonym)

Paraphrase the sentence.

Discuss the word:
- Visual clues
- Letter patterns
- Tricky parts

Use the word in a new sentence.

Balanced Literacy • Fourth Grade • Skidmore & Graber
Kagan Publishing • 1 (800) 933-2667 • www.KaganOnline.com

Sentence Cards for Vocabulary Spinner
RoundTable Consensus

Instructions: Copy one set of cards per team. Cut apart.

Sentence Cards for Vocabulary Spinner

The two basketball teams were <u>rivals</u> for the championship.

Sentence Cards for Vocabulary Spinner

The drink of water <u>quenched</u> my thirst.

Sentence Cards for Vocabulary Spinner

The store gave me a full <u>refund</u> on my returned purchase.

Sentence Cards for Vocabulary Spinner

When you look at how many tennis matches Tim has won, you would never know that he is a <u>novice</u>.

Sentence Cards for Vocabulary Spinner

My dad has a 45-minute <u>commute</u> to work.

Sentence Cards for Vocabulary Spinner

The bully was <u>overbearing</u> to the younger boys.

Blank Sentence Cards for Vocabulary Spinner
RoundTable Consensus

Instructions: Use blank cards to create sentence cards.

Blank Sentence Cards for Vocabulary Spinner	Blank Sentence Cards for Vocabulary Spinner	Blank Sentence Cards for Vocabulary Spinner

Blank Sentence Cards for Vocabulary Spinner	Blank Sentence Cards for Vocabulary Spinner	Blank Sentence Cards for Vocabulary Spinner

ROUNDTABLE CONSENSUS ACTIVITY

Comprehension Puzzles

After teammates have read the same text, teammates place puzzle pieces on a puzzle mat. Each puzzle piece has a prompt for students to review the reading. Three different puzzle blacklines are provided: 1) retelling fiction, 2) retelling nonfiction, and 3) nonfiction text features.

Activity Steps

1. Each team receives a set of puzzle pieces and a puzzle mat. The puzzle pieces are mixed up and placed facedown in the center of team (except for the Retelling [Fiction] puzzle pieces, which need to be selected in the order of their numbers 1–8).

2. Student #1 selects one puzzle piece, reads the prompt, and gives an answer. For example, if the puzzle piece is "Titles," the student states the title. The student checks for consensus.

3. Teammates show agreement or lack of agreement with thumbs up or down.

4. If there is agreement, the student places the puzzle piece on the matching section on the puzzle mat. If not, teammates discuss the response until there is agreement. If no agreement is reached, the puzzle piece is set aside to be discussed later.

5. The next student selects the next puzzle piece and the process is continued until the team completes the puzzle.

STRUCTURE
RoundTable Consensus

Blacklines

- Retelling (Fiction) Puzzle Pieces...209
- Retelling (Fiction) Puzzle Mat..210
- Retelling (Nonfiction) Puzzle Pieces 211
- Retelling (Nonfiction) Puzzle Mat 212
- Text Feature (Nonfiction) Puzzle Pieces..................................213
- Text Feature (Nonfiction) Puzzle Mat.......................................214

COMPREHENSION Blackline

Retelling (Fiction) Puzzle Pieces
RoundTable Consensus

Instructions: Copy one puzzle for each teams. Cut puzzle pieces apart.

2. Characters

3. Setting

4. Problem

8. Solution

7. Event

1. Title

5. Event

6. Event

Retelling (Fiction)

Balanced Literacy • Fourth Grade • Skidmore & Graber
Kagan Publishing • 1 (800) 933-2667 • www.KaganOnline.com

Retelling (Fiction) Puzzle Mat
RoundTable Consensus

Instructions: Copy one puzzle mat for each team.

| 1 | 2 | 3 | 4 | 5 | 6 | 7 | 8 |

210 Balanced Literacy • Fourth Grade • Skidmore & Graber
Kagan Publishing • 1 (800) 933-2667 • www.KaganOnline.com

Retelling (Nonfiction) Puzzle Pieces
RoundTable Consensus

Instructions: Copy one puzzle for each teams. Cut puzzle pieces apart.

- Detail
- Detail
- Text Feature
- Detail
- Detail
- Information from Picture
- Heading (Main Idea)
- Text Feature
- Key Vocabulary Words

Retelling (Nonfiction) Puzzle Mat
RoundTable Consensus

Instructions: Copy one puzzle mat for each team.

COMPREHENSION Blackline

Text Feature (Nonfiction) Puzzle Pieces
RoundTable Consensus

Instructions: Copy one puzzle for each teams. Cut puzzle pieces apart.

(Bolded, Italicized, Colored, or Stylized) Word	Text Feature (Nonfiction)
Table of Contents	Text Feature (Nonfiction)
Timeline	Text Feature (Nonfiction)
Heading	Text Feature (Nonfiction)
Index	Text Feature (Nonfiction)
Map	Text Feature (Nonfiction)
Photograph with Caption	Text Feature (Nonfiction)
Glossary	Text Feature (Nonfiction)
Bullets	Text Feature (Nonfiction)
Label	Text Feature (Nonfiction)
Boxed Item or Sidebar	Text Feature (Nonfiction)
Graph or Diagram	Text Feature (Nonfiction)

Balanced Literacy • Fourth Grade • Skidmore & Graber
Kagan Publishing • 1 (800) 933-2667 • www.KaganOnline.com

Text Feature (Nonfiction) Puzzle Mat
RoundTable Consensus

Instructions: Copy one puzzle mat for each team.

SOLO & RALLYCOACH Activity

Anticipation Guide

Before reading a text, individuals mark "true" or "false" predictions on an Anticipation Guide Form. Students read the text independently and mark their answers and page number where the answer was found on the "after reading" section. Partners then take turns sharing their answers and proving them from the text. Students are allowed to adjust answers after discussion with partner.

Activity Steps

1. Using an Anticipation Guide Student Form, the teacher fills in statements relating to the reading, some true and some false. (See the Anticipation Guide Sample on page 217–219.)

2. Individuals receive an Anticipation Guide Form and a book or article to read.

3. Before reading the text, each individual marks true or false predictions for each statement on the form by checking the "true" or "false" box in the "Before Reading" column.

4. Students read the assigned article or book independently.

5. After reading the text, individuals read the statements on the Anticipation Guide, finding and recording the related text page.

6. Partners take turns sharing their answers and proving them from the text. Students are allowed to adjust their answers after discussion with partner.

7. Partners alternate roles for each statement.

STRUCTURE
Solo & RallyCoach

Blacklines

- Anticipation Guide Samples 216–219
- Anticipation Guide—Blank Student Form 220

Anticipation Guide Answer Form
Solo and RallyCoach

Solo Before Reading (True / False)	*Ranger Rick* March 2004 pp. 32–34 "Reptile Safari!"	RallyCoach After Reading (Pg. / True / False)
✓ /	1. A herpetologist is a scientist who studies snakes, turtles, lizards, and frogs.	32 / ✓ /
✓ /	2. When looking under a rock for a snake, tilt the rock away from you.	33 / / ✓
/ ✓	3. A "noose" is a hook used at the end of a fishing pole to help catch lizards.	34 / ✓ /
✓ /	4. Collared lizards can run on their hind legs.	35 / ✓ /
/ ✓	5. When reptile hunting, it is not necessary to put rocks and logs back like you found them.	32 / / ✓
✓ /	6. Snakes usually move around during the hottest part of the day.	36 / / ✓
✓ /	7. Wild animals should be released where you find them.	36 / ✓ /
✓ /	8. Deserts are only cool in the morning.	36 / / ✓
✓ /	9. A GPS (Global Positioning System) Unit is an instrument that uses satellite signals to tell you exactly where you are.	36 / ✓ /
/ ✓	10. Matthew's father wrote a field guide about snakes, turtles, and lizards that live in the northwestern part of North America.	36 / ✓ /

What is a question that you would like to ask your partner?

What is "roadhunting" and when is the best time of the day to do it?

Anticipation Guide Student Form
Solo and RallyCoach

Solo Before Reading		*Ranger Rick* March 2004 pp. 32–34 "Reptile Safari!"	RallyCoach After Reading		
True	False		Pg.	True	False
		1. A herpetologist is a scientist who studies snakes, turtles, lizards, and frogs.			
		2. When looking under a rock for a snake, tilt the rock away from you.			
		3. A "noose" is a hook used at the end of a fishing pole to help catch lizards.			
		4. Collared lizards can run on their hind legs.			
		5. When reptile hunting, it is not necessary to put rocks and logs back like you found them.			
		6. Snakes usually move around during the hottest part of the day.			
		7. Wild animals should be released where you find them.			
		8. Deserts are only cool in the morning.			
		9. A GPS (Global Positioning System) Unit is an instrument that uses satellite signals to tell you exactly where you are.			
		10. Matthew's father wrote a field guide about snakes, turtles, and lizards that live in the northwestern part of North America.			

What is a question that you would like to ask your partner?

Anticipation Guide Answer Form
Solo and RallyCoach

Solo Before Reading True	Solo Before Reading False	*Ranger Rick* February 2005 pp. 16–19 "Saving Saigas"	Pg.	RallyCoach After Reading True	RallyCoach After Reading False
✓		1. The saiga is a relative of the elephant.	16		✓
✓		2. Dust causes a major problem for the saiga and its elephant-like nose.	17		✓
✓		3. The saiga can run up to 43 miles per hour.	17	✓	
	✓	4. Saigas live only in China.	18		✓
✓		5. People have caused saigas to become endangered.	17	✓	
	✓	6. Saiga horns are being ground up and used for medicine.	18	✓	
	✓	7. Young saigas spend most of their day sleeping.	19	✓	
✓		8. Saigas are killed mainly for their fur coats.	17–18		✓
✓		9. Saiga meat is not edible.	18		✓
✓		10. Only the male saiga grows horns.	18	✓	

11. The section "Hope for Saigas" is written in which text structure?
    (cause-effect, problem-solution, description, comparison, sequencing)
    problem-solution

12. This article is which text type?
    (narrative, expository, technical, persuasive)
    expository

Anticipation Guide Student Form
Solo and RallyCoach

Solo Before Reading		*Ranger Rick* February 2005 pp. 16–19 "Saving Saigas"	RallyCoach Before Reading		
True	False		Pg.	True	False
		1. The saiga is a relative of the elephant.			
		2. Dust causes a major problem for the saiga and its elephant-like nose.			
		3. The saiga can run up to 43 miles per hour.			
		4. Saigas live only in China.			
		5. People have caused saigas to become endangered.			
		6. Saiga horns are being ground up and used for medicine.			
		7. Young saigas spend most of their day sleeping.			
		8. Saigas are killed mainly for their fur coats.			
		9. Saiga meat is not edible.			
		10. Only the male saiga grows horns.			

11. The section "Hope for Saigas" is written in which text structure?
    (cause-effect, problem-solution, description, comparison, sequencing)

12. This article is which text type?
    (narrative, expository, technical, persuasive)

Anticipation Guide Blank Student Form
Solo and RallyCoach

Solo Before Reading			RallyCoach After Reading		
True	False		Pg.	True	False
		1.			
		2.			
		3.			
		4.			
		5.			
		6.			
		7.			
		8.			
		9.			
		10.			

Q: Do you have a question to ask the group?

LISTEN-SKETCH-DRAFT Activity

Sketching for Comprehension

Students listen to the teacher, sketch the important details, share their sketches, then draft a main idea of the statement.

Activity Steps

1. Each student is given the Listen-Sketch-Draft form.
2. The teacher presents the first chunk of information while students listen carefully.
3. The teacher stops presenting and calls for each student to sketch the most important details in the first "sketch" box.
4. Students share their sketches using RoundRobin or Timed Pair Share.
5. Students draft a main idea statement in the first "draft" box.
6. The process is repeated for additional chunks of information.
7. When all chunks of information have been presented, students draft a summary in the bottom box.
8. Students compare their summaries with a partner or teammate.

STRUCTURE
Listen-Sketch-Draft

Blacklines

- Listen-Sketch-Draft Sample 222
- Listen-Sketch-Draft Form 223

Listen-Sketch-Draft
Sample Form

Important to Remember (Sketch)	Main Idea (Draft)
[sketch of burrow tunnels]	Prairie dogs live in burrows on the prairie.
[sketch of prairie dog barking]	Prairie dogs have a sharp bark that warns other prairie dogs.
Predators: • coyotes • bobcats • ferrets • hawks/eagles	Prairie dogs have many enemies.

Summary Statement:
Prairie dogs live on the prairie in underground burrows. They watch for their enemies and "bark" to warn other prairie dogs to be careful.

Listen-Sketch-Draft Form

Instructions: Copy for each student.

Important to Remember (Sketch)	Main Idea (Draft)

Summary Statement:

TIMED PAIR SHARE Activity

Story Predictions

Students manipulate cards with possible characters, settings, problems, and solutions to the text on the prediction mat. They confirm or adjust their predictions during reading and after reading the selection. Partners take timed turns listening and sharing about their Prediction Mats.

Activity Steps

1. The teacher creates Story Element Cards corresponding to the story the class will read. (One sample set is provided.)

2. Each student receives a Prediction Mat and a set of story cards.

3. As the story is read, students are stopped periodically and given time to make story predictions by manipulating their Story Cards on their Prediction Mats. Stories can be read using:
   - Teacher read aloud
   - RallyRobin reading (partners take turns)
   - Independent reading

4. After each prediction adjustment, students are each given one minute to share their prediction with a partner.

STRUCTURE
Timed Pair Share

Blacklines

- Prediction Mat..225
- Blank Story Element Cards for Prediction Mat................226
- *Escape North: The Story of Harriet Tubman*
  Story Element Cards for Prediction Mat..........................227

Prediction Mat
Timed Pair Share

Instructions: Copy for each student.

Characters	Setting

Problem	Solution

Important Words

Blank Story Element Cards for Prediction Mat
Timed Pair Share

Instructions: Teacher writes possible story elements in these boxes and makes copies for each student.

Story Element Cards for Prediction Mat
Timed Pair Share
Escape North: The Story of Harriet Tubman by Monica Kulling

Instructions: Copy for each student. Cut apart.

Harriet Tubman	slaves	freedom	moss
1851	tobacco plantation	Araminta Ross	Choptank River
Pennsylvania	north star	Underground Railroad	Daddy Ben
law	runaways	sleeping spells	Fugitive Slave Act
Quaker woman	water	shoes	gun
Civil War	Abraham Lincoln	"Stand Together"	"Go Down, Moses"

Jot Thoughts & Sorting Activity

Sort It Out

Teammates cover a mat with ideas about what they just read on small sticky notes. Then they sort the ideas into categories. This is a great way to promote active listening and processing of reading content.

Activity Steps

1. After reading a text, each team receives a Recall Mat, a Sorting Mat, four different colored pencils, and a pad of sticky notes.

2. Students recall things from the text, write the idea or event on a sticky note, and announce it as they place the sticky note on the Recall Mat.

3. After students have numerous sticky notes on the Recall Mat, they pull out their Sorting Mat.

4. Teams discuss possible categories for their Sorting Mat. Once they reach consensus on the category names, they write them on the Sorting Mat.

5. Students take turns reading each sticky note and placing it on the Sorting Mat.

Optional Writing Activity: Students use the information on the sorting mat to write about the text. For expository writing each category can be formed into a heading and paragraph. For narrative writing each category can be ordered into a sequenced story.

STRUCTURE
Jot Thoughts & Sorting

Blacklines

- Recall Mat 229
- Sorting Mat 230

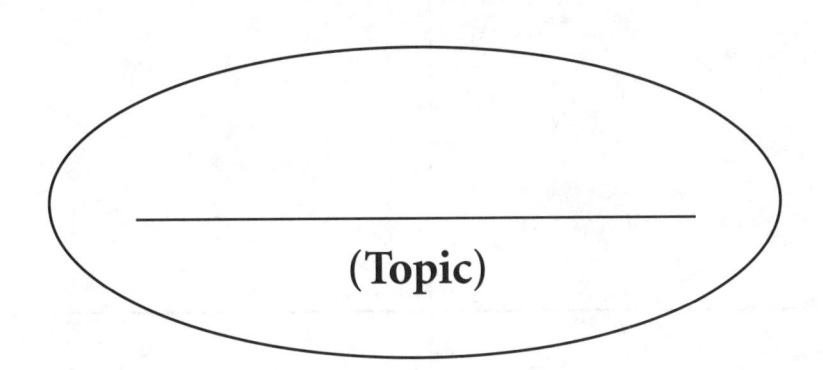

Recall Mat

Jot Thoughts

Instructions: Copy one mat per team. Use to generate ideas for Sorting Mat.

_____
(Topic)

Sorting Mat
Jot Thoughts

Instructions: Copy one mat per team. Use to sort ideas from Recall Mat.

TRAVELING HEADS TOGETHER

Activity

Idioms and Morals

Students discuss in teams the meaning of various idioms and fable morals in a fun and energizing format.

Activity Steps

1. Students form teams.
2. The teacher shares an idiom or fable moral by reading it and displaying it on the overhead.
3. Students individually write what it means.
4. Teammates stand at their team desk, put their heads together, and discuss what the statement means.
5. Students sit back down when ready.
6. The teacher calls a student number and says how many teams to move ahead.
7. The student called travels to the new team.
8. Students who rotated share their team's ideas with their new team.
9. The teacher then leads a group discussion of the statement's meaning.
10. The process is repeated for each new idiom or moral.

STRUCTURE
Traveling Heads Together

Blacklines

- Idioms 232–234
- Idiom Answer Sheet 235
- Fable Morals..236–237

Idioms
Traveling Heads Together

Instructions: Teacher makes an overhead of this page and shares one idiom for each round of the activity.

- Hold your horses!

- That's just ducky!

- She pulled the wool over his eyes.

- He squirreled it away.

- There's an elephant in the room.

- Don't ruffle any feathers.

- My head is full of cobwebs.

- Don't count your chickens before they hatch.

- She clammed up.

- Stop hounding me.

Idioms
Traveling Heads Together

Instructions: Teacher makes an overhead of this page and shares one idiom for each round of the activity.

- His bark is worse than his bite.

- This place is going to the dogs.

- Something smells fishy.

- Who will bell the cat?

- Keep him on a short leash.

- That's a feather in his cap.

- She's on a fishing expedition.

- I had to eat crow.

- I rule the roost!

- He gets up with the chickens.

Idioms
Traveling Heads Together

Instructions: Teacher makes an overhead of this page and shares one idiom for each round of the activity.

- Don't put all your eggs in one basket.

- You can lead a horse to water, but you can't make him drink.

- I have butterflies in my stomach.

- You could've knocked me down with a feather.

- We threw in the towel.

- That will happen when pigs fly.

- Keep your chin up.

- She's a quick study.

- He's feeling under the weather.

- She was feeling down in the dumps.

Idioms—Answer Sheet
Traveling Heads Together

Idiom	Explanation of Idiom
Hold your horses!	Be patient.
That's just ducky!	That's just great!
She pulled the wool over his eyes.	She fooled him.
He squirreled it away.	He saved it for later.
There's an elephant in the room.	There's a big problem nobody wants to face.
Don't ruffle any feathers.	Don't upset anyone.
My head is full of cobwebs.	I can't think straight.
Don't count your chickens before they hatch.	You can't plan on having something until you actually get it.
She clammed up.	She refused to talk.
Stop hounding me.	Stop pestering me.
His bark is worse than his bite.	He's not as fierce as he seems.
This place is going to the dogs.	Things are getting worse and worse.
Something smells fishy.	I suspect wrongdoing.
Who will bell the cat?	Who will face danger for the good of us all?
Keep him on a short leash.	Don't give him too much freedom.
That's a feather in his cap.	That's an achievement.
She's on a fishing expedition.	She's trying to get information.
I had to eat crow.	I had to admit I was wrong.
I rule the roost!	I'm the boss.
He gets up with the chickens.	He wakes up early in the morning.
Don't put all your eggs in one basket.	Spread out your risk in more than one place.
You can lead a horse to water, but you can't make him drink.	You can't force someone to take advice.
I have butterflies in my stomach.	I feel nervous.
You could've knocked me down with a feather.	I was very surprised.
We threw in the towel.	We gave up.
That will happen when pigs fly.	That will never happen.
Keep your chin up.	Remain brave and don't worry.
She's a quick study.	She learns new things quickly and easily.
He's feeling under the weather.	He is sick.
She was feeling down in the dumps.	She was feeling sad.

Fable Morals
Traveling Heads Together

Instructions: Teacher makes an overhead of this page and shares one fable moral for each round of the activity.

- Good looks aren't everything.

- It is easy to be brave from a safe distance.

- Every tale is not to be believed.

- He who plays a trick must be prepared to take a joke.

- Trouble comes from the direction we least expect it.

- Fine feathers don't make fine birds.

- Quality is better than quantity.

- The hero is brave in deeds as well as words.

- Even the wildest can be tamed by love.

- There is always someone worse off than yourself.

- Let well enough alone.

Fable Morals
Traveling Heads Together

Instructions: Teacher makes an overhead of this page and shares one fable moral for each round of the activity.

- It is best to prepare for the days of necessity.

- Do not attempt too much at once.

- Never trust your enemy.

- One man's pleasure may be another's pain.

- Whatever you do, do with all your might.

- Never trust a friend that deserts you in a pinch.

- Two wrongs do not make a right.

- If it's not broken, don't fix it.

- Misery loves company.

- A liar deceives no one but himself.

- Every man should be content to mind his own business.

RallyCoach Activity

Idiom Meanings

Partners take turns matching idioms with their meanings.

Activity Seps

1. Each pair receives an Idiom Mat and a set of Idiom Cards. (Two separate sets are provided.) They spread out the Idiom Cards so they can read them all.
2. Partner A chooses an idiom card (bold font) and a matching meaning card. Partner A places the cards across from each other in the correct columns on the Idiom Mat.
3. Partner B watches, listens, checks, and praises.
4. Partner B chooses an idiom card and a matching meaning card. Partner B places the cards across from each other in the correct columns on the Idiom Mat.
5. Partner A watches, listens, checks, and praises.
6. The process is continued until the pair fills out the Idiom Mat.

STRUCTURE
RallyCoach

Blacklines

- Idiom Mat 239
- Idiom Cards (Set 1) 240
- Idiom Cards (Set 2) 241

Idiom Mat
RallyCoach

Instructions: Copy for each pair of students.

Idiom	Meaning

Idiom Cards—Set 1 for Mat
RallyCoach

Instructions: Copy one set of cards for each pair of students. Cut apart.

Idiom Cards—Set 1	Idiom Cards—Set 1
smell a rat	to spot signs of a problem
step on it	to hurry
tall order	large expectation
sit on the fence	undecided
under the weather	ill; not feeling well
eager beaver	a person with extreme enthusiasm
push one's buttons	to make someone angry
put out fires	to take care of problems
raise the roof	to cause an uproar
rocky start	a beginning with problems

Idiom Cards—Set 2 for Mat
RallyCoach

Instructions: Copy one set of cards for each pair of students. Cut apart.

Idiom Cards—Set 2	Idiom Cards—Set 2
selling like hotcakes	selling quickly
top banana	person in charge
sit tight	to take no action
by the skin of one's teeth	barely made it
take under one's wing	to take care of someone
under the sun	everywhere
chicken out	to back away from an experience out of fear
chill out	to completely relax
chip in	to help out
in a jam	in trouble

FIND-THE-FICTION Activity

Idiom Cards–True or False?

Students pick out the fictitious statement, explaining an idiom from a set of three statements.

Activity Steps

1. Teammates each choose one idiom card.
2. Teammates each write three statements about the meaning of the idiom on one side of their markerboards: two true, one false.
3. One student on each team stands, then reads his or her statements to teammates.
4. Without consulting teammates, each student writes down his or her own best guess as to which statement is false on the empty side of the markerboard.
5. Teammates RoundRobin and defend their "best guess." Teams attempt to reach consensus.
6. Teammates announce their guess(es).
7. The standing student announces the false statement.
8. Students celebrate: The standing student congratulates teammates who guessed correctly. Teammates who were fooled congratulate the standing student.
9. The next teammate stands to share. The process is repeated from Step 2.

Variation: Teammates write three statements about the meaning of the idiom: one true, two false. Teammates find the true statement.

STRUCTURE
Find-the-Fiction

Blacklines

- Idioms 243–245

Idiom Cards — True or False?
Find-the-Fiction

Instructions: Copy one set of cards for each team. Cut apart.

Idioms — True or False?	Idioms — True or False?
Hold your horses.	That's just ducky.
She pulled the wool over his eyes.	He squirreled it away.
There's an elephant in the room.	Don't ruffle any feathers.
My head is full of cobwebs.	Don't count your chickens before they hatch.
She clammed up.	Stop hounding me.

Idiom Cards — True or False?
Find-the-Fiction

Instructions: Copy one set of cards for each team. Cut apart.

Idioms — True or False?

His bark is worse than his bite.

Idioms — True or False?

This place is going to the dogs.

Idioms — True or False?

Something smells fishy.

Idioms — True or False?

Who will bell the cat?

Idioms — True or False?

Keep him on a short leash.

Idioms — True or False?

That's a feather in his cap.

Idioms — True or False?

She's on a fishing expedition.

Idioms — True or False?

I had to eat crow.

Idioms — True or False?

I rule the roost.

Idioms — True or False?

He gets up with the chickens.

Idiom Cards—True or False?
Find-the-Fiction

Instructions: Copy one set of cards for each team. Cut apart.

Idioms—True or False?

Don't put all your eggs in one basket.

Idioms—True or False?

You can lead a horse to water, but you can't make him drink.

Idioms—True or False?

I have butterflies in my stomach.

Idioms—True or False?

You could've knocked me down with a feather.

Idioms—True or False?

We threw in the towel.

Idioms—True or False?

That will happen when pigs fly.

Idioms—True or False?

Keep your chin up.

Idioms—True or False?

She's a quick study.

Idioms—True or False?

He's feeling under the weather.

Idioms—True or False?

She was feeling down in the dumps.

Balanced Literacy

Comprehension
Word Study
Fluency
Writing

Word Study

Word Study

Effective word study instruction involves both decoding words and deriving meaning from words (vocabulary). Word study allows students to take words apart while reading and put word parts together while writing. Word-solving strategies help students learn important concepts related to decoding, spelling, and understanding vocabulary. As students participate in word study activities, they become aware of relationships between sounds, letters, letter combinations, and word parts. Various cooperative activities in this book provide opportunities for students to practice application of word study skills and decoding strategies for effective reading and writing.

Following the framework of balanced literacy allows the teacher to scaffold instruction through use of explicit teaching during read/write alouds and shared reading/writing to explain strategies used to decode words and understand their meanings. Scaffolding continues during guided reading/writing as the teacher monitors and provides feedback to students applying word-solving skills and strategies. Support is withdrawn as students independently apply these skills and strategies successfully.

Table of Word Study Resources

Balanced Literacy

Page(s)	Resources	Aloud	Shared	Guided	Independent	Literature Circles
Word Study Descriptions and Lists						
254	Word Study Resources/Materials Descriptions					
255	Spelling Strategies	●	●	●	●	●
256	Prefix and Suffix Word List	●	●	●	●	●
258	Contraction List	●	●	●	●	●
259	Homophone List	●	●	●	●	●
262	Homograph List	●	●	●	●	●

Table of Word Study Activities and Lessons

Page(s)	Activities/Lessons	Blacklines	Balanced Literacy				
			Aloud	Shared	Guided	Independent	Literature Circles
264	Partner Word Study Activities		●	●	●	●	●
268	Team Word Study Activities		●	●	●	●	●
272	Class Word Study Activities		●	●	●	●	●
273	**Making Words Lesson Plans**						
274	**Lesson 1:** *Yourself*						
274	**RallyCoach Activity**						
275	Activity 1: Making Words	• Teacher Transparency Form • Student Form	●	●	●	●	
276	**Find My Rule Activity**						
276	Activity 2: Sorting	• Teacher Transparency Form • Find My Rule Mat	●	●	●	●	
277	**RallyCoach Activity**						
277	Activity 3: Transfer		●	●	●	●	
280	**Lesson 2:** *Rainforest*						
280	**RallyCoach Activity**						
280	Activity 1: Making Words	• Teacher Transparency Form • Student Form	●	●	●	●	
281	**Find My Rule Activity**						
281	Activity 2: Sorting	• Teacher Transparency Form • Find My Rule Mat	●	●	●	●	
281	**RallyCoach Activity**						
281	Activity 3: Transfer		●	●	●	●	

Table of Word Study Activities and Lessons (continued)

Balanced Literacy

Page(s)	Activities/Lessons	Resources	Aloud	Shared	Guided	Independent	Literature Circles
284	**Lesson 3: *Relationship***						
284	**RallyCoach Activity**						
284	Activity 1: Making Words	• Teacher Transparency Form • Planning Form • Student Form	●	●	●	●	
285	**Find My Rule Activity**						
285	Activity 2: Sorting	• Teacher Transparency Form • Find My Rule Mat	●	●	●	●	
285	**RallyCoach Activity**						
285	Activity 3: Transfer		●	●	●	●	
291	**Find Someone Who Activities**						
292	All About Prefixes	• Worksheet		●	●		
293	Skill Review #1	• Worksheet		●	●		
294	Skill Review #2	• Worksheet		●	●		
295	Skill Review #3	• Worksheet		●	●		
296	Find Someone Who	• Form		●	●		
297	**Quiz-Quiz-Trade Activities**						
298	Contractions	• Question/Answer Cards		●	●		
305	Silent Letters	• Question/Answer Cards		●	●		
312	Letter Patterns (ar, er, ir, or, ur)	• Question/Answer Cards		●	●		
319	Letter Patterns (au, aw, ou, ow)	• Question/Answer Cards		●	●		
327	Letter Patterns (ie, ei)	• Question/Answer Cards		●	●		
334	Prefixes (anti-, dis-, ex-, non-, under-)	• Question/Answer Cards		●	●		
342	Prefixes (anti-, dis-, ex-, non-, under-) Suffixes (-en, -ful, -less, -ment, -ness)	• Question/Answer Cards		●	●		

Table of Word Study Activities and Lessons (continued)

Page(s)	Activities/Lessons	Blacklines	Balanced Literacy				
			Aloud	Shared	Guided	Independent	Literature Circles
349	Letter Patterns (Their, There, They're)	• Question/Answer Cards		●	●		
356	**RallyCoach Activities**						
357	Prefixes (anti-, dis-, ex-, non-, under)	• Cube • Worksheet • Answer Sheet		●	●		
360	Suffixes (-ful, -en, less, -ment, -ness)	• Cube • Worksheet • Answer Sheet		●	●		
365	Antonyms and Synonyms	• Cube • Worksheet • Answer Sheet		●	●		
368	Contractions	• Spinner • Worksheet		●	●		
370	Adding Endings	• Spinner • Worksheet • Answer Sheet		●	●		
373	Hard g, Soft g	• Sorting Mat • Word Cards		●	●		
377	**Showdown Activities**						
378	Prefixes (anti-, dis-, ex-, non-, under-)	• Team Cards • Student Cards		●	●		
382	Antonyms, Synonyms, Homophones	• Team Cards • Student Cards		●	●		
389	**Numbered Heads Together Activity**						
390	Word Wall Words	• Word List • Word Wall Cards • Additional Word Wall Cards • Blank Word Wall Cards	●	●	●	●	

252 Balanced Literacy • Fourth Grade • Skidmore & Graber
Kagan Publishing • 1 (800) 933-2667 • www.KaganOnline.com

Word Study Resources

Word Study Resource Descriptions

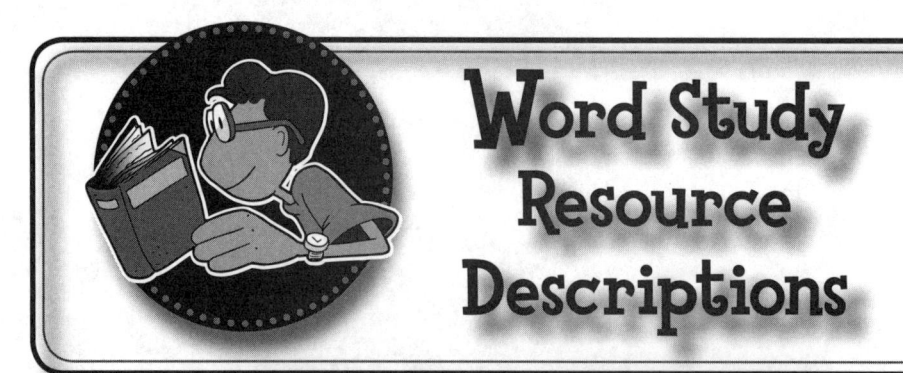

Resources/Materials Descriptions

Spelling Strategies (p. 255)
The goal of word study is to spell words correctly in everyday writing. Spelling strategies, which students should learn to use, are listed as a resource. Several of the Kagan activities in this book reinforce these spelling strategies.

Prefix and Suffix Word List (pp. 256–257)
This resource lists several prefixes and suffixes, their meanings, and word examples.

Contraction List (p. 258)
This contraction list includes contractions made with *am, are, had, would, have, is, has, not, us,* and *will*.

Homophone List (p. 259)
Homophones are words that are spelled differently, but sound the same such as *rain, rein, reign*. This homophone list is a classroom resource for teachers and students.

Homograph List (p. 262)
This resource lists homographs, which are words written the same way, but which have different meanings and different pronunciations. For example, bow (to bend the head, knee, or body) and bow (a knot having two loops and two ends).

Word Study Activities (pp. 263–272)
These word study activities are arranged according to partner, team, and class activities. The Kagan cooperative learning structure, activity name, and a brief description are included.

Word Study Spelling Strategies

Visualize it.	**Try it several ways. Which way looks right?**
Stretch it out. Listen to the sounds. · Letter patterns · Endings · Prefixes	**Ask a friend.**
Circle the word. Come back later.	**Check the Word Wall.**
Use what you already know. (analogy) Blue → Glue	**Use a dictionary or spell check.**

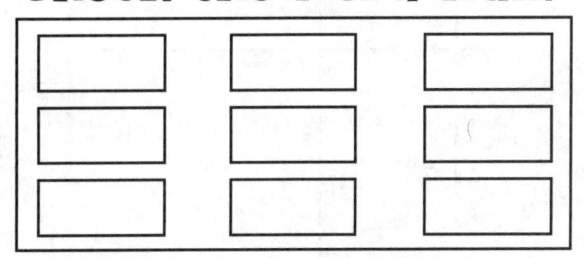

Word Study Prefix and Suffix Word List

Teacher Resources

Prefixes			
	anti–	"against"	antibiotic, antiterrorism, antidote, antifreeze, antisocial, antiseptic, antithesis, antibody, antitrust, anticlimax, antihistamine
	dis–	"not"	dislike, displace, disgrace, disarm, disobey, disorder, discontinue, disperse, distaste, disagree, dissatisfied, disconnect, disrespect, dissatisfy, disarray, disloyal, dismiss, disappear, discard, disinfect, disorganized, disbelief, discolor, disable, discourage, discount, disrepair
	ex-	"out of" "is no longer"	explain, exhale, express, exclusive, expulsion, exceed, explosion, exit, exclaim, excite, excommunicate, excrete, exodus, explore, expose, express, extend, extinct, extract, extra, exude, expensive, expect, excuse, expert, exterior, expire, excursion, extinguish, extreme, expensive, ex-president
	non–	"not" "without"	nonsense, nonrefundable, nonnegotiable, nondairy, nonsmoker, nonreturnable, nonexistent, nonskid, nonresident, nondescript, nondenominational, noncommissioned, nonstop, nonstandard, nonprofit, nonsupport, nonconformist, nonviolence
	under–	"beneath" "below" "too little"	underachieve, underage, underarm, underbid, underbrush, undercarriage, undercharge, underclassman, underclothes, undercoat, undercover, undercurrent, undercut, understate, underdeveloped, underdog, underestimate, underfoot, undergarment, undergo, undertaking, undergraduate, underground, underhand, underlying, undermine, underneath, underpass, underprivileged, underscore, undersea, undersell, undershirt, underside, understaffed, understand

Word Study Prefix and Suffix Word List
(continued)

Teacher Resources

Suffixes		
-ful	"full of" "having a lot of"	mouthful, beautiful, wonderful, colorful, wishful, cheerful, hopeful, painful, powerful, useful, grateful, pitiful, meaningful, joyful, pocketful, basketful, plateful, armful, doubtful, flavorful, playful, regretful, revengeful, spoonful, spiteful, tasteful, handful, mouthful, plentiful, thankful, useful, delightful, faithful, stressful, thoughtful, youthful, wasteful, careful, disgraceful, fearful, graceful, peaceful, sorrowful, successful, trustful, delightful, prideful
-en	"to make" "made of" "after"	sharpen, soften, lengthen, shorten, sweeten, harden, lighten, weaken, tighten, whiten, stiffen, lessen, freshen, darken, blacken, redden, strengthen, golden, silken, woolen, wooden, frozen
-less	"without"	fearless, wireless, pointless, senseless, spotless, weightless, careless, motherless, ageless, useless, aimless, blameless, boneless, endless, priceless, coreless, tasteless, timeless, painless, needless, breathless, stainless, reckless, worthless, thankless, soundless, lifeless, speechless, sleepless, homeless, cheerless, hairless, sightless, shapeless, mindless, sleeveless
-ment	"in a state of" "result of"	government, movement, agreement, punishment, employment, encouragement, commitment, development, arrangement, excitement, banishment, achievement, advertisement, argument, involvement, settlement, tournament, amazement, statement, measurement, merriment
-ness	"state of" "quality of"	goodness, quietness, forgiveness, happiness, loudness, sickness, darkness, kindness, fitness, willingness, sadness, tenderness, usefulness, carefulness, heaviness, suddenness, toughness, laziness, wilderness

Word Study Contraction List

Teacher Resources

am
I'm

are
they're
we're
you're

had / would
I'd
it'd
she'd
there'd
they'd

have
could've
I've
might've
should've
they've
we've
would've
you've

is / has
here's
he's
it's
she's
that's
there's
what's
where's

not
aren't
can't
couldn't
didn't
doesn't
don't
hadn't
hasn't
haven't
isn't
mustn't
needn't
shouldn't
wouldn't

us
let's

will
I'll
it'll
he'll
she'll
that'll
they'll
we'll
you'll

Word Study Homophone List

Teacher Resources

accept/except	bough/bow	creak/creek	genes/jeans
ad/add	boy/buoy	cymbal/symbol	great/grate
affect/effect	break/brake	days/daze	groan/grown
ail/ale	brews/bruise	dear/deer	guessed/guest
aisle/I'll/isle	bridal/bridle	dew/do/due	hail/hale
all/awl	buy/by/bye	die/dye	hall/haul
aloud/allowed	capital/capitol	doe/dough	hare/hair
alter/altar	carat/caret/carrot	dual/duel	hay/hey
ant/aunt	caught/cot	earn/urn	heal/heel/he'll
arc/ark	ceiling/sealing	ewe/yew/you	hear/here
ate/eight	cell/sell	eye/I	heard/herd
aye/eye/I	cellar/seller	fair/fare	hi/high
bale/bail	cent/sent/scent	fairy/ferry	higher/hire
ball/bawl	cents/scents/sense	feat/feet	him/hymn
base/bass	cereal/serial	find/fined	hoarse/horse
be/bee	cheap/cheep	fir/fur	hole/whole
bear/bare	chews/choose	flair/flare	holy/wholly
beat/beet	chili/chilly	flea/flee	hour/our
beau/bow	choral/coral	flew/flue/flue	idle/idol
berry/bury	chord/cord	flour/flower	in/inn
billed/build	chute/shoot	foaled/fold	Jim/gym
bite/byte	cite/sight/site	for/fore/four	knead/need
blue/blew	close/clothes	foreword/forward	knew/new
boar/bore	coarse/course	forth/fourth	knight/night
board/bored	core/corps	foul/fowl	knit/nit
bold/bowled	council/counsel	gate/gait	knot/not

Balanced Literacy • Fourth Grade • Skidmore & Graber
Kagan Publishing • 1 (800) 933-2667 • www.KaganOnline.com

Word Study Homophone List (continued)

Teacher Resources

know/no	pair/pare/pear	red/read	
knows/nose	past/passed	right/rite/write	
lead/led	patience/patients	ring/wring	
leak/leek	pause/paws	road/rode/rowed	
lessen/lesson	peace/piece	role/roll	
lie/lye	peal/peel	root/route	
links/lynx	pearl/purl	rose/rows	
load/lode	pedal/peddle	rote/wrote	
loot/lute	peek/peak	rough/ruff	
made/maid	peer/pier	rye/wry	
mail/male	pi/pie	sail/sale	
main/Maine/mane	plane/plain	scene/seen	
Mary/marry/merry	plum/plumb	sea/see	
meat/meet	pole/poll	seam/seam	
might/mite	pour/pore	sew/so/sow	
mind/mined	praise/prays/preys	shear/sheer	
missed/mist	pray/prey	shoe/shoo	
moose/mousse	presence/presents	shone/shown	
none/nun	prince/prints	side/sighed	
oar/or/ore	principal/principle	sole/soul	
oh/owe	profit/prophet	some/sum	
one/won	quarts/quartz	son/sun	
overdo/overdue	rain/reign/rein	stair/stare	
paced/paste	raise/rays/raze	stake/steak	
pail/pale	rap/wrap	stationary/stationery	
pain/pane	real/reel	steal/steel	

Word Study Homophone List (continued)

Teacher Resources

straight/strait	wait/weight
suite/sweet	waive/wave
sundae/Sunday	ware/wear/where
tacks/tax	wave/waive
tail/tale	way/weigh/whey
tea/tee	we/wee
team/teem	weak/week
teas/tease/tees	weather/whether
their/there/they're	weave/we've
theirs/there's	we'd/weed
threw/through	were/whirr
throne/thrown	which/witch
thyme/time	whine/wine
tide/tied	who's/whose
to/too/two	woe/whoa
toad/towed	wood/would
told/tolled	worn/warn
tow/toe	yoke/yolk
troop/troupe	you/ewe
vain/vane/vein	you'll/Yule
vale/veil	your/you're
vary/very	
vial/vile	
wade/weighed	
wail/whale	
waist/waste	

Word Study Homograph List

Teacher Resources

bow	bend; part of a ship	live	broadcast at time of occurrence
bow	a knot with two loops and ends; arched weapon	live	having life
tear	rip	minute	60 seconds
tear	fluid in eye	minute	tiny
row	a fight	putting	golfing
row	in a line; to move a boat with oars	putting	placing
project	undertaking	reside	live somewhere
project	hurl	reside	put outside on building again
record	a list; round musical disk	refuse	do not accept
record	to write down	refuse	garbage
bass	fish	wind	moving air
bass	low musical sound	wind	to coil up
invalid	ill person	desert	dry place
invalid	wrong	desert	abandon
job	task	mow	place to keep hay in barn
Job	book	mow	cut the grass
lead	heavy metal	Herb	man's name
lead	show the way	herb	plant
moped	motorized bike	resign	quit
moped	was gloomy	resign	sign again
sewer	one who sews	present	gift
sewer	pipe or drain to carry off waste	present	give
dove	bird	read	to say words from print (present tense)
dove	jump off	read	to say words from print (past tense)
resort	sort again	perfect	exactly correct
resort	vacation spot	perfect	to make correct
polish	shine	close	shut
Polish	from Poland	close	not far
does	female deer	separate	not connected
does	form of to do	separate	to divide into parts
wound	injury		
wound	coiled up		

Word Study Activities and Lessons

Partner Word Study Activities

Match My Word

Structure: Match Mine

Use stand-up folders as buddy barriers. The teacher shows Partner A a slip of paper with a word study word on it. Partner A writes the word on a small dry-erase board, which Partner B cannot see. Partner A tells Partner B how to spell the word on his or her dry-erase board. The directions may include how to form the letters, but the letter names may not be said. Partners switch roles for the next word.

Big Words/Little Words

Structure: RallyCoach

The teacher makes individual letter cards for words. These are packaged in separate bags. Partners take a bag and take turns making as many different words as they can using the letters from the bag. Each word is recorded. A mystery word can be made by using all the letters in the bag.

Computer Typing

Structure: RallyCoach

Partners use a word list to take turns giving each other words to type on a word-processing program on the computer. They change the font style and sizes, so each word looks different. Print out the words to see the finished product.

Foamy Fun

Structure: RallyCoach

Partners sit side by side. The teacher squirts a heap of shaving cream on a protected surface. One at a time, the teacher calls out the word study words. The partners use their fingertips to write the word in the foam. Partners check and praise each other.

Hand Spelling

Structure: RallyCoach

Partner A traces the letters of a word in the palm of Partner B's hand. Partner A says the name of the traced word. Partners take turns tracing the word, praising, coaching, and naming the word. Partners try identifying the word while looking and then with eyes closed.

Illustrating Words

Structure: RallyCoach

Partners take turns giving each other a word from a list. Partner A gives Partner B a word. Partner B writes the word and draws a picture to represent the word. Partner B then explains the picture and spells the word aloud without looking. Partner A praises and coaches. Partner B then gives a word to Partner A. Each word has its own box on the paper.

Partner Word Study Activities
(continued)

Inflatable Ball Spelling

Structure: RallyCoach

Use an inflatable ball with letters printed on it. (You may purchase one with letters already on it or make your own by printing letters with a permanent marker.) Partners take turns tossing the ball back and forth. When the catcher gets the ball, he or she lifts one hand and sees which letter is under it. As quickly as possible, he or she says a word beginning with that letter and spells it. Together partners decide if the word is correctly spelled and record it on paper.

Memory

Structure: RallyCoach

Partners work together to make two identical word cards for each word on the list. Partners check each other's word cards. The cards are mixed up and placed facedown in rows. Partner A turns over two cards, saying the words. If the cards are a match, he or she removes them, spells the word without looking, and takes another turn. If they are not a match, the cards are turned facedown, and Partner B has a turn. Partners praise and coach each other.

Letter Ladders

Structure: RallyCoach

Partners are given a set of letter cards (one of every consonant and several of every vowel). Partners take turns making new words by changing one letter at a time. The teacher begins by giving the first word (for example, *hat*). Partner A may change the *h* to *c* to make a new word (*cat*) above the first word. Partner B may then change the *t* to *n* to make *can*. Challenge partners to see how tall they can make their ladders.

Prefixes and Suffixes

Structure: RallyCoach

Partners use a container filled with base words. They take turns adding various prefixes or suffixes provided by the teacher to make new words, which are recorded on paper. Partners check, then coach or praise. (examples: *non*—nonskid, nonstop, nonresident)

On My Back

Structure: RallyCoach

Partner A sits on a chair without a back. Partner B stands in back with a list of words. Partner B "draws" the letters to spell a word on the back of Partner A. Partner A writes the word on paper. Partner B praises and coaches. Partners switch roles.

Partner Word Study Activities
(continued)

Roll a Word

Structure: RallyCoach

Prepare two large dice by writing prefixes (suffixes) on one and base words on the other. Partners take turns rolling both dice. If a word is rolled, partners praise and both write the word. If the roll does not make a word, the partner rolls the die again until a word is rolled.

Sit and Spell

Structure: RallyCoach

The teacher writes a word list on the chalkboard. Students sit in two lines facing one another, so that only one line of students can see the word list. Students identify their partners, who are directly across from them. Partners A, who can see the words, are the "callers." Partners B are the "spellers." A caller reads a word aloud and listens carefully as the partner spells the word. If an incorrect spelling is given, the caller repeats the word and the partners spell it together. If a correct spelling is given, the partner praises. Partners switch roles for the next word.

Spelling Takes a Hit

Structure: RallyCoach

Partner A gives Partner B a word to spell by using a flyswatter to "hit" letters printed on a shower curtain hung on a wall. Partner A praises and coaches. Partners take turns giving the word and "hitting" the letters.

Study Buddies

Structure: RallyCoach

Partners take turns giving each other words to spell. A form with three columns is used. Partner A gives a word to Partner B to write in the first column. If the word is spelled correctly the first time, Partner A gives another word, which is written in a new first column. If the word is not spelled correctly, Partner B tries again in the second column. If that word is not correct, Partner A coaches by showing the word. Partner B writes it again in the third column. At any point that the word is correctly spelled, the partner is given a smiley face by the word. Partners switch roles when the words on the list have been spelled correctly or when the teacher indicates it is time to switch roles.

Water Spelling

Structure: RallyCoach

Partner A gives Partner B a word to spell on the sidewalk using a paintbrush and a container of water. Partner A praises and coaches. Partners take turns giving the word and "painting" it. (Note: Water sticks—plastic tubes with sponges on the ends—may also be used to "paint" words on the chalkboard.)

Partner Word Study Activities
(continued)

Word Search

Structure: RallyCoach

Students use graph paper to create their own word searches, including the words they are focusing on for that week. Students form partners. Using one partner's word search, partners take turns circling one hidden word at a time. Each partner has a different colored pencil. Partners coach and praise. When one word search is completed, the other one is used.

Tic-Tac-Toe — Three Words in a Row

Structure: RallyRobin

Each set of partners is given a set of word cards, a Tic-Tac-Toe worksheet, and two different colors or types of counters. Partner A picks up a card and reads it to Partner B. If Partner B correctly spells the word, he or she places a counter on any open square of the game board. If Partner B gives an incorrect response, Partner A correctly spells the word and coaches Partner B to spell the word correctly. The word card is placed at the bottom of the pile and no counter is placed on the game board. Partner A now has a turn to spell the next word. Partners try to place three counters in a row (horizontally, vertically, or diagonally). Partners celebrate.

Prefix/Suffix Race

Structure: RallyTable

Partners have a die with each side labeled with different prefixes or suffixes. Partner A rolls the die and announces the prefix or suffix rolled. For example, if the die lands on "dis-," Partner A could write *disable*. Partner B could write *disorganized*. Partners continue to alternate generating written words. When neither partner can think of another word in the category, the letter die is rolled again and new words are generated.

Spelling Toss

Structure: RallyToss

Partners spell a word while tossing a ball back and forth. Each partner says the next letter of the word until the word is spelled.

Word Toss Game

Structure: RallyToss

Partner A tosses a ball to Partner B at the same time as saying a word. Partner B writes the word on paper and spells it aloud to Partner A. Partner A praises or coaches. Continue by switching roles.

Team Word Study Activities

Spelling Detective

Structure: CenterPiece

Each team needs a page from a newspaper for each team member and one for the center. Each team member has a different colored pencil. The teacher calls out a word pattern and students look for a word on their newspaper page, which fits the pattern, and circle it. Students then trade their paper with the one in the center. Students continue circling words which fit the pattern until the teacher calls a new word pattern (examples: silent *e*, -ing ending, suffix –ment, etc.).

Add On Relay

Structure: RoundTable

A team forms a line facing the chalkboard. Teammate #1 gives a word. Teammate #2 goes to the chalkboard and writes the first letter of the word, returning to the line and handing the chalk to Teammate #3, who writes the second letter of the word. Continue in this manner, until the word is spelled. If a student sees that a team member has made a spelling error, he or she may use a turn to correct the error. Teammate #2 gives the second word. (A markerboard could also be used.)

Scrambled Word Problem Solving

Structure: Jigsaw Problem Solving

Each team is given a bag with the individual letters of a word. Teammates each take a letter or letters, until all the letters are taken. Student #1 states his or her letter and where it goes in the sequence. Teammates check, coach, and move letters. Process continues with each teammate until word is spelled correctly. When the word is spelled correctly, the team receives a new bag with a new word.

Forming Plurals

Structure: RoundTable

Each team needs a set of laminated cards with a plural ending written on the top (for example: es, s, ves), a set of word cards (singular words), a beanbag, and a different colored transparency pen for each student. Lay out the set of word cards on the floor. Teammate #1 tosses the beanbag at the cards. He or she picks up the card that the beanbag landed on, says the word, and uses a transparency pen to write the word in its plural form on the correct plural ending card. The word card goes in a discard pile. The other teammates take turns tossing the beanbag and writing the plural forms of the words on the plural ending cards.

Word Family Lists

Structure: Jot Thoughts

Teammates cover the table with words, belonging to a word family, written on slips of paper. Each student writes one word per slip of paper and announces the word before placing it in the middle of the table. Each added word needs to be new. (Variation: words that begin or end the same; words that were made plural by adding *es*, words ending with -ing, etc.)

Team Word Study Activities (continued)

Colorful Team Spelling

Structure: RoundTable

Each team member has a different colored pencil or marker. The teacher gives a word. The team passes a paper around the table. Each student adds one letter to spell the word and passes the paper on to the next student until the word is spelled.

Sentence Writing

Structure: RoundTable

Each student on the team has a different colored pencil. Each person adds a word to a paper, which is passed around the table. The words need to form a complete sentence. When the sentence is completed, the sentence is read to the other teams. Each word study word for the week that is used correctly in the sentence is worth one point for class goal.

Guess the Letters

Structure: Talking Chips

Use a large dry-erase board or chalkboard, that all team members can see. Teammate #1 looks at a list of words and chooses one word. He or she makes a line for each letter of the word (_ _ _ _). The other team members take turns putting a talking chip in the middle of the table and guessing a letter or the word. If the word is not guessed and all the talking chips have been used, teammates pick up their talking chips and begin guessing again. When the word has been identified, Teammate #2 chooses a new word. Continue until all teammates have had an opportunity to choose a word.

Do You Know My Word?

Structure: Showdown

One teammate spells aloud a word. Once the word is spelled, teammates pick up a marker and spell the word on individual dry-erase boards. When the Showdown Captain calls, "Showdown," teammates hold up their boards and show their spellings and name the word. They then celebrate or coach.

Find the Errors

Structure: Simultaneous RoundTable

Each team has four teacher-made sentence strips with spelling errors (one for each student). Each student has a different colored pencil. The papers are passed around the table, with each student correcting one error before passing the paper to the next student. Keep passing the sentences around until all the errors have been corrected.

Base Word Web

Structure: RoundTable

Each team works together to create a base word web. A large piece of paper is placed in the center of the team with the base word written in the middle (for example: *use, stop, color*). Each student has a different colored marker. Teammates take turns adding new words to the web by adding a prefix or suffix to the base word. The team needs to agree on the spelling of the word before the person writes.

Balanced Literacy • Fourth Grade • Skidmore & Graber
Kagan Publishing • 1 (800) 933-2667 • www.KaganOnline.com

Team Word Study Activities (continued)

Body Spelling

Structure: Team Formations

Each team receives a word on a card. Their task is to use their bodies to spell the word. Each person on the team must be part of the spelling. Other teams guess what word was spelled.

Movement Spelling

Structure: Team Formations

The teacher calls out a word. Each team decides on a repetitive movement to use with each letter. For example, one team may decide to hop on one foot for each letter of the word as they spell it. Teams spell the word for the other teams, after practicing their words and movements at least three times. (Variation: Teams may use a different movement for each letter of the word.)

Spelling Cheerleaders

Structure: Team Formations

Students in teams act out the given word with their bodies, showing the tall letters (stretching tall with hands over heads), short letters (putting arms straight out or on hips), and tail letters (squatting or touching toes). For example, "Give me a ____. Give me an ____. Give me a ____."

Machine Spelling

Structure: Team Line-Ups

Each student on a team becomes one letter of the word being spelled. They line up in order. The word is spelled orally with each student saying his or her word while making a body motion. The team becomes a "word machine." Teams demonstrate their machines to the other teams.

Word Line-Ups

Structure: Team Line-Ups

Each team receives a stack of scrambled letters, which spell a word. Each teammate takes one of the letters. (Teammates may need to take more than one letter or share a letter, depending on the length of the word.) Each team tries to be the first to line up holding the letters in the correct order to spell the word. (If a team member has two letters, which are not positioned side by side in the word, the team will need to be creative in solving the problem.) Teams share their words with other teams.

Word Practice

Structure: Team-Pair-Solo

Teams work together to spell a word. Then teams divide into pairs and spell the same word. They compare with the other pair. Finally, individuals spell the word. They come back together as a team and compare. They celebrate or coach and begin the process with a new word.

Team Word Study Activities (continued)

Spelling Word Collage

Structure: Team Word-Webbing

Roll out a large piece of paper on the floor or tape one to a wall for each team. Each student has a different colored marker. In a set amount of time, each student tries to fit in as many word study words as possible on the paper to create a colorful word collage.

Pick a Letter, Any Letter

Structure: Think-Write-RoundRobin

Each team has a bag of letters. Teammate #1 chooses a letter from the bag without looking and announces the letter to the team, placing it in the middle. Each student thinks about possible words beginning with that letter and then makes a list of words beginning with that letter on individual dry-erase boards. Time is called after a preset time limit. Teammates take turns RoundRobin sharing one of the words on their lists. If a shared word is also on their lists, students may put a mark by it. Words shared aloud must be new words not previously shared. Continue sharing until all new words have been shared. If a teammate does not have a new word on the list to share, he or she may try to come up with another word.

Spelling Walk

Structure: Traveling Heads Together

Teams huddle to make sure all can spell a given word correctly. Use dry-erase boards to practice writing the word. When everyone is confident they can spell the word, the dry-erase boards are cleared and the team sits down. The teacher calls a number and the student with that number travels to a new team with his or her cleared dry-erase board and a marker. At the new team, the student shares the spelling of the word by writing it on the dry-erase board.

Spelling Toss

Structure: Turn Toss

Teammates toss a ball to each other. As each teammate catches the ball, he or she contributes a letter to the spelling of a word called out by the teacher. Teammates continue until the word is spelled. The teacher then gives a new word.

Class Word Study Activities

Add a Plural Word

Structure: Find Someone Who

Students have bingo sheets with one singular word written in each square. They circulate throughout the room looking for a partner who can change the singular word into a plural word. If both partners agree on the spelling, the paper's owner writes the plural word and the other partner signs his or her name in the square.

Spell My Word

Structure: Inside-Outside Circle

Students form two circles facing each other. Each student has a word list. As either the outside or the inside circle moves one space, students face new partners. Partners take turns having their partner spell a word from the list. Rotate.

What's My Word?

Structure: Who Am I?

Students attempt to determine their secret word (taped on their back) by circulating and asking "yes/no" questions of classmates. They are allowed three questions per classmate (or unlimited questions until they receive a "no" response). They then find a new classmate to question. When the student guesses his or her word, the student becomes a consultant to give clues to those who have not yet found their identity.

Jumping Words

Structure: Take Off, Touch Down

Give each student a word card. The teacher calls out a vowel sound. If the student's word contains the vowel sound, he or she stands or jumps up. Standing students share their words simultaneously. Teacher and class check for accuracy. The teacher continues to call vowel sounds as students listen for the vowel sound in their words. Variation: The teacher calls out a word and students jump up when they hear a word that rhymes with the word on their word card.

How Many?

Structure: Mix-Freeze-Group

Students make groups with a specific number of students corresponding to answers to questions, asked by the teacher, such as:
- # of total letters in a given word
- # of vowels in a word
- # of a specific letter in a word
- # of syllables in a word

(For example, if the answer to the question is four, when the teacher calls, "Show me," students show the number 4 with their fingers on their chests, quickly form groups of four, and kneel down. Students not finding a group should meet in a predetermined part of the room in "Lost and Found.")

Making Words Lesson Plans

On the following pages are three lessons designed to help students think about the sounds they hear in words and the letter patterns that make up those sounds. They all involve making words from one longer word. The steps for the three lessons are the same. In each of the three lessons, students proceed through three activities:

- **Activity 1: Making Words (RallyCoach)**
- **Activity 2: Sorting (Find My Rule)**
- **Activity 3: Transfer (RallyCoach)**

Since the steps are the same for all three lesson, we will provide a full description of Lesson 1, then just provide the necessary substitutions for Lessons 2 and 3.

Each lesson has its own set of blacklines, but they all share the Find My Rule Mat on page 288. Also, you will find two forms to plan and create your own Making Words lessons.

- **Making Words Planning Form (p. 289)**
- **Making Words Student Form (p. 290)**

The Magic Word
When done with each lesson, challenge pairs to see if they can discover the "Magic Word." The magic word is the word made from all the letters from each set of student letters.
The magic words from each lesson are:
Lesson 1: yourself
Lesson 2: rainforest
Lesson 3: relationship

Helpful Hints:
- These activities may be done in one day or two days at the beginning of the week. Making Words may be done on day one and the Sorting and Transfer activities on day two.
- Mailing envelopes or plastic sandwich baggies will help students keep their materials organized and accessible.
- These activities are most beneficial when the teacher selects or designs lessons that reinforce letter patterns the students are needing to know or strengthen for their reading and writing.
- All letters on the Making Words form are put in alphabetical order with vowels first, followed by consonants.

Making Words Lessons

- Lesson 1: Making Words: *Yourself* 274
- Lesson 2: Making Words: *Rainforest* 280
- Lesson 3: Making Words: *Relationship* 284

WORD STUDY Lessons

Making Words
Lesson 1: *Yourself*

Activity 1: Making Words

In pairs, students take turns manipulating letter cards to make words.

Activity 1 Steps

STRUCTURE
RallyCoach

1. The teacher makes a transparency of the Making Words (*Yourself*) page and cuts out the letters and words.

2. Each pair receives one set of the following letters, *e, o, u, f, l, r, s, y* (the letters from the word *yourself*), from the blackline.

3. The teacher asks students to make words as described in the table on page 275, Words to Make from *Yourself*. The teacher reviews the teaching points as indicated on the table.

4. Partner A makes the first word, while Partner B coaches if necessary.

5. The teacher makes the word on the overhead projector.

6. Students write the word in a box on their student form. They will use these words in Activity 2.

7. Partners take turns for each new word and the process is repeated.

Blacklines

- Making Words (*Yourself*) Teacher Transparency Form..........278
- Making Words Student Form 279

Words to Make from *Yourself*

Directions	Word	Teaching Point
Make: *us*	us	
Add a letter to make a new word	use	Discuss how silent *e* changes vowel.
Make: *yes*	yes	
Make: *sly*	sly	Y as a vowel No vowels = long /i/ words.
Change the beginning letter and make a new word.	fly	
Make: *self*	self	
Make: *for* I am going to the store *for* milk.	for	Discuss *or* letter pattern.
Add a silent *e* and make a new word	fore	Discuss homophones. Discuss meaning of *fore*.
Make another homophone for this pair.	four	
Replace the *f* with another letter and spell a new word.	your	Discuss letter patterns to help decode or write words.
Replace the *y* with another letter.	sour	Discuss the two sounds for *our*.
Take away the *s* and you will have a new word.	our	Remind students to try *our* pattern both ways when decoding words.
Make: *lousy*	lousy	Y as vowel Vowels in the word, y = long /e/
Make: *sure*	sure	What is tricky about this word?
Add a suffix to this word.	surely	Discuss taking off suffix to decode. Remind them not to take off the silent *e* when adding *ly*.
Take off the *ly*. Replace the 'u' with another vowel.	sore	Discuss "Which way looks right—*sor* or *sore*?"
Add the *ly* suffix to this word.	sorely	What did you need to remember when adding the suffix?
Make: *fury*	fury	Discuss /ur/ letter pattern.
Make: *rule*	rule	
Make: *rely*	rely	Y with a vowel doesn't work on this word.
Make: *rose*	rose	
Make: *rosy*	rosy	Discuss dropping silent *e* before adding *y*. "Which way looks right—*rosey*, *rosy*?"
Use all the letters to make the magic word.	yourself	Discuss compound words.

Activity 2: Sorting

The teacher places words in two different columns on the overhead projector. The challenge is for students to discover the teacher's rules for sorting the words this way. This activity draws the students' attention to visual clues and letter patterns.

Activity 2 Steps

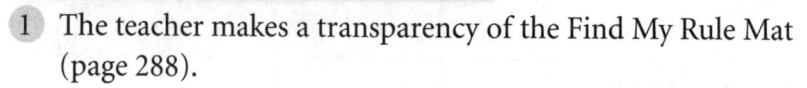

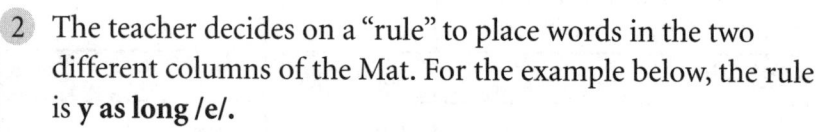

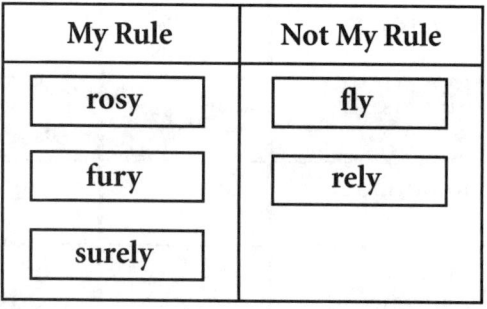

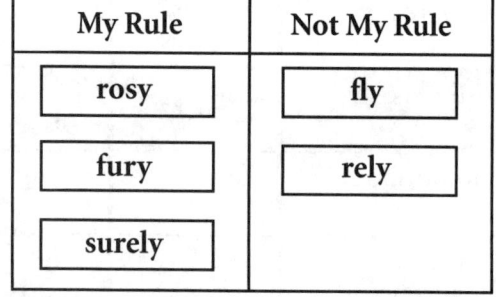

1. The teacher makes a transparency of the Find My Rule Mat (page 288).

2. The teacher decides on a "rule" to place words in the two different columns of the Mat. For the example below, the rule is **y as long /e/**.

My Rule	Not My Rule
rosy	fly
fury	rely
surely	

3. The teacher places one word in each column, and asks, "What is my rule?"

4. Students RallyRobin with their shoulder partners to determine what the rule may be.

5. The teacher adds the next two words, one in each column, and asks again, "What is my rule?"

6. Students RallyRobin again.

7. This continues until students think they know the rule. The teacher calls on students to verbalize the rule. If correct, the teacher congratulates the students, if incorrect the process continues.

8. When done, the activity may be repeated with a new rule. Other rule examples are listed at left.

9. After practice, students can cut apart their word boxes from Activity 1, step 6. They can create their own word sorts and have a partner find the rule.

STRUCTURE
Find My Rule

Ideas for Rules

- homophones
- ending -ly
- y as a long /i/
- y as a long /e/
- /ou/ letter pattern

Blacklines

- Making Words (*Yourself*) Teacher Transparency Form..............278
- Find My Rule Mat..............288

Activity 3: Transfer

The teacher displays a word card on the overhead projector and discusses the letter pattern. Then the teacher says, "If you can spell this word, you can also spell..." Students work in pairs to spell the new word. This activity helps students "use what they know" from one word and transfer it to a new word that they are trying to read or write.

STRUCTURE
RallyCoach

Activity 3 Steps

1. The teacher places a word card on the overhead projector.
2. The teacher states, "If you can spell this word, you can also spell…." (See the examples below.)
3. Partner A spells the word while Partner B watches, checks, and coaches as needed.
4. The teacher spells the new word for the class, and students praise their partners for correct spelling.
5. Students switch roles of Speller and Coach for each new word.

Using What You Know

If you can spell…	Then you can spell…
self	shelf, elf
our	flour, hour, sour
sore	more, store, core
sly	dry, pry, try, shy
rose	close, hose, nose, chose

Making Words (*Yourself*) Teacher Transparency Form

Instructions: Make a transparency of this page. Cut out letters and words to use during Activity 1: Making Words and with Activity 2: Sorting.

e	o	u	f	l	r	s	y
us	self	sour	sore	rose			
use	for	our	sorely	rosy			
yes	fore	lousy	fury	yourself			
sly	four	sure	rule				
fly	your	surely	rely				

278 Balanced Literacy • Fourth Grade • Skidmore & Graber
Kagan Publishing • 1 (800) 933-2667 • www.KaganOnline.com

Making Words (e, o, u, f, l, r, s, y) Student Form

Instructions: Make one copy per student. Cut apart letters to use during Activity 1: Making Words. Cut apart boxes after words are added to use during Activity 2: Sorting.

e   o   u   f   l   r   s   y

Lesson 2: *Rainforest*
Activity 1: Making Words

The steps for this activity are the same as Lesson 1, Activity 1 but substitute the following words to make from the letters in *Rainforest*.

Words to Make from *Rainforest*

Directions	Word	Teaching Point
Make: *stain*	stain	Discuss /ai/ letter pattern.
Make: *train*	train	/ai/ letter pattern Decoding blends: Cover up from the vowel to the end of the word, say blend, then uncover and say the rest.
Make: *for*	for	
Add an ending consonant.	fort	
Take off the *t* and add a silent *e*.	fore	Discuss meaning. (forehead, forearm, before)
Replace the *f* with a *t*.	tore	Discuss /ore/ letter pattern.
Replace the *t* with another consonant.	sore	Remind the students to use letter patterns to read/write.
Add a *t* somewhere in the word to make a new word.	store	
Replace the *r* with another letter.	stone	Silent *e* makes long /o/.
Make: *fat*	fat	
Add a silent *e*.	fate	What does the silent *e* do?
Make: *rat*	rat	
Make: *rate*	rate	What did you add? How did you know?
Make: *into*	into	
Make: *roar* I have never heard a lion roar.	roar	Discuss /oa/ letter pattern.
Make: *soar* Have you seen an eagle soar?	soar	
Make: *seat*	seat	Discuss /ea/ letter pattern.
Change the beginning letter and make a new word.	neat	

Directions	Word	Teaching Point
Replace the *n* with a blend.	treat	
Make: *rest*	rest	Discuss the /est/ pattern.
Change the beginning letter.	nest	
Make: *fin*	fin	
Make the vowel long.	fine	How did you know to do that?
Make: *rise*	rise	
Make: *risen*	risen	
Use all the letters and make the magic word.	rainforest	Discuss letter patterns that helped them spell the word. Discuss compound words.

Activity 2: Sorting

The steps for this activity are the same as Lesson 1, Activity 2. Below is an example for Find My Rule using the Rainforest words and additional ideas for Find My Rule.

Ideas for Rules
- homophones
- letter patterns: /eat/, /ore/, /est/, /ai/
- silent /e/ words
- short vowel words
- long vowel words
- compound words

My Rule	Not My Rule
fine	fat
rise	soar
rate	

Example: silent /e/ words

Activity 3: Transfer

The steps for this activity are the same as Lesson 1, Activity 3, except use the following words to spell.

Using What You Know
If you can spell…	Then you can spell…
tore	more, core, chore
fine	spine, swine, line
stain	drain, main, strain
stone	phone, lone, shone
rest	best, west, crest

Making Words (*Rainforest*) Teacher Transparency Form

Instructions: Make a transparency of this page. Cut out letters and words to use during Activity 1: Making Words.

t	fore	fat	roar	rest	risen
s	fort	stone	into	treat	rise
r	for	store	rate	neat	fine
r	for	store	rate	neat	fine
n	train	sore	rat	seat	fin
f					
o	stain	tore	fate	soar	nest	rainforest
i					
e					
a					

Making Words (a, e, i, o, f, n, r, r, s, t)
Student Form

Instructions: Make one copy per student. Cut apart letters to use during Activity 1: Making Words. Cut apart boxes after words are added to use during Activity 2: Sorting.

Balanced Literacy • Fourth Grade • Skidmore & Graber

Lesson 3: Relationship
Activity 1: Making Words

The steps for this activity are the same as Lesson 1, Activity 1 but substitute the following words to make from the letters in Relationship.

Words to Make from *Relationship*

Directions	Word	Teaching Point
Make: *hat*	hat	
Add one letter to spell *hate*.	hate	Silent *e* changes vowel sound.
Change the beginning to an *r*. What is the new word?	rate	Use the word in a sentence to clarify meaning.
Replace the *r* with an *l*. Now what is the new word?	late	
Add an ending letter.	later	
Take away the *r* at the end and add an *s* at the beginning. What is the new word?	slate	Use the word in a sentence to clarify meaning.
Make: *stripe*	stripe	How did you know to add a silent *e* at the end?
Make: *shape*	shape	
Make: *stone*	stone	Discuss the two ways to make long /o/. (oa, o-e) Which way looks right (*stone* or *stoan*)?
Make: *oil*	oil	Discuss the /oi/ sound.
Add a letter to spell *soil*.	soil	What is a synonym for *soil*?
Add a letter to make a new word.	spoil	
Make: *loan*	loan	How did you know how to spell this word?
Make this word plural.	loans	
Take away the *s* and add *er*.	loaner	Discuss the -er suffix meaning: one who...
Make: *neat*	neat	Discuss the /ea/ letter pattern.
Replace the *n* with another letter to make a new word.	heat	
Make: *leash*	leash	
Take away the *sh* and add a different letter. What is the new word?	lean	Use the word in a sentence to clarify meaning.
Make: *tale* The boy told a wild tale to the teacher.	tale	Use the word in a sentence to clarify meaning
Make a homonym for *tale*.	tail	
Make: *pie*	pie	Discuss the /ie/ letter pattern.

Words to Make from *Relationship* (continued)

Directions	Word	Teaching Point
Replace the beginning letter to make a new word.	lie	
Make: *tile*	tile	Discuss the two ways to make long /i/.
Make: *ratio* Use a 1:1 ratio of water and vinegar to mop the floor.	ratio	
Add an *n* to the end of the word to make a new word.	ration	Use the word in a sentence to clarify meaning.
Make: *ship*	ship	
Add a prefix to *ship* to make a new word.	reship	Discuss prefix meaning of *pre*: again.
Use all the letters to make the magic word.	relationship	Discuss the letter patterns that helped spell this word.

Activity 2: Sorting

The steps for this activity are the same as Lesson 1, Activity 2. Below is an example for Find My Rule using the Relationship words and additional ideas for Find My Rule.

Ideas for Rules
- silent /e/ words
- /ea/ words
- /oi/ words
- /oa/ words
- words that begin with blends
- /ie/ words

My Rule	Not My Rule
slate	oil
stone	neat
tile	

Example: silent /e/ words

Activity 3: Transfer

The steps for this activity are the same as Lesson 1, Activity 3, except use the following words to spell.

Using What You Know
If you can spell…	Then you can spell…
soil	foil, coil, toil
tile	pile, smile, file
ration	nation, vacation, station
reship	restate, retile, reshape

Making Words (*Relationship*) Teacher Transparency Form

Instructions: Make a transparency of this page. Cut out letters and words to use during Activity 1: Making Words.

a e i i o h l n p r s t					
hat	later	oil	loaner	tale	ratio
hate	late	stone	loans	lean	tile	relationship
slate	rate	shape	loan	leash	lie	reship
soil	stripe	spoil	heat	pie	ship
hat	slate	soil	neat	tail	ration

Making Words (a, e, i, i, o, h, l, n, p, r, s, t)
Student Form

Instructions: Make one copy per student. Cut apart letters to use during Activity 1: Making Words. Cut apart boxes after words are added to use during Activity 2: Sorting.

a | e | i | i | o | h | l | n | p | r | s | t

Find My Rule Mat for Making Words

Instructions: Make a transparency of this mat for Activity 2: Sorting. Make copies for each pair of students for Activity 2: Sorting.

My Rule	Not My Rule

Balanced Literacy • Fourth Grade • Skidmore & Graber
Kagan Publishing • 1 (800) 933-2667 • www.KaganOnline.com

Making Words Planning Form

Letters: _____

Magic Word: _____

Part 1: Making Words (RallyTable)

Instructions: Use this planning form to create additional Making Words lessons.

Directions	Word	Teaching Point

Part 2: Sorting (Find My Rule)	Sort For:

Part 3: Transfer (RallyCoach)	Using What You Know

Making Words
Student Form

Instructions: Use this planning form to create the letters and words for additional Making Words lessons.

FIND SOMEONE WHO Activity

Who Knows?

Students mix about the room, finding others who can help them fill out their Find Someone Who word study worksheets.

Activity Steps

1. Every student receives a Find Someone Who worksheet.
2. Students mix around the room until they find a partner.
3. In pairs, Partner A asks a question from the worksheet; Partner B responds. Partner A records the answer on his or her worksheet.
4. Partner B checks and initials the answer.
5. Partner B asks a question. Partner A responds. Partner B records the answer on his or her worksheet.
6. Partner A checks and initials the answer.
7. Partners shake hands, part, and raise a hand again as they search for a new partner.
8. Students repeat the process until they complete their worksheets.
9. When their worksheets are completed, students sit down; seated students may be approached by others as a resource.
10. In teams, students compare answers; if there is disagreement or uncertainty, they raise four hands to ask a team question.

STRUCTURE
Find Someone Who

Blacklines

- All About Prefixes 292
- Skill Review #1
  Possessives, Misspelled Words, Prefixes, Homophones,
  Silent Letters, Contractions 293
- Skill Review #2
  Two Sounds of g, au/aw, Homophones, Correct Spelling, Prefixes,
  Compound Words 294
- Skill Review #3
  Cause and Effect, Similes, Making Words, Figurative Language 295
- Blank Form 296

All About Prefixes!
Find Someone Who

Name _____

Instructions: Copy one page per student.

All About Prefixes!

Draw lines to connect the prefixes with their meanings.

dis- • • beneath, below, too little

under- • • against

anti- • • not

Initials

All About Prefixes!

Circle the word which means "not arranged."

nonstop   disorganized   impolite   disloyal

Initials

All About Prefixes!

Read the sentence below and circle each word with a prefix.

After defrosting the disorganized refrigerator, we discarded the spoiled foods.

Initials

All About Prefixes!

Draw lines to connect the prefixes with their meanings.

non- • • out of, is no longer

ex- • • not, without

Initials

All About Prefixes!

Add a prefix (dis, anti, under, non)

_____ skid

_____ continue

_____ brush

_____ freeze

_____ appear

Initials

All About Prefixes!

Circle the prefix in each word.

discolor

express

undercharge

nonprofit

discourage

undershirt

nonresident

disable

Initials

Skill Review #1
Find Someone Who

Name _____

Instructions: Copy one page per student.

Possessives

Circle the possessive words.

Maria's
he's
friend's
it's
puppies
fish's

Initials

Add a Prefix

under = beneath, below, too little
dis = not

_____ connect

_____ ground

_____ clothes

_____ like

Initials

Silent Letters

Circle the silent letters.

knight   sword

rhyme   listen

Initials

Misspelled Words

Circle the misspelled words.

Wich way did you sea them go win thay drove buy?

Initials

Homophones

Match the pairs.

piece	pail
pale	pare
pane	pain
pair	peace

Initials

Contractions

Write the contractions for these words.

should not   _____

they will   _____

there is   _____

Initials

Skill Review #2
Find Someone Who

Name _____

Instructions: Copy one page per student.

Two Sounds of g

g or j

gardener	g or j
Germany	g or j
gerbil	g or j
goblet	g or j
angry	g or j
dodge	g or j

Initials

au or aw?

au or aw?

spr_____ling

bec_____se

d_____ghter

str_____berry

Initials

Homophones

Match the Homophones

waive	wear
weight	wave
ware	wait

Initials

Which Looks Correct?

Circle the correct spelling.

brief / breif	their / thier
freind / friend	piece / peice
believe / beleive	

Initials

Prefixes

Add a prefix.

under- = beneath, below, too little   anti- = against
non- = not, is no longer   dis- = not

_____ stop   _____ connect

_____ social   _____ infect

_____ arm   _____ smoker

Initials

Make Compound Words

Make Compound Words

thunder	knee	
mate	scraper	sky
cap	team	storm

_____ _____

_____ _____

_____ _____

Initials

Skill Review #3
Find Someone Who

Name _____

Instructions: Copy one page per student.

Cause and Effect

Which is the Cause? Which is the Effect?

The wind blew forcefully all night long.   Cause   or   Effect

A tree branch fell on the house roof.   Cause   or   Effect

Initials

Cause and Effort

Which is the Cause? Which is the Effect?

We decided to pack up our gear and go home.   Cause   or   Effect

After three hours of fishing, we hadn't caught any fish.   Cause   or   Effect

Initials

Similes

Complete the similes.

prickly as _____

noisy like _____

Initials

Making Words

Use these letters to make five words.

a e i l m n r t

_____ _____

_____

_____

Initials

Figurative Language

Match the term with the definition.

alliteration   •   • a word that sounds like what it is describing

simile   •   • a comparison

idiom   •   • repetition of the same letter at the beginning of two or more words

onomatopoeia •   • a familiar phrase that means something other than what it literally says

Initials

Find Someone Who Form

Name _____

Instructions: Use this form to create questions for additional activities.

Initials

Initials

Initials

Initials

Initials

Initials

Initials

QUIZ-QUIZ-TRADE Activity

Partner Word Study Practice

Students quiz a partner, get quizzed by a partner, and then trade cards to repeat the process with a new partner.

Activity Steps

1. Each student receives a card with a question on the front and answer on the back.
2. All students stand up, put a hand up, and pair up.
3. Partner A quizzes Partner B.
4. Partner B answers.
5. Partner A checks the answer on back and praises or coaches.
6. Partners switch roles and quiz again.
7. After they have quizzed both ways, partners trade cards, and raise their hands to find a new partner. The partner quizzing and trading proceeds for numerous pairings.

STRUCTURE
Quiz-Quiz-Trade

Front

Letter Patterns
Question
Say the word. Which way looks right?
a) boil
b) boyl

Back

Letter Patterns
Answer
Say the word. Which way looks right?
a) boil

Blacklines

- Contractions 298–304
- Silent Letters 305–311
- Letter Patterns (ar, er, ir, or, ur) 312–318
- Letter Patterns (au, aw, ou, ow) 319–326
- Letter Patterns (ie, ei) 327–333
- Prefixes (anti-, dis-, ex-, non-, under-) 334–341
- Prefixes and Suffixes 342–348
- Their, There, They're 349–355

Contractions
Quiz-Quiz-Trade

Instructions: Copy enough cards so each student has one card. Cut on dotted lines and fold in half.

Contractions	Contractions
Spell the contraction (aloud or on paper). **Question** What contraction can be made with these two words? **she had**	**Answer** **she'd**
Spell the contraction (aloud or on paper). **Question** What contraction can be made with these two words? **there had**	**Answer** **there'd**
Spell the contraction (aloud or on paper). **Question** What contraction can be made with these two words? **they had**	**Answer** **they'd**
Spell the contraction (aloud or on paper). **Question** What contraction can be made with these two words? **I would**	**Answer** **I'd**

Contractions
Quiz-Quiz-Trade

Instructions: Copy enough cards so each student has one card. Cut on dotted lines and fold in half.

Contractions
Spell the contraction (aloud or on paper).
Question
What contraction can be made with these two words?

it would

Contractions
Answer

it'd

Contractions
Spell the contraction (aloud or on paper).
Question
What contraction can be made with these two words?

she would

Contractions
Answer

she'd

Contractions
Spell the contraction (aloud or on paper).
Question
What contraction can be made with these two words?

there would

Contractions
Answer

there'd

Contractions
Spell the contraction (aloud or on paper).
Question
What contraction can be made with these two words?

I had

Contractions
Answer

I'd

Balanced Literacy • Fourth Grade • Skidmore & Graber
Kagan Publishing • 1 (800) 933-2667 • www.KaganOnline.com

Contractions
Quiz-Quiz-Trade

Instructions: Copy enough cards so each student has one card. Cut on dotted lines and fold in half.

Contractions	Contractions
Spell the contraction (aloud or on paper). **Question** What contraction can be made with these two words? **it had**	**Answer** **it'd**
Spell the contraction (aloud or on paper). **Question** What contraction can be made with these two words? **they are**	**Answer** **they're**
Spell the contraction (aloud or on paper). **Question** What contraction can be made with these two words? **you are**	**Answer** **you're**
Spell the contraction (aloud or on paper). **Question** What contraction can be made with these two words? **need not**	**Answer** **needn't**

Contractions
Quiz-Quiz-Trade

Instructions: Copy enough cards so each student has one card. Cut on dotted lines and fold in half.

Contractions	Contractions
Spell the contraction (aloud or on paper). **Question** What contraction can be made with these two words? **must not**	**Answer** **mustn't**
Spell the contraction (aloud or on paper). **Question** What contraction can be made with these two words? **might have**	**Answer** **might've**
Spell the contraction (aloud or on paper). **Question** What contraction can be made with these two words? **let us**	**Answer** **let's**
Spell the contraction (aloud or on paper). **Question** What contraction can be made with these two words? **I will**	**Answer** **I'll**

Contractions
Quiz-Quiz-Trade

Instructions: Copy enough cards so each student has one card. Cut on dotted lines and fold in half.

Contractions

Spell the contraction (aloud or on paper).

Question

What contraction can be made with these two words?

it will

Contractions

Answer

it'll

Contractions

Spell the contraction (aloud or on paper).

Question

What contraction can be made with these two words?

he will

Contractions

Answer

he'll

Contractions

Spell the contraction (aloud or on paper).

Question

What contraction can be made with these two words?

she will

Contractions

Answer

she'll

Contractions

Spell the contraction (aloud or on paper).

Question

What contraction can be made with these two words?

that will

Contractions

Answer

that'll

Contractions
Quiz-Quiz-Trade

Instructions: Copy enough cards so each student has one card. Cut on dotted lines and fold in half.

Contractions	Contractions
Spell the contraction (aloud or on paper). **Question** What contraction can be made with these two words? **they will**	**Answer** **they'll**
Spell the contraction (aloud or on paper). **Question** What contraction can be made with these two words? **we will**	**Answer** **we'll**
Spell the contraction (aloud or on paper). **Question** What contraction can be made with these two words? **you will**	**Answer** **you'll**
Spell the contraction (aloud or on paper). **Question** What contraction can be made with these two words? **you have**	**Answer** **you've**

Balanced Literacy • Fourth Grade • Skidmore & Graber
Kagan Publishing • 1 (800) 933-2667 • www.KaganOnline.com

Contractions
Quiz-Quiz-Trade

Instructions: Copy enough cards so each student has one card. Cut on dotted lines and fold in half.

Contractions	Contractions
Spell the contraction (aloud or on paper). **Question** What contraction can be made with these two words? **could have**	**Answer** **could've**
Spell the contraction (aloud or on paper). **Question** What contraction can be made with these two words? **would have**	**Answer** **would've**
Spell the contraction (aloud or on paper). **Question** What contraction can be made with these two words? **we have**	**Answer** **we've**
Spell the contraction (aloud or on paper). **Question** What contraction can be made with these two words? **I have**	**Answer** **I've**

Silent Letters
Quiz-Quiz-Trade

Instructions: Copy enough cards so each student has one card. Cut on dotted lines and fold in half.

Silent Letters — Question	Silent Letters — Answer
Say the word. Which consonant is silent? **comb**	**b** com__b__
Say the word. Which consonant is silent? **scene**	**c** __s__cene
Say the word. Which consonant is silent? **rhyme**	**h** r__h__yme
Say the word. Which consonant is silent? **Knee**	**k** __K__nee

Balanced Literacy • Fourth Grade • Skidmore & Graber
Kagan Publishing • 1 (800) 933-2667 • www.KaganOnline.com

Silent Letters
Quiz-Quiz-Trade

Instructions: Copy enough cards so each student has one card. Cut on dotted lines and fold in half.

Silent Letters	Silent Letters
Question Say the word. Which consonant is silent? **could**	**Answer** $\boxed{l}$ cou_l_d
Question Say the word. Which consonant is silent? **whole**	**Answer** $\boxed{w}$ _w_hole
Question Say the word. Which consonant is silent? **sword**	**Answer** $\boxed{w}$ s_w_ord
Question Say the word. Which consonant is silent? **island**	**Answer** $\boxed{s}$ i_s_land

Word Study Blackline

Silent Letters
Quiz-Quiz-Trade

Instructions: Copy enough cards so each student has one card. Cut on dotted lines and fold in half.

Silent Letters

Question

Say the word.
Which consonant is silent?

know

Silent Letters

Answer

| k |

Know

Silent Letters

Question

Say the word.
Which consonant is silent?

listen

Silent Letters

Answer

| t |

listen

Silent Letters

Question

Say the word.
Which consonant is silent?

gnat

Silent Letters

Answer

| g |

gnat

Silent Letters

Question

Say the word.
Which consonant is silent?

half

Silent Letters

Answer

| l |

half

Balanced Literacy • Fourth Grade • Skidmore & Graber
Kagan Publishing • 1 (800) 933-2667 • www.KaganOnline.com

Silent Letters
Quiz-Quiz-Trade

Instructions: Copy enough cards so each student has one card. Cut on dotted lines and fold in half.

Silent Letters

Question

Say the word.
Which consonant is silent?

calf

Silent Letters

Answer

| l |

calf

Silent Letters

Question

Say the word.
Which consonant is silent?

wrap

Silent Letters

Answer

| w |

wrap

Silent Letters

Question

Say the word.
Which consonant is silent?

two

Silent Letters

Answer

| w |

two

Silent Letters

Question

Say the word.
Which consonant is silent?

watch

Silent Letters

Answer

| t |

watch

Word Study Blackline

Silent Letters
Quiz-Quiz-Trade

Instructions: Copy enough cards so each student has one card. Cut on dotted lines and fold in half.

Silent Letters

Question

Say the word.
Which consonant is silent?

wren

Silent Letters

Answer

| w |

w̲ren

Silent Letters

Question

Say the word.
Which consonant is silent?

often

Silent Letters

Answer

| t |

of̲ten

Silent Letters

Question

Say the word.
Which consonant is silent?

calm

Silent Letters

Answer

| l |

cal̲m

Silent Letters

Question

Say the word.
Which consonant is silent?

edge

Silent Letters

Answer

| d |

ed̲ge

Balanced Literacy • Fourth Grade • Skidmore & Graber
Kagan Publishing • 1 (800) 933-2667 • www.KaganOnline.com

Silent Letters
Quiz-Quiz-Trade

Instructions: Copy enough cards so each student has one card. Cut on dotted lines and fold in half.

Silent Letters

Question

Say the word.
Which consonant is silent?

hymn

Silent Letters

Answer

n

hymn

Silent Letters

Question

Say the word.
Which consonant is silent?

lamb

Silent Letters

Answer

b

lamb

Silent Letters

Question

Say the word.
Which consonant is silent?

ghost

Silent Letters

Answer

h

ghost

Silent Letters

Question

Say the word.
Which consonant is silent?

bridge

Silent Letters

Answer

d

bridge

Silent Letters
Quiz-Quiz-Trade

Instructions: Copy enough cards so each student has one card. Cut on dotted lines and fold in half.

Silent Letters	Silent Letters
Question Say the word. Which consonant is silent? **walk**	**Answer** **l** wa_l_k
Question Say the word. Which consonant is silent? **wrinkle**	**Answer** **w** _w_rinkle
Question Say the word. Which consonant is silent? **sign**	**Answer** **g** si_g_n
Question Say the word. Which consonant is silent? **soften**	**Answer** **t** sof_t_en

Balanced Literacy • Fourth Grade • Skidmore & Graber
Kagan Publishing • 1 (800) 933-2667 • www.KaganOnline.com

Letter Patterns: ar, er, ir, or, ur
Quiz-Quiz-Trade

Instructions: Copy enough cards so each student has one card. Cut on dotted lines and fold in half.

Letter Patterns: ar, er, ir, or, ur

Question
Say the word.
Which way looks right?

a) curly
b) cerly
c) cirly

Letter Patterns: ar, er, ir, or, ur

Answer

a) curly

Letter Patterns: ar, er, ir, or, ur

Question
Say the word.
Which way looks right?

a) formal
b) farmal
c) fermal

Letter Patterns: ar, er, ir, or, ur

Answer

a) formal

Letter Patterns: ar, er, ir, or, ur

Question
Say the word.
Which way looks right?

a) distirb
b) disterb
c) disturb

Letter Patterns: ar, er, ir, or, ur

Answer

c) disturb

Letter Patterns: ar, er, ir, or, ur

Question
Say the word.
Which way looks right?

a) tertilla
b) tortilla
c) tartilla

Letter Patterns: ar, er, ir, or, ur

Answer

b) tortilla

Letter Patterns:
ar, er, ir, or, ur
Quiz-Quiz-Trade

Instructions: Copy enough cards so each student has one card. Cut on dotted lines and fold in half.

Letter Patterns: ar, er, ir, or, ur

Question
Say the word.
Which way looks right?

a) whurlwind
b) wherlwind
c) whirlwind

Letter Patterns: ar, er, ir, or, ur

Answer

c) whirlwind

Letter Patterns: ar, er, ir, or, ur

Question
Say the word.
Which way looks right?

a) emirging
b) emerging
c) emorging

Letter Patterns: ar, er, ir, or, ur

Answer

b) emerging

Letter Patterns: ar, er, ir, or, ur

Question
Say the word.
Which way looks right?

a) answered
b) answired
c) answared

Letter Patterns: ar, er, ir, or, ur

Answer

a) answered

Letter Patterns: ar, er, ir, or, ur

Question
Say the word.
Which way looks right?

a) fernace
b) furnace
c) fornace

Letter Patterns: ar, er, ir, or, ur

Answer

b) furnace

Letter Patterns: ar, er, ir, or, ur
Quiz-Quiz-Trade

Instructions: Copy enough cards so each student has one card. Cut on dotted lines and fold in half.

Letter Patterns: ar, er, ir, or, ur

Question
Say the word.
Which way looks right?
a) creatares
b) creatures
c) creatores

Letter Patterns: ar, er, ir, or, ur

Answer

b) creatures

Letter Patterns: ar, er, ir, or, ur

Question
Say the word.
Which way looks right?
a) misunderstand
b) misundarstand
c) misundorstand

Letter Patterns: ar, er, ir, or, ur

Answer

a) misunderstand

Letter Patterns: ar, er, ir, or, ur

Question
Say the word.
Which way looks right?
a) shuttored
b) shuttared
c) shuttered

Letter Patterns: ar, er, ir, or, ur

Answer

c) shuttered

Letter Patterns: ar, er, ir, or, ur

Question
Say the word.
Which way looks right?
a) hernessed
b) harnessed
c) hurnessed

Letter Patterns: ar, er, ir, or, ur

Answer

b) harnessed

Letter Patterns: ar, er, ir, or, ur
Quiz-Quiz-Trade

Instructions: Copy enough cards so each student has one card. Cut on dotted lines and fold in half.

Letter Patterns: ar, er, ir, or, ur

Question
Say the word.
Which way looks right?

a) infurmation
b) infermation
c) information

Letter Patterns: ar, er, ir, or, ur

Answer

c) information

Letter Patterns: ar, er, ir, or, ur

Question
Say the word.
Which way looks right?

a) twurling
b) twirling
c) tworling

Letter Patterns: ar, er, ir, or, ur

Answer

b) twirling

Letter Patterns: ar, er, ir, or, ur

Question
Say the word.
Which way looks right?

a) corpenters
b) cerpenters
c) carpenters

Letter Patterns: ar, er, ir, or, ur

Answer

c) carpenters

Letter Patterns: ar, er, ir, or, ur

Question
Say the word.
Which way looks right?

a) forward
b) forwird
c) forwerd

Letter Patterns: ar, er, ir, or, ur

Answer

a) forward

Letter Patterns: ar, er, ir, or, ur
Quiz-Quiz-Trade

Instructions: Copy enough cards so each student has one card. Cut on dotted lines and fold in half.

Letter Patterns: ar, er, ir, or, ur

Question
Say the word.
Which way looks right?

a) ordinery
b) ordinary
c) ordinory

Letter Patterns: ar, er, ir, or, ur

Answer

b) ordinary

Letter Patterns: ar, er, ir, or, ur

Question
Say the word.
Which way looks right?

a) passport
b) passpart
c) passpert

Letter Patterns: ar, er, ir, or, ur

Answer

a) passport

Letter Patterns: ar, er, ir, or, ur

Question
Say the word.
Which way looks right?

a) performed
b) purformed
c) porformed

Letter Patterns: ar, er, ir, or, ur

Answer

a) performed

Letter Patterns: ar, er, ir, or, ur

Question
Say the word.
Which way looks right?

a) ferniture
b) furniture
c) firniture

Letter Patterns: ar, er, ir, or, ur

Answer

b) furniture

Letter Patterns:
ar, er, ir, or, ur
Quiz-Quiz-Trade

Instructions: Copy enough cards so each student has one card. Cut on dotted lines and fold in half.

Letter Patterns: ar, er, ir, or, ur

Question
Say the word.
Which way looks right?

a) burger
b) berger
c) barger

Letter Patterns: ar, er, ir, or, ur

Answer

a) burger

Letter Patterns: ar, er, ir, or, ur

Question
Say the word.
Which way looks right?

a) disturbed
b) distirbed
c) disterbed

Letter Patterns: ar, er, ir, or, ur

Answer

a) disturbed

Letter Patterns: ar, er, ir, or, ur

Question
Say the word.
Which way looks right?

a) carrect
b) correct
c) currect

Letter Patterns: ar, er, ir, or, ur

Answer

b) correct

Letter Patterns: ar, er, ir, or, ur

Question
Say the word.
Which way looks right?

a) transfurm
b) transfarm
c) transform

Letter Patterns: ar, er, ir, or, ur

Answer

c) transform

Letter Patterns: ar, er, ir, or, ur
Quiz-Quiz-Trade

Instructions: Copy enough cards so each student has one card. Cut on dotted lines and fold in half.

Letter Patterns: ar, er, ir, or, ur

Question
Say the word.
Which way looks right?

a) accorate
b) accerate
c) accurate

Letter Patterns: ar, er, ir, or, ur

Answer

c) accurate

Letter Patterns: ar, er, ir, or, ur

Question
Say the word.
Which way looks right?

a) afterwurds
b) afterwords
c) afterwards

Letter Patterns: ar, er, ir, or, ur

Answer

c) afterwards

Letter Patterns: ar, er, ir, or, ur

Question
Say the word.
Which way looks right?

a) parform
b) perform
c) porform

Letter Patterns: ar, er, ir, or, ur

Answer

b) perform

Letter Patterns: ar, er, ir, or, ur

Question
Say the word.
Which way looks right?

a) gorillas
b) girillas
c) gurillas

Letter Patterns: ar, er, ir, or, ur

Answer

a) gorillas

Letter Patterns:
au, aw, ou, ow
Quiz-Quiz-Trade

Instructions: Copy enough cards so each student has one card. Cut on dotted lines and fold in half.

Letter Patterns: au, aw, ou, ow

Question

Say the word.
Which way looks right?

a) astronaut
b) astronawt

Letter Patterns: au, aw, ou, ow

Answer

a) astronaut

Letter Patterns: au, aw, ou, ow

Question

Say the word.
Which way looks right?

a) lawndry
b) laundry

Letter Patterns: au, aw, ou, ow

Answer

b) laundry

Letter Patterns: au, aw, ou, ow

Question

Say the word.
Which way looks right?

a) autograph
b) awtograph

Letter Patterns: au, aw, ou, ow

Answer

a) autograph

Letter Patterns: au, aw, ou, ow

Question

Say the word.
Which way looks right?

a) awtomatic
b) automatic

Letter Patterns: au, aw, ou, ow

Answer

b) automatic

Balanced Literacy • Fourth Grade • Skidmore & Graber
Kagan Publishing • 1 (800) 933-2667 • www.KaganOnline.com

Letter Patterns: au, aw, ou, ow
Quiz-Quiz-Trade

Instructions: Copy enough cards so each student has one card. Cut on dotted lines and fold in half.

Letter Patterns: au, aw, ou, ow

Question

Say the word.
Which way looks right?

a) applesauce
b) applesawce

Letter Patterns: au, aw, ou, ow

Answer

a) applesauce

Letter Patterns: au, aw, ou, ow

Question

Say the word.
Which way looks right?

a) lawnch
b) launch

Letter Patterns: au, aw, ou, ow

Answer

b) launch

Letter Patterns: au, aw, ou, ow

Question

Say the word.
Which way looks right?

a) audience
b) awdience

Letter Patterns: au, aw, ou, ow

Answer

a) audience

Letter Patterns: au, aw, ou, ow

Question

Say the word.
Which way looks right?

a) awtumn
b) autumn

Letter Patterns: au, aw, ou, ow

Answer

b) autumn

Letter Patterns: au, aw, ou, ow
Quiz-Quiz-Trade

Instructions: Copy enough cards so each student has one card. Cut on dotted lines and fold in half.

Letter Patterns: au, aw, ou, ow

Question

Say the word.
Which way looks right?

a) seesaw
b) seesau

Letter Patterns: au, aw, ou, ow

Answer

a) seesaw

Letter Patterns: au, aw, ou, ow

Question

Say the word.
Which way looks right?

a) sprauling
b) sprawling

Letter Patterns: au, aw, ou, ow

Answer

b) sprawling

Letter Patterns: au, aw, ou, ow

Question

Say the word.
Which way looks right?

a) clawed
b) claued

Letter Patterns: au, aw, ou, ow

Answer

a) clawed

Letter Patterns: au, aw, ou, ow

Question

Say the word.
Which way looks right?

a) awning
b) auning

Letter Patterns: au, aw, ou, ow

Answer

a) awning

Balanced Literacy • Fourth Grade • Skidmore & Graber
Kagan Publishing • 1 (800) 933-2667 • www.KaganOnline.com

Letter Patterns: au, aw, ou, ow
Quiz-Quiz-Trade

Instructions: Copy enough cards so each student has one card. Cut on dotted lines and fold in half.

Letter Patterns: au, aw, ou, ow

Question

Say the word.
Which way looks right?

a) gnawing
b) gnauing

Letter Patterns: au, aw, ou, ow

Answer

a) gnawing

Letter Patterns: au, aw, ou, ow

Question

Say the word.
Which way looks right?

a) yowl
b) youl

Letter Patterns: au, aw, ou, ow

Answer

a) yowl

Letter Patterns: au, aw, ou, ow

Question

Say the word.
Which way looks right?

a) rawhide
b) rauhide

Letter Patterns: au, aw, ou, ow

Answer

a) rawhide

Letter Patterns: au, aw, ou, ow

Question

Say the word.
Which way looks right?

a) yauning
b) yawning

Letter Patterns: au, aw, ou, ow

Answer

b) yawning

Letter Patterns: au, aw, ou, ow
Quiz-Quiz-Trade

Instructions: Copy enough cards so each student has one card. Cut on dotted lines and fold in half.

Letter Patterns: au, aw, ou, ow

Question

Say the word.
Which way looks right?

a) announce
b) annownce

Letter Patterns: au, aw, ou, ow

Answer

a) announce

Letter Patterns: au, aw, ou, ow

Question

Say the word.
Which way looks right?

a) cowntdown
b) countdown

Letter Patterns: au, aw, ou, ow

Answer

b) countdown

Letter Patterns: au, aw, ou, ow

Question

Say the word.
Which way looks right?

a) boundary
b) bowdary

Letter Patterns: au, aw, ou, ow

Answer

a) boundary

Letter Patterns: au, aw, ou, ow

Question

Say the word.
Which way looks right?

a) lowder
b) louder

Letter Patterns: au, aw, ou, ow

Answer

b) louder

Letter Patterns: au, aw, ou, ow
Quiz-Quiz-Trade

Instructions: Copy enough cards so each student has one card. Cut on dotted lines and fold in half.

Letter Patterns: au, aw, ou, ow

Question

Say the word.
Which way looks right?

a) checkout
b) checkowt

Letter Patterns: au, aw, ou, ow

Answer

a) checkout

Letter Patterns: au, aw, ou, ow

Question

Say the word.
Which way looks right?

a) arownd
b) around

Letter Patterns: au, aw, ou, ow

Answer

b) around

Letter Patterns: au, aw, ou, ow

Question

Say the word.
Which way looks right?

a) mountaintops
b) mowtaintops

Letter Patterns: au, aw, ou, ow

Answer

a) mountaintops

Letter Patterns: au, aw, ou, ow

Question

Say the word.
Which way looks right?

a) owch
b) ouch

Letter Patterns: au, aw, ou, ow

Answer

b) ouch

Balanced Literacy • Fourth Grade • Skidmore & Graber
Kagan Publishing • 1 (800) 933-2667 • www.KaganOnline.com

Letter Patterns:
au, aw, ou, ow
Quiz-Quiz-Trade

Instructions: Copy enough cards so each student has one card. Cut on dotted lines and fold in half.

Letter Patterns: au, aw, ou, ow

Question

Say the word.
Which way looks right?

a) towels
b) touels

Letter Patterns: au, aw, ou, ow

Answer

a) towels

Letter Patterns: au, aw, ou, ow

Question

Say the word.
Which way looks right?

a) houls
b) howls

Letter Patterns: au, aw, ou, ow

Answer

b) howls

Letter Patterns: au, aw, ou, ow

Question

Say the word.
Which way looks right?

a) powdered
b) poudered

Letter Patterns: au, aw, ou, ow

Answer

a) powdered

Letter Patterns: au, aw, ou, ow

Question

Say the word.
Which way looks right?

a) shouers
b) showers

Letter Patterns: au, aw, ou, ow

Answer

b) showers

Balanced Literacy • Fourth Grade • Skidmore & Graber
Kagan Publishing • 1 (800) 933-2667 • www.KaganOnline.com

Letter Patterns: au, aw, ou, ow
Quiz-Quiz-Trade

Instructions: Copy enough cards so each student has one card. Cut on dotted lines and fold in half.

Letter Patterns: au, aw, ou, ow

Question

Say the word.
Which way looks right?

a) hometown
b) hometoun

Letter Patterns: au, aw, ou, ow

Answer

a) hometown

Letter Patterns: au, aw, ou, ow

Question

Say the word.
Which way looks right?

a) couardly
b) cowardly

Letter Patterns: au, aw, ou, ow

Answer

b) cowardly

Letter Patterns: au, aw, ou, ow

Question

Say the word.
Which way looks right?

a) scowled
b) scouled

Letter Patterns: au, aw, ou, ow

Answer

a) scowled

Letter Patterns: au, aw, ou, ow

Question

Say the word.
Which way looks right?

a) cauliflouer
b) cauliflower

Letter Patterns: au, aw, ou, ow

Answer

b) cauliflower

Word Study Blackline

Letter Patterns: ie, ei
Quiz-Quiz-Trade

Instructions: Copy enough cards so each student has one card. Cut on dotted lines and fold in half.

Letter Patterns: ie, ei

Question

Say the word.
Which way looks right?

a) brief
b) breif

Letter Patterns: ie, ei

Answer

a) brief

Letter Patterns: ie, ei

Question

Say the word.
Which way looks right?

a) theif
b) thief

Letter Patterns: ie, ei

Answer

a) thief

Letter Patterns: ie, ei

Question

Say the word.
Which way looks right?

a) their
b) thier

Letter Patterns: ie, ei

Answer

a) their

Letter Patterns: ie, ei

Question

Say the word.
Which way looks right?

a) friend
b) freind

Letter Patterns: ie, ei

Answer

a) friend

Balanced Literacy • Fourth Grade • Skidmore & Graber
Kagan Publishing • 1 (800) 933-2667 • www.KaganOnline.com

Letter Patterns: ie, ei
Quiz-Quiz-Trade

Instructions: Copy enough cards so each student has one card. Cut on dotted lines and fold in half.

Letter Patterns: ie, ei

Question

Say the word.
Which way looks right?

a) chief
b) cheif

Letter Patterns: ie, ei

Answer

a) chief

Letter Patterns: ie, ei

Question

Say the word.
Which way looks right?

a) cieling
b) ceiling

Letter Patterns: ie, ei

Answer

b) ceiling

Letter Patterns: ie, ei

Question

Say the word.
Which way looks right?

a) eight
b) ieght

Letter Patterns: ie, ei

Answer

a) eight

Letter Patterns: ie, ei

Question

Say the word.
Which way looks right?

a) peice
b) piece

Letter Patterns: ie, ei

Answer

b) piece

Letter Patterns: ie, ei
Quiz-Quiz-Trade

Instructions: Copy enough cards so each student has one card. Cut on dotted lines and fold in half.

Letter Patterns: ie, ei

Question

Say the word.
Which way looks right?

a) reciept
b) receipt

Letter Patterns: ie, ei

Answer

b) receipt

Letter Patterns: ie, ei

Question

Say the word.
Which way looks right?

a) believe
b) beleive

Letter Patterns: ie, ei

Answer

a) believe

Letter Patterns: ie, ei

Question

Say the word.
Which way looks right?

a) wiegh
b) weigh

Letter Patterns: ie, ei

Answer

b) weigh

Letter Patterns: ie, ei

Question

Say the word.
Which way looks right?

a) priest
b) preist

Letter Patterns: ie, ei

Answer

a) priest

Letter Patterns: ie, ei
Quiz-Quiz-Trade

Instructions: Copy enough cards so each student has one card. Cut on dotted lines and fold in half.

Letter Patterns: ie, ei

Question

Say the word.
Which way looks right?

a) yeild
b) yield

Letter Patterns: ie, ei

Answer

b) yield

Letter Patterns: ie, ei

Question

Say the word.
Which way looks right?

a) nieghbor
b) neighbor

Letter Patterns: ie, ei

Answer

b) neighbor

Letter Patterns: ie, ei

Question

Say the word.
Which way looks right?

a) rein
b) rien

Letter Patterns: ie, ei

Answer

a) rein

Letter Patterns: ie, ei

Question

Say the word.
Which way looks right?

a) feild
b) field

Letter Patterns: ie, ei

Answer

b) field

Letter Patterns: ie, ei
Quiz-Quiz-Trade

Instructions: Copy enough cards so each student has one card. Cut on dotted lines and fold in half.

Letter Patterns: ie, ei

Question

Say the word.
Which way looks right?

a) weird
b) wierd

Letter Patterns: ie, ei

Answer

a) weird

Letter Patterns: ie, ei

Question

Say the word.
Which way looks right?

a) greif
b) grief

Letter Patterns: ie, ei

Answer

b) grief

Letter Patterns: ie, ei

Question

Say the word.
Which way looks right?

a) breifcase
b) briefcase

Letter Patterns: ie, ei

Answer

b) briefcase

Letter Patterns: ie, ei

Question

Say the word.
Which way looks right?

a) niece
b) neice

Letter Patterns: ie, ei

Answer

a) niece

Letter Patterns: ie, ei
Quiz-Quiz-Trade

Instructions: Copy enough cards so each student has one card. Cut on dotted lines and fold in half.

Letter Patterns: ie, ei

Question

Say the word.
Which way looks right?

a) veil
b) viel

Letter Patterns: ie, ei

Answer

a) veil

Letter Patterns: ie, ei

Question

Say the word.
Which way looks right?

a) iether
b) either

Letter Patterns: ie, ei

Answer

b) either

Letter Patterns: ie, ei

Question

Say the word.
Which way looks right?

a) shriek
b) shreik

Letter Patterns: ie, ei

Answer

a) shriek

Letter Patterns: ie, ei

Question

Say the word.
Which way looks right?

a) sliegh
b) sleigh

Letter Patterns: ie, ei

Answer

b) sleigh

Letter Patterns: ie, ei
Quiz-Quiz-Trade

Instructions: Copy enough cards so each student has one card. Cut on dotted lines and fold in half.

Letter Patterns: ie, ei

Question

Say the word.
Which way looks right?

a) recieve
b) receive

Letter Patterns: ie, ei

Answer

b) receive

Letter Patterns: ie, ei

Question

Say the word.
Which way looks right?

a) hieght
b) height

Letter Patterns: ie, ei

Answer

b) height

Letter Patterns: ie, ei

Question

Say the word.
Which way looks right?

a) leisure
b) liesure

Letter Patterns: ie, ei

Answer

a) leisure

Letter Patterns: ie, ei

Question

Say the word.
Which way looks right?

a) freight
b) frieght

Letter Patterns: ie, ei

Answer

a) freight

Prefixes
(anti-, dis-, ex-, non-, under-)
Quiz-Quiz-Trade

Instructions: Copy enough cards so each student has one card. Cut on dotted lines and fold in half.

Prefixes (anti-, dis-, ex-, non-, under-)

Question

What does this word mean?

antifreeze

Prefixes (anti-, dis-, ex-, non-, under-)

Answer

something which protects **against** freezing

Prefixes (anti-, dis-, ex-, non-, under-)

Question

What does this word mean?

disconnect

Prefixes (anti-, dis-, ex-, non-, under-)

Answer

not hooked up or joined

Prefixes (anti-, dis-, ex-, non-, under-)

Question

What does this word mean?

explosion

Prefixes (anti-, dis-, ex-, non-, under-)

Answer

a sudden outburst; coming **out of** forcefully

Prefixes (anti-, dis-, ex-, non-, under-)

Question

What does this word mean?

disobey

Prefixes (anti-, dis-, ex-, non-, under-)

Answer

not obeying or following directions

Prefixes
(anti-, dis-, ex-, non-, under-)
Quiz-Quiz-Trade

Instructions: Copy enough cards so each student has one card. Cut on dotted lines and fold in half.

Prefixes (anti-, dis-, ex-, non-, under-)

Question

What does this word mean?

disloyal

Prefixes (anti-, dis-, ex-, non-, under-)

Answer

<u>not</u> loyal;
not faithful or trustworthy

Prefixes (anti-, dis-, ex-, non-, under-)

Question

What does this word mean?

discontinue

Prefixes (anti-, dis-, ex-, non-, under-)

Answer

<u>not</u> continuing or going on

Prefixes (anti-, dis-, ex-, non-, under-)

Question

What does this word mean?

displaced

Prefixes (anti-, dis-, ex-, non-, under-)

Answer

<u>not</u> in the right place

Prefixes (anti-, dis-, ex-, non-, under-)

Question

What does this word mean?

antibacterial

Prefixes (anti-, dis-, ex-, non-, under-)

Answer

<u>against</u> the growth of bacteria

Prefixes
(anti-, dis-, ex-, non-, under-)
Quiz-Quiz-Trade

Instructions: Copy enough cards so each student has one card. Cut on dotted lines and fold in half.

Prefixes (anti-, dis-, ex-, non-, under-)

Question

What does this word mean?

nonsmoker

Prefixes (anti-, dis-, ex-, non-, under-)

Answer

someone who does **not** smoke

Prefixes (anti-, dis-, ex-, non-, under-)

Question

What does this word mean?

nonreturnable

Prefixes (anti-, dis-, ex-, non-, under-)

Answer

something that is **not** able to be returned

Prefixes (anti-, dis-, ex-, non-, under-)

Question

What does this word mean?

nonstop

Prefixes (anti-, dis-, ex-, non-, under-)

Answer

not ending or stopping

Prefixes (anti-, dis-, ex-, non-, under-)

Question

What does this word mean?

understaffed

Prefixes (anti-, dis-, ex-, non-, under-)

Answer

too little staff or help

Prefixes
(anti-, dis-, ex-, non-, under-)
Quiz-Quiz-Trade

Instructions: Copy enough cards so each student has one card. Cut on dotted lines and fold in half.

Prefixes (anti-, dis-, ex-, non-, under-)

Question

What does this word mean?

underfoot

Prefixes (anti-, dis-, ex-, non-, under-)

Answer

beneath someone's feet or where someone is trying to walk

Prefixes (anti-, dis-, ex-, non-, under-)

Question

What does this word mean?

disbelief

Prefixes (anti-, dis-, ex-, non-, under-)

Answer

not believing; **not** accepting as true

Prefixes (anti-, dis-, ex-, non-, under-)

Question

What does this word mean?

nonresident

Prefixes (anti-, dis-, ex-, non-, under-)

Answer

not a resident; **not** living there

Prefixes (anti-, dis-, ex-, non-, under-)

Question

What does this word mean?

antiseptic

Prefixes (anti-, dis-, ex-, non-, under-)

Answer

against infection or disease

Prefixes
(anti-, dis-, ex-, non-, under-)
Quiz-Quiz-Trade

Instructions: Copy enough cards so each student has one card. Cut on dotted lines and fold in half.

Prefixes (anti-, dis-, ex-, non-, under-)

Question

What does this word mean?

nonviolent

Prefixes (anti-, dis-, ex-, non-, under-)

Answer

not using violence or force

Prefixes (anti-, dis-, ex-, non-, under-)

Question

What does this word mean?

undercurrent

Prefixes (anti-, dis-, ex-, non-, under-)

Answer

a current **beneath** the surface of the water

Prefixes (anti-, dis-, ex-, non-, under-)

Question

What does this word mean?

undersell

Prefixes (anti-, dis-, ex-, non-, under-)

Answer

to sell for **too little**

Prefixes (anti-, dis-, ex-, non-, under-)

Question

What does this word mean?

undershirt

Prefixes (anti-, dis-, ex-, non-, under-)

Answer

a shirt worn **beneath** other clothes

Prefixes
(anti-, dis-, ex-, non-, under-)
Quiz-Quiz-Trade

Instructions: Copy enough cards so each student has one card. Cut on dotted lines and fold in half.

Prefixes (anti-, dis-, ex-, non-, under-)

Question

What does this word mean?

express

Prefixes (anti-, dis-, ex-, non-, under-)

Answer

to press **out of**

Prefixes (anti-, dis-, ex-, non-, under-)

Question

What does this word mean?

excommunicate

Prefixes (anti-, dis-, ex-, non-, under-)

Answer

is no longer communicated with

Prefixes (anti-, dis-, ex-, non-, under-)

Question

What does this word mean?

antiterrorism

Prefixes (anti-, dis-, ex-, non-, under-)

Answer

against terrorism

Prefixes (anti-, dis-, ex-, non-, under-)

Question

What does this word mean?

dissatisfied

Prefixes (anti-, dis-, ex-, non-, under-)

Answer

not satisfied or **not** pleased

Prefixes
(anti-, dis-, ex-, non-, under-)
Quiz-Quiz-Trade

Instructions: Copy enough cards so each student has one card. Cut on dotted lines and fold in half.

Prefixes (anti-, dis-, ex-, non-, under-)

Question

What does this word mean?

ex-president

Prefixes (anti-, dis-, ex-, non-, under-)

Answer

no longer the president

Prefixes (anti-, dis-, ex-, non-, under-)

Question

What does this word mean?

nonprofit

Prefixes (anti-, dis-, ex-, non-, under-)

Answer

not for profit;
not to make money

Prefixes (anti-, dis-, ex-, non-, under-)

Question

What does this word mean?

underage

Prefixes (anti-, dis-, ex-, non-, under-)

Answer

below the required age

Prefixes (anti-, dis-, ex-, non-, under-)

Question

What does this word mean?

underscore

Prefixes (anti-, dis-, ex-, non-, under-)

Answer

a line or score **underneath** something

Prefixes
(anti-, dis-, ex-, non-, under-)
Quiz-Quiz-Trade

Instructions: Copy enough cards so each student has one card. Cut on dotted lines and fold in half.

Prefixes (anti-, dis-, ex-, non-, under-)

Question

What does this word mean?

disorganized

Prefixes (anti-, dis-, ex-, non-, under-)

Answer

not arranged or organized

Prefixes (anti-, dis-, ex-, non-, under-)

Question

What does this word mean?

antisocial

Prefixes (anti-, dis-, ex-, non-, under-)

Answer

acting **against** others; rude

Prefixes (anti-, dis-, ex-, non-, under-)

Question

What does this word mean?

disagree

Prefixes (anti-, dis-, ex-, non-, under-)

Answer

not agreeing or **not** having the same opinion

Prefixes (anti-, dis-, ex-, non-, under-)

Question

What does this word mean?

underground

Prefixes (anti-, dis-, ex-, non-, under-)

Answer

beneath or **below** the ground

Prefixes (anti-, dis-, -ex-, non-, under-)
Suffixes (-en, -ful, -less, -ment, -ness)
Quiz-Quiz-Trade

Instructions: Copy enough cards so each student has one card. Cut on dotted lines and fold in half.

Prefixes (anti-, dis-, -ex-, non-, under-)
Suffixes (-en, -ful, -less, -ment, -ness)

Which one of the following is a real word which means . . . ?

Question

something that protects against freezing

- a) antibiotic
- b) nonstop
- c) antifreeze

Prefixes (anti-, dis-, -ex-, non-, under-)
Suffixes (-en, -ful, -less, -ment, -ness)

Answer

something that protects against freezing

c) antifreeze

Prefixes (anti-, dis-, -ex-, non-, under-)
Suffixes (-en, -ful, -less, -ment, -ness)

Which one of the following is a real word which means . . . ?

Question

no longer the president

- a) ex-president
- b) noncommissioned
- c) nonpresident

Prefixes (anti-, dis-, -ex-, non-, under-)
Suffixes (-en, -ful, -less, -ment, -ness)

Answer

no longer the president

a) ex-president

Prefixes (anti-, dis-, -ex-, non-, under-)
Suffixes (-en, -ful, -less, -ment, -ness)

Which one of the following is a real word which means . . . ?

Question

not ordered

- a) exordered
- b) disordered
- c) nonordered

Prefixes (anti-, dis-, -ex-, non-, under-)
Suffixes (-en, -ful, -less, -ment, -ness)

Answer

not ordered

b) disordered

Prefixes (anti-, dis-, -ex-, non-, under-)
Suffixes (-en, -ful, -less, -ment, -ness)

Which one of the following is a real word which means . . . ?

Question

not violent or mean

- a) disviolent
- b) exviolent
- c) nonviolent

Prefixes (anti-, dis-, -ex-, non-, under-)
Suffixes (-en, -ful, -less, -ment, -ness)

Answer

not violent or mean

c) nonviolent

Prefixes (anti-, dis-, -ex-, non-, under-)
Suffixes (-en, -ful, -less, -ment, -ness)
Quiz-Quiz-Trade

Instructions: Copy enough cards so each student has one card. Cut on dotted lines and fold in half.

Prefixes (anti-, dis-, -ex-, non-, under-)
Suffixes (-en, -ful, -less, -ment, -ness)

Which one of the following is a real word which means . . . ?

Question

showing no respect

a) anti-respect
b) dislike
c) disrespect

Prefixes (anti-, dis-, -ex-, non-, under-)
Suffixes (-en, -ful, -less, -ment, -ness)

Answer

showing no respect

c) disrespect

Prefixes (anti-, dis-, -ex-, non-, under-)
Suffixes (-en, -ful, -less, -ment, -ness)

Which one of the following is a real word which means . . . ?

Question

beneath the bushes or plant growth

a) underbrush
b) underfoot
c) brushless

Prefixes (anti-, dis-, -ex-, non-, under-)
Suffixes (-en, -ful, -less, -ment, -ness)

Answer

beneath the bushes or plant growth

a) underbrush

Prefixes (anti-, dis-, -ex-, non-, under-)
Suffixes (-en, -ful, -less, -ment, -ness)

Which one of the following is a real word which means . . . ?

Question

not stopping

a) antistop
b) nonstop
c) stopless

Prefixes (anti-, dis-, -ex-, non-, under-)
Suffixes (-en, -ful, -less, -ment, -ness)

Answer

not stopping

b) nonstop

Prefixes (anti-, dis-, -ex-, non-, under-)
Suffixes (-en, -ful, -less, -ment, -ness)

Which one of the following is a real word which means . . . ?

Question

without milk or milk products

a) antidairy
b) dairyness
c) nondairy

Prefixes (anti-, dis-, -ex-, non-, under-)
Suffixes (-en, -ful, -less, -ment, -ness)

Answer

without milk or milk products

c) nondairy

Balanced Literacy • Fourth Grade • Skidmore & Graber
Kagan Publishing • 1 (800) 933-2667 • www.KaganOnline.com

Prefixes (anti-, dis-, -ex-, non-, under-)
Suffixes (-en, -ful, -less, -ment, -ness)
Quiz-Quiz-Trade

Instructions: Copy enough cards so each student has one card. Cut on dotted lines and fold in half.

Prefixes (anti-, dis-, -ex-, non-, under-)
Suffixes (-en, -ful, -less, -ment, -ness)

Which one of the following is a real word which means . . . ?

Question

worn beneath clothes or garments

a) nongarment
b) underfoot
c) undergarment

Prefixes (anti-, dis-, -ex-, non-, under-)
Suffixes (-en, -ful, -less, -ment, -ness)

Answer

worn beneath clothes or garments

c) undergarment

Prefixes (anti-, dis-, -ex-, non-, under-)
Suffixes (-en, -ful, -less, -ment, -ness)

Which one of the following is a real word which means . . . ?

Question

having too little staff or people to work

a) understaffed
b) nonstaffed
c) staffness

Prefixes (anti-, dis-, -ex-, non-, under-)
Suffixes (-en, -ful, -less, -ment, -ness)

Answer

having too little staff or people to work

a) understaffed

Prefixes (anti-, dis-, -ex-, non-, under-)
Suffixes (-en, -ful, -less, -ment, -ness)

Which one of the following is a real word which means . . . ?

Question

without sense

a) dissense
b) nonsense
c) undersense

Prefixes (anti-, dis-, -ex-, non-, under-)
Suffixes (-en, -ful, -less, -ment, -ness)

Answer

without sense

b) nonsense

Prefixes (anti-, dis-, -ex-, non-, under-)
Suffixes (-en, -ful, -less, -ment, -ness)

Which one of the following is a real word which means . . . ?

Question

not living there or not a resident

a) residentless
b) disresident
c) nonresident

Prefixes (anti-, dis-, -ex-, non-, under-)
Suffixes (-en, -ful, -less, -ment, -ness)

Answer

not living there or not a resident

c) nonresident

Prefixes (anti-, dis-, -ex-, non-, under-)
Suffixes (-en, -ful, -less, -ment, -ness)
Quiz-Quiz-Trade

Instructions: Copy enough cards so each student has one card. Cut on dotted lines and fold in half.

Prefixes (anti-, dis-, -ex-, non-, under-) Suffixes (-en, -ful, -less, -ment, -ness)

Which one of the following is a real word which means . . . ?

Question

without fear

a) fearful
b) fearless
c) antifear

Prefixes (anti-, dis-, -ex-, non-, under-) Suffixes (-en, -ful, -less, -ment, -ness)

Answer

without fear

b) fearless

Prefixes (anti-, dis-, -ex-, non-, under-) Suffixes (-en, -ful, -less, -ment, -ness)

Which one of the following is a real word which means . . . ?

Question

in a state of being amazed

a) amazement
b) amazeness
c) amazen

Prefixes (anti-, dis-, -ex-, non-, under-) Suffixes (-en, -ful, -less, -ment, -ness)

Answer

in a state of being amazed

a) amazement

Prefixes (anti-, dis-, -ex-, non-, under-) Suffixes (-en, -ful, -less, -ment, -ness)

Which one of the following is a real word which means . . . ?

Question

a state of being sick

a) sickment
b) sickness
c) sickful

Prefixes (anti-, dis-, -ex-, non-, under-) Suffixes (-en, -ful, -less, -ment, -ness)

Answer

a state of being sick

b) sickness

Prefixes (anti-, dis-, -ex-, non-, under-) Suffixes (-en, -ful, -less, -ment, -ness)

Which one of the following is a real word which means . . . ?

Question

without sound

a) soundful
b) nonsound
c) soundless

Prefixes (anti-, dis-, -ex-, non-, under-) Suffixes (-en, -ful, -less, -ment, -ness)

Answer

without sound

c) soundless

Balanced Literacy • Fourth Grade • Skidmore & Graber
Kagan Publishing • 1 (800) 933-2667 • www.KaganOnline.com

Prefixes (anti-, dis-, -ex-, non-, under-)
Suffixes (-en, -ful, -less, -ment, -ness)
Quiz-Quiz-Trade

Instructions: Copy enough cards so each student has one card. Cut on dotted lines and fold in half.

Prefixes (anti-, dis-, -ex-, non-, under-)
Suffixes (-en, -ful, -less, -ment, -ness)

Which one of the following is a real word which means...?

Question

to make weak

  a) weakless
  b) weaken
  c) weakment

Prefixes (anti-, dis-, -ex-, non-, under-)
Suffixes (-en, -ful, -less, -ment, -ness)

Answer

to make weak

b) weaken

Prefixes (anti-, dis-, -ex-, non-, under-)
Suffixes (-en, -ful, -less, -ment, -ness)

Which one of the following is a real word which means...?

Question

made of wool

  a) woolen
  b) woolful
  c) woolness

Prefixes (anti-, dis-, -ex-, non-, under-)
Suffixes (-en, -ful, -less, -ment, -ness)

Answer

made of wool

a) woolen

Prefixes (anti-, dis-, -ex-, non-, under-)
Suffixes (-en, -ful, -less, -ment, -ness)

Which one of the following is a real word which means...?

Question

without bones

  a) exbone
  b) boneless
  c) nonbone

Prefixes (anti-, dis-, -ex-, non-, under-)
Suffixes (-en, -ful, -less, -ment, -ness)

Answer

without bones

b) boneless

Prefixes (anti-, dis-, -ex-, non-, under-)
Suffixes (-en, -ful, -less, -ment, -ness)

Which one of the following is a real word which means...?

Question

having a plate that is full of something

  a) platement
  b) plateness
  c) plateful

Prefixes (anti-, dis-, -ex-, non-, under-)
Suffixes (-en, -ful, -less, -ment, -ness)

Answer

having a plate that is full of something

c) plateful

Prefixes (anti-, dis-, -ex-, non-, under-)
Suffixes (-en, -ful, -less, -ment, -ness)
Quiz-Quiz-Trade

Instructions: Copy enough cards so each student has one card. Cut on dotted lines and fold in half.

Prefixes (anti-, dis-, -ex-, non-, under-)
Suffixes (-en, -ful, -less, -ment, -ness)

Which one of the following is a real word which means . . . ?

Question

having a lot of stress

a) antistress
b) stressful
c) nonstress

Prefixes (anti-, dis-, -ex-, non-, under-)
Suffixes (-en, -ful, -less, -ment, -ness)

Answer

having a lot of stress

b) stressful

Prefixes (anti-, dis-, -ex-, non-, under-)
Suffixes (-en, -ful, -less, -ment, -ness)

Which one of the following is a real word which means . . . ?

Question

without taste or flavor

a) tasteless
b) nontaste
c) tasteful

Prefixes (anti-, dis-, -ex-, non-, under-)
Suffixes (-en, -ful, -less, -ment, -ness)

Answer

without taste or flavor

a) tasteless

Prefixes (anti-, dis-, -ex-, non-, under-)
Suffixes (-en, -ful, -less, -ment, -ness)

Which one of the following is a real word which means . . . ?

Question

having a lot of something in your hand

a) handless
b) handful
c) handy

Prefixes (anti-, dis-, -ex-, non-, under-)
Suffixes (-en, -ful, -less, -ment, -ness)

Answer

having a lot of something in your hand

b) handful

Prefixes (anti-, dis-, -ex-, non-, under-)
Suffixes (-en, -ful, -less, -ment, -ness)

Which one of the following is a real word which means . . . ?

Question

quality of being fit or in shape

a) fitless
b) fitten
c) fitness

Prefixes (anti-, dis-, -ex-, non-, under-)
Suffixes (-en, -ful, -less, -ment, -ness)

Answer

quality of being fit or in shape

c) fitness

Balanced Literacy • Fourth Grade • Skidmore & Graber
Kagan Publishing • 1 (800) 933-2667 • www.KaganOnline.com

Prefixes (anti-, dis-, -ex-, non-, under-)
Suffixes (-en, -ful, -less, -ment, -ness)
Quiz-Quiz-Trade

Instructions: Copy enough cards so each student has one card. Cut on dotted lines and fold in half.

Prefixes (anti-, dis-, -ex-, non-, under-) Suffixes (-en, -ful, -less, -ment, -ness)

Which one of the following is a real word which means . . . ?

Question

to make longer

a) lengthment
b) lengthen
c) lengthful

Prefixes (anti-, dis-, -ex-, non-, under-) Suffixes (-en, -ful, -less, -ment, -ness)

Answer

to make longer

b) lengthen

Prefixes (anti-, dis-, -ex-, non-, under-) Suffixes (-en, -ful, -less, -ment, -ness)

Which one of the following is a real word which means . . . ?

Question

having a lot of waste

a) wasteful
b) underwaste
c) wasteness

Prefixes (anti-, dis-, -ex-, non-, under-) Suffixes (-en, -ful, -less, -ment, -ness)

Answer

having a lot of waste

a) wasteful

Prefixes (anti-, dis-, -ex-, non-, under-) Suffixes (-en, -ful, -less, -ment, -ness)

Which one of the following is a real word which means . . . ?

Question
in the state of being employed or having a job

a) employness
b) employment
c) employful

Prefixes (anti-, dis-, -ex-, non-, under-) Suffixes (-en, -ful, -less, -ment, -ness)

Answer

in the state of being employed or having a job

b) employment

Prefixes (anti-, dis-, -ex-, non-, under-) Suffixes (-en, -ful, -less, -ment, -ness)

Which one of the following is a real word which means . . . ?

Question

having a lot of fear

a) fearless
b) fearment
c) fearful

Prefixes (anti-, dis-, -ex-, non-, under-) Suffixes (-en, -ful, -less, -ment, -ness)

Answer

having a lot of fear

c) fearful

Their, There, They're
Quiz-Quiz-Trade

Instructions: Copy enough cards so each student has one card. Cut on dotted lines and fold in half.

Their, There, They're

Question
Some people take naps when _____ tired.

  a) their
  b) there
  c) they're

Their, There, They're

Answer
Some people take naps when **they're** tired.

c) they're

Their, There, They're

Question
Are _____ any cookies left from the party?

  a) their
  b) there
  c) they're

Their, There, They're

Answer
Are **there** any cookies left from the party?

b) there

Their, There, They're

Question
The people took _____ seats before the concert began.

  a) their
  b) there
  c) they're

Their, There, They're

Answer
The people took **their** seats before the concert began.

a) their

Their, There, They're

Question
_____ leaving on vacation today.

  a) Their
  b) There
  c) They're

Their, There, They're

Answer
They're leaving on vacation today.

c) They're

Their, There, They're
Quiz-Quiz-Trade

Instructions: Copy enough cards so each student has one card. Cut on dotted lines and fold in half.

Their, There, They're

Question
Dad puts the dishes away after _____ washed.
- a) their
- b) there
- c) they're

Their, There, They're

Answer
Dad puts the dishes away after <u>they're</u> washed.

c) they're

Their, There, They're

Question
Some people grow vegetables in _____ gardens.
- a) their
- b) there
- c) they're

Their, There, They're

Answer
Some people grow vegetables in <u>their</u> gardens.

a) their

Their, There, They're

Question
Will _____ be snow tomorrow?
- a) their
- b) there
- c) they're

Their, There, They're

Answer
Will <u>there</u> be snow tomorrow?

b) there

Their, There, They're

Question
_____ the best musicians I have heard.
- a) Their
- b) There
- c) They're

Their, There, They're

Answer
<u>They're</u> the best musicians I have heard.

c) They're

Their, There, They're
Quiz-Quiz-Trade

Instructions: Copy enough cards so each student has one card. Cut on dotted lines and fold in half.

Their, There, They're

Question
The eagles landed on _____ perch at the zoo.

 a) their
 b) there
 c) they're

Their, There, They're

Answer
The eagles landed on **their** perch at the zoo.

a) their

Their, There, They're

Question
Friday _____ going to bake a cake.

 a) their
 b) there
 c) they're

Their, There, They're

Answer
Friday **they're** going to bake a cake.

c) they're

Their, There, They're

Question
Many workers relax after _____ jobs.

 a) their
 b) there
 c) they're

Their, There, They're

Answer
Many workers relax after **their** jobs.

a) their

Their, There, They're

Question
The paper is over _____.

 a) their
 b) there
 c) they're

Their, There, They're

Answer
The paper is over **there**.

b) there

Balanced Literacy • Fourth Grade • Skidmore & Graber
Kagan Publishing • 1 (800) 933-2667 • www.KaganOnline.com

Their, There, They're
Quiz-Quiz-Trade

Instructions: Copy enough cards so each student has one card. Cut on dotted lines and fold in half.

Their, There, They're

Question
Sometimes dogs bark when _____ lonely.

   a) their
   b) there
   c) they're

Their, There, They're

Answer
Sometimes dogs bark when **they're** lonely.

c) they're

Their, There, They're

Question
_____ are five turtles sun-bathing on the logs.

   a) Their
   b) There
   c) They're

Their, There, They're

Answer
There are five turtles sun-bathing on the logs.

b) There

Their, There, They're

Question
_____ are numerous ducks swimming on the lake.

   a) Their
   b) There
   c) They're

Their, There, They're

Answer
There are numerous ducks swimming on the lake.

b) There

Their, There, They're

Question
Pet owners should look after _____ animals.

   a) their
   b) there
   c) they're

Their, There, They're

Answer
Pet owners should look after **their** animals.

a) their

Their, There, They're
Quiz-Quiz-Trade

Instructions: Copy enough cards so each student has one card. Cut on dotted lines and fold in half.

Their, There, They're

Question
The students studied _____ notes for the test.

- a) their
- b) there
- c) they're

Their, There, They're

Answer
The students studied **their** notes for the test.

a) their

Their, There, They're

Question
_____ new house is located at the edge of the city.

- a) Their
- b) There
- c) They're

Their, There, They're

Answer
Their new house is located at the edge of the city.

a) Their

Their, There, They're

Question
In July _____ planning to visit relatives in another state.

- a) their
- b) there
- c) they're

Their, There, They're

Answer
In July **they're** planning to visit relatives in another state.

c) they're

Their, There, They're

Question
Ben and Cindy will drive _____ van to work.

- a) their
- b) there
- c) they're

Their, There, They're

Answer
Ben and Cindy will drive **their** van to work.

a) their

Their, There, They're
Quiz-Quiz-Trade

Instructions: Copy enough cards so each student has one card. Cut on dotted lines and fold in half.

Their, There, They're

Question
John and Ted took turns mowing _____ lawn.

a) their
b) there
c) they're

Their, There, They're

Answer
John and Ted took turns mowing <u>their</u> lawn.

a) their

Their, There, They're

Question
_____ will be a meeting for the newly formed committee.

a) Their
b) There
c) They're

Their, There, They're

Answer
<u>There</u> will be a meeting for the newly formed committee.

b) There

Their, There, They're

Question
After practicing, _____ going to sing in the opera.

a) their
b) there
c) they're

Their, There, They're

Answer
After practicing, <u>they're</u> going to sing in the opera.

c) they're

Their, There, They're

Question
Please put the stack of books over _____ on the counter.

a) their
b) there
c) they're

Their, There, They're

Answer
Please put the stack of books over <u>there</u> on the counter.

b) there

Their, There, They're
Quiz-Quiz-Trade

Instructions: Copy enough cards so each student has one card. Cut on dotted lines and fold in half.

Their, There, They're

Question
Since it is raining outside, _____ going to visit friends.

a) their
b) there
c) they're

Their, There, They're

Answer
Since it is raining outside, <u>they're</u> going to visit friends.

c) they're

Their, There, They're

Question
Where does _____ cat sleep during the day?

a) their
b) there
c) they're

Their, There, They're

Answer
Where does <u>their</u> cat sleep during the day?

a) their

Their, There, They're

Question
_____ running in the race at the end of the week.

a) Their
b) There
c) They're

Their, There, They're

Answer
<u>They're</u> running in the race at the end of the week.

c) They're

Their, There, They're

Question
Will _____ be a meeting after school today?

a) their
b) there
c) they're

Their, There, They're

Answer
Will <u>there</u> be a meeting after school today?

b) there

RALLYCOACH Activity

Coach Me

Three different types of word study RallyCoach activities are provided: 1) cube, 2) spinner, and 3) sorting mat. Using the materials provided, one partner completes the task while the other is the coach. They switch roles for each new problem.

Activity Steps

1. Depending on the activity below, each pair receives either a cube and a worksheet, a spinner and a worksheet, or a sorting mat and word cards.

2. First Partner A completes the task.
   - Cube: Partner rolls cube and uses result to fill in worksheet.
   - Spinner: Partner spins spinner and uses result to fill in worksheet.
   - Sorting Mat: Partner picks a word card and sorts it on the mat.

3. Partner B watches and listens, checks, and praises.

4. Then, Partner B rolls the cube, spins the spinner, or selects the next word card. Partner B completes the next problem.

5. Partner A watches and listens, checks, and praises.

6. The process continues until they complete their worksheet or sort all word cards.

STRUCTURE
RallyCoach

Blacklines

- Prefix Cube and Worksheet (anti-, dis-, ex-, non-, under-) 357–258
- Prefix Answer Sheet (anti-, dis-, ex-, non-, under-) 359
- Suffix Cube and Worksheets (-ful, -en, -less, -ment, -ness) 360–362
- Suffix Answer Sheets (-ful, -en, -less, -ment, -ness) 363–364
- Antonym and Synonym Cube and Worksheet 365–366
- Antonym and Synonym Answer Sheet 367
- Contraction Spinner and Worksheet (have, had, will) 368–369
- Adding Endings Spinner and Worksheet (-ing, -ed, -s) 370–371
- Adding Endings Answer Sheet 372
- Hard *g* and Soft *g* Sorting Mat and Word Cards 373–376

Prefix Cube
(anti-, dis-, ex-, non-, under-)
RallyCoach

Instructions: Copy the cube pattern onto cardstock for each pair. Cut out, fold, and tape together to form a cube. Partners take turns rolling the cube. The student rolling the cube chooses one incomplete word on the worksheet to make a word.

anti-

dis-

ex-

non-

under-

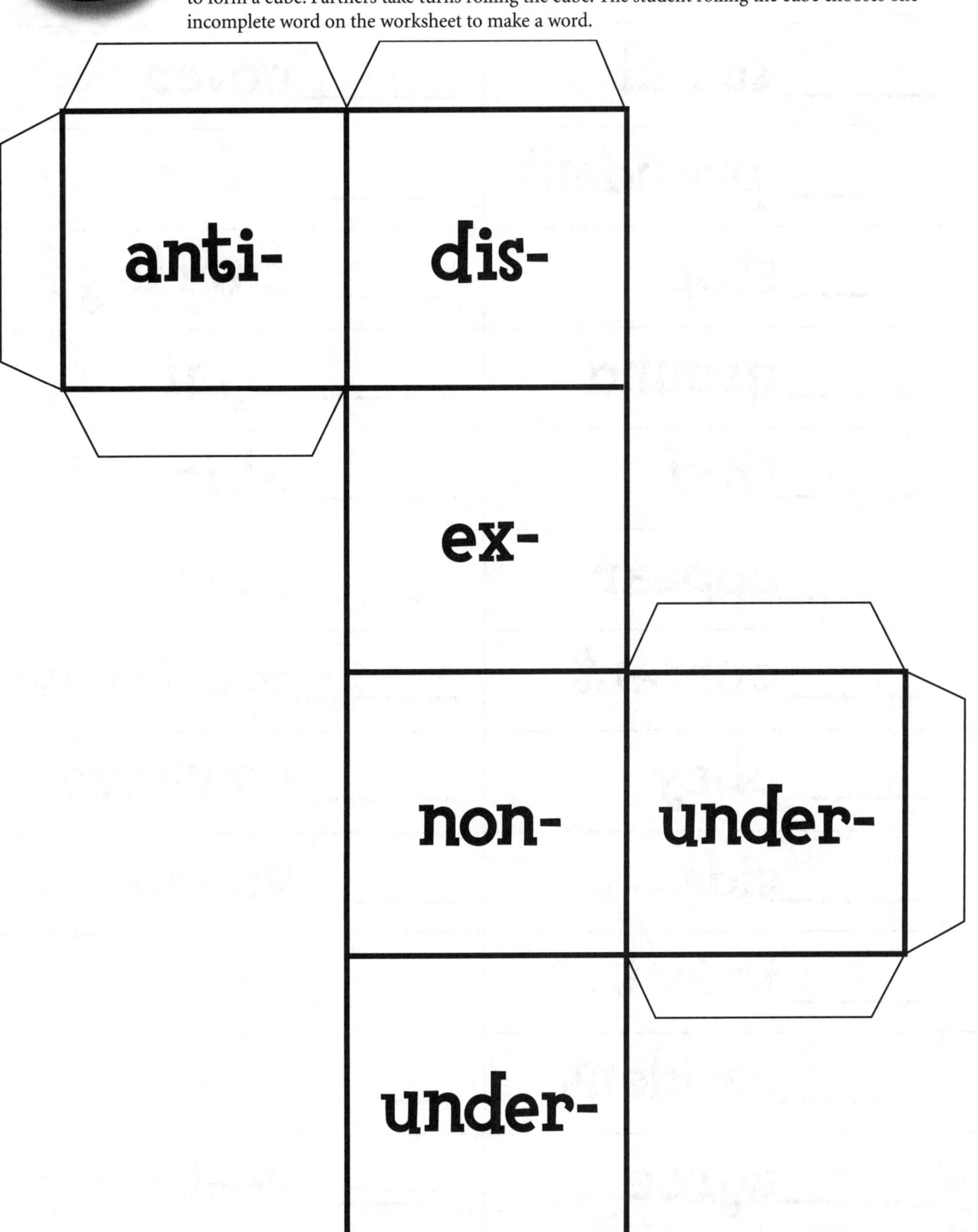

under-

Prefix Worksheet
(anti-, dis-, ex-, non-, under-)
RallyCoach

Instructions: Partners use worksheet with prefix cube.

_____ social	_____ cover
_____ -president	_____ color
_____ stop	_____ carriage
_____ ground	_____ loyal
_____ skid	_____ able
_____ appear	_____ shirt
_____ current	_____ communicate
_____ obey	_____ continue
_____ side	_____ violence
_____ infect	_____ foot
_____ resident	_____ dairy
_____ agree	_____ coat

Prefix Answer Sheet
(anti-, dis-, ex-, non-, under-)
RallyCoach

antisocial	undercover
ex-president	discolor
nonstop	undercarriage
underground	disloyal
nonskid	disable
disappear	undershirt
undercurrent	excommunicate
disobey	discontinue
underside	nonviolence
disinfect	underfoot
nonresident	nondairy
disagree	undercoat

Suffix Cube
(-ful, -en, -less, -ment, -ness)
RallyCoach

Instructions: Copy the cube pattern onto cardstock for each pair. Cut out, fold, and tape together to form a cube. Partners take turns rolling the cube. The student rolling the cube chooses one incomplete word on the worksheet to make a word.

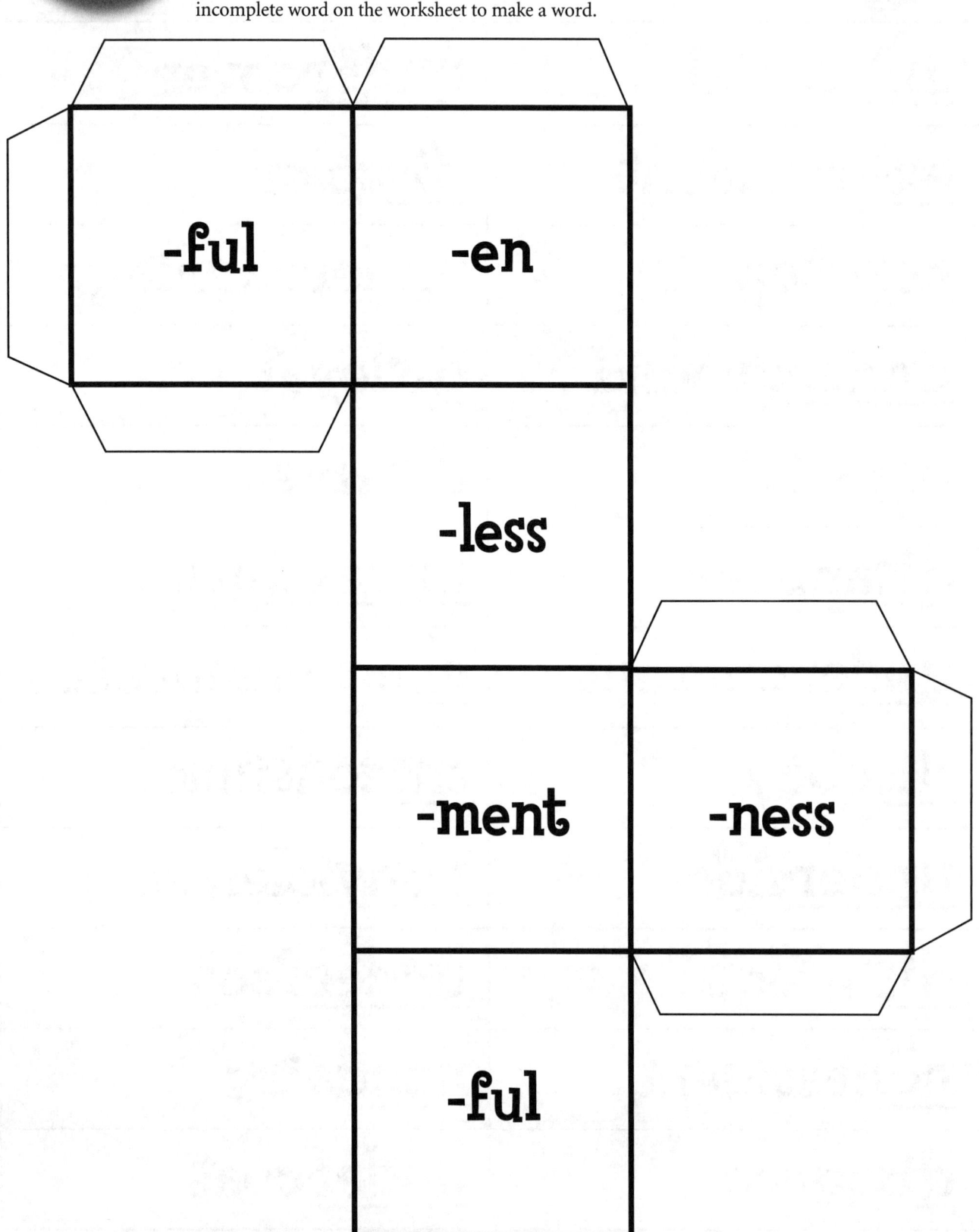

-ful

-en

-less

-ment

-ness

-ful

Suffix Worksheet
(-ful, -en, -less, -ment, -ness)
RallyCoach

Instructions: Partners use worksheet with suffix cube.

govern_____	point_____
good_____	stiff_____
weak_____	taste_____
hope_____	waste_____
hand_____	peace_____
short_____	less_____
wool_____	sleep_____
pain_____	speech_____
thank_____	play_____
amaze_____	mouth_____
kind_____	sick_____
develop_____	forgive_____

Suffix Worksheet
(-ful, -en, -less, -ment, -ness)
RallyCoach

Instructions: Partners use worksheet with prefix cube.
Rule: When adding an ending to a word that ends with *y*, change the *y* to *i* when it is preceded by a consonant. This does not apply to the ending *-ing*.

move_____	sharp_____
cheer_____	employ_____
white_____	spoon_____
success_____	pocket_____
sweet_____	plenty_____
merry_____	thought_____
home_____	beauty_____
advertise_____	sleeve_____
quiet_____	heavy_____
care_____	achieve_____
stress_____	happy_____
pity_____	fresh_____

Suffix Answer Sheet
(-ful, -en, -less, -ment, -ness)
RallyCoach

govern**ment**	point**less**
good**ness**	stiff**en**
weak**en**	taste**less**
hope**ful**	waste**ful**
hand**ful**	peace**ful**
short**en**	less**en**
wool**en**	sleep**less**
pain**ful**	speech**less**
thank**less**	play**ful**
amaze**ment**	mouth**ful**
kind**ness**	sick**ness**
develop**ment**	forgive**ness**

Suffix Answer Sheet (continued)
(-ful, -en, -less, -ment, -ness)
RallyCoach

move**ment**	sharp**en**
cheer**ful**	employ**ment**
whit**en**	spoon**ful**
success**ful**	pocket**ful**
sweet**en**	plenti**ful**
merri**ment**	thought**ful**
home**less**	beauti**ful**
advertise**ment**	sleeve**less**
quiet**ness**	heavi**ness**
care**ful**	achieve**ment**
stress**ful**	happi**ness**
piti**ful**	fresh**en**

Antonym-Synonym Cube
RallyCoach

Instructions: Copy the cube pattern onto cardstock for each pair. Cut out, fold, and tape to form a cube. Partners take turns rolling the cube. The student rolling the cube chooses a pair of words on the worksheet that fits the description "antonyms" or "synonyms."

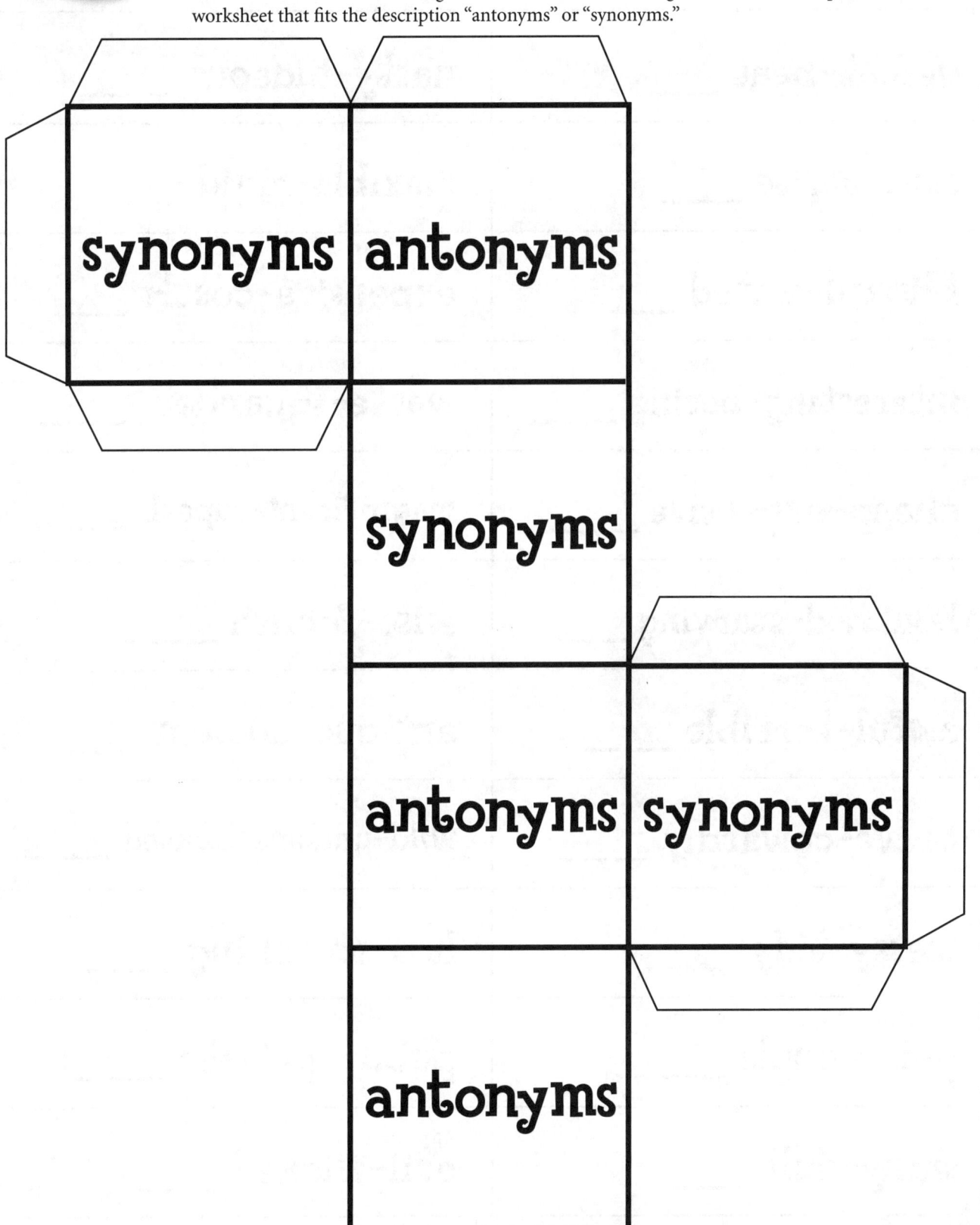

synonyms | antonyms

synonyms

antonyms | synonyms

antonyms

Antonym-Synonym Worksheet
RallyCoach

Instructions: Partners use worksheet with Antonym-Synonym Cube. Write *A* if the word pair are antonyms. Write *S* if the word pair are synonyms.

defeat-beat ____	nasty-hideous ____
save-waste ____	flexible-rigid ____
blissful-elated ____	expensive-costly ____
interesting-boring ____	waste-squander ____
cheap-expensive ____	magnificent-superb ____
famished-starving ____	wise-foolish ____
awful-terrible ____	antique-ancient ____
brave-cowardly ____	wild-undomesticated ____
messy-tidy ____	hot-scorching ____
pair-couple ____	public-private ____
shiny-dull ____	evil-wicked ____

Antonym-Synonym Answer Sheet
RallyCoach

defeat-beat	**S**	nasty-hideous	**S**
save-waste	**A**	flexible-rigid	**A**
blissful-elated	**S**	expensive-costly	**S**
interesting-boring	**A**	waste-squander	**S**
cheap-expensive	**A**	magnificent-superb	**S**
famished-starving	**S**	wise—foolish	**A**
awful-terrible	**S**	antique—ancient	**S**
brave-cowardly	**A**	wild-undomesticated	**S**
messy-tidy	**A**	hot-scorching	**S**
pair-couple	**S**	public-private	**A**
shiny-dull	**A**	evil-wicked	**S**

Contraction Spinner
RallyCoach

Instructions: Copy the spinner onto cardstock for each pair. Add a plastic/metal spinner in the middle or use a spinner made from a paper clip and a pencil. (To make a paper clip spinner: Place a paper clip over the center of the spinner. Place the pencil point on the center point of the spinner through the paper clip. Using the other hand, spin the paper clip around the pencil point.) Partners take turns spinning. The student spinning chooses an incomplete word on the worksheet to form a word.

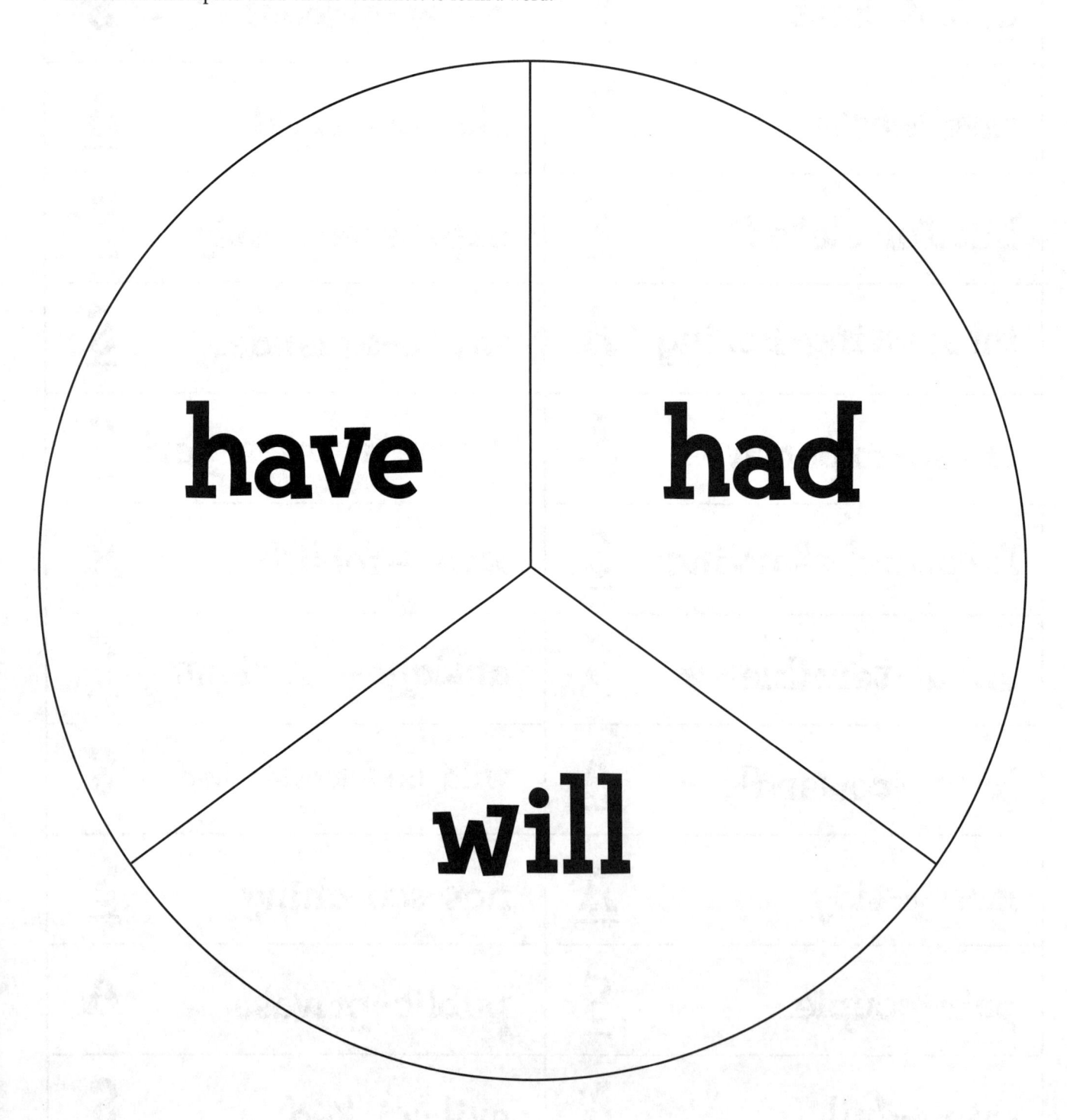

have

had

will

Contraction Worksheet
RallyCoach

Instructions: Partners use worksheet with Contraction Spinner. Partners write word from Spinner in first column. The two words are written as a contraction in the second column.

Word from Spinner	Contraction
you _____	_____
I _____	_____
would _____	_____
they _____	_____
she _____	_____
that _____	_____
we _____	_____
should _____	_____
might _____	_____
it _____	_____
there _____	_____
he _____	_____

Adding Endings Spinner
RallyCoach

Instructions: Copy the spinner onto cardstock for each pair. Add a plastic/metal spinner in the middle or use a spinner made from a paper clip and a pencil. (To make a paper clip spinner: Place a paper clip over the center of the spinner. Place the pencil point on the center point of the spinner through the paper clip. Using the other hand, spin the paper clip around the pencil point.) Partners take turns spinning. The student spinning follows the direction indicated by the spin and applies it to one word from the worksheet to form a new word.

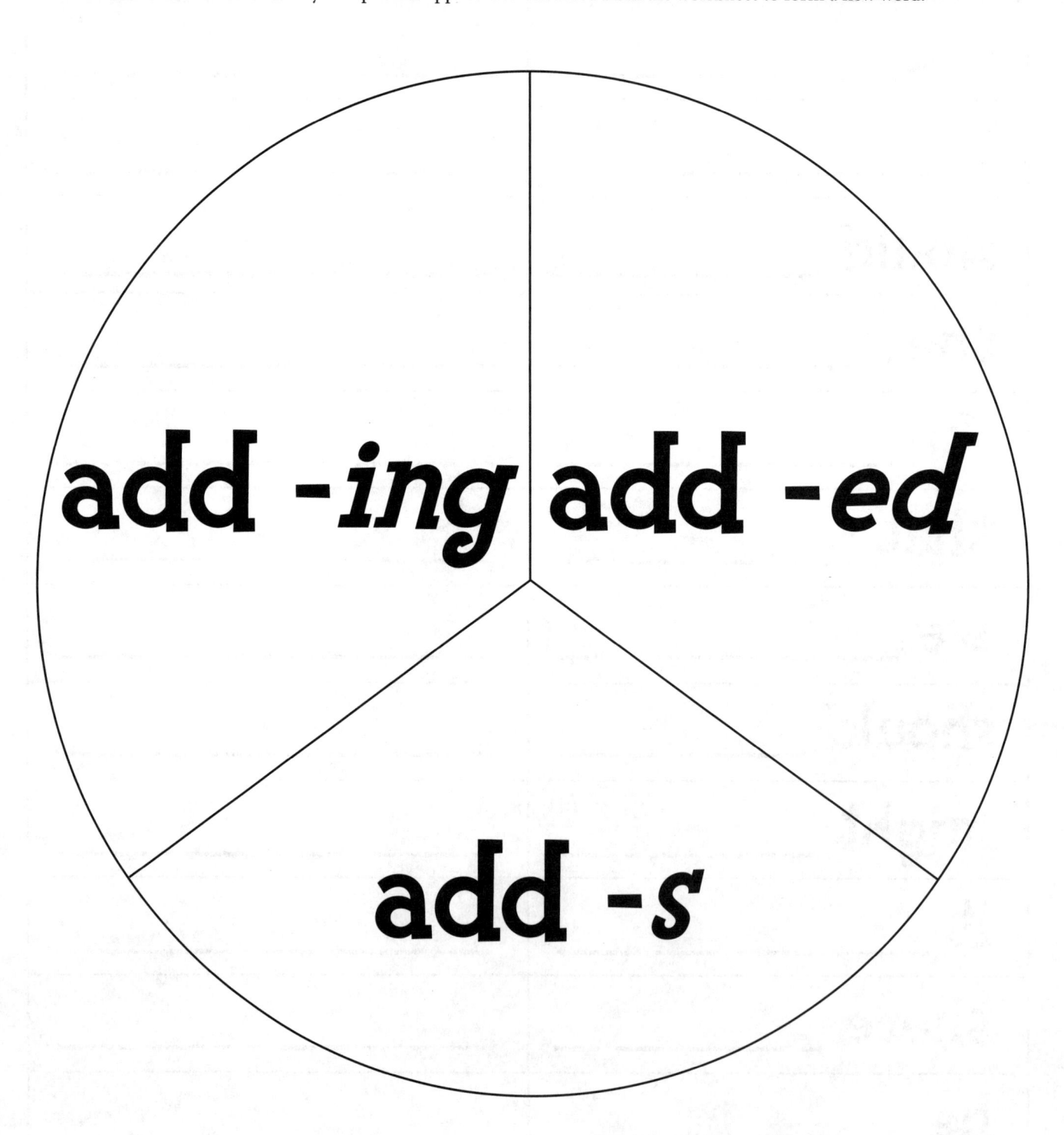

- add *-ing*
- add *-ed*
- add *-s*

Adding Endings Worksheet
RallyCoach

Instructions: Partners use worksheet with Spinner (adding -ing, -ed, -s).
Rule: When adding an ending to a word that ends with *y*, change the *y* to *i* when it is preceded by a consonant. This does not apply to the ending *-ing*.

carry_____	reply_____
try_____	empty_____
apply_____	hurry_____
dry_____	marry_____
supply_____	vary_____
study_____	party_____
pry_____	copy_____
magnify_____	bury_____
cry_____	hurry_____
worry_____	pity_____

Adding Endings Answer Sheet
RallyCoach

word	possible answers	word	possible answers
carry	carrying, carried, carries	**reply**	replying, replied, replies
try	trying, tried, tries	**empty**	emptying, emptied, empties
apply	applying, applied, applies	**hurry**	hurrying, hurried, hurries
dry	drying, dried, dries	**marry**	marrying, married, marries
supply	supplying, supplied, supplies	**vary**	varying, varied, varies
study	studying, studied, studies	**party**	partying, partied, parties
pry	prying, pried, pries	**copy**	copying, copied, copies
magnify	magnifying, magnified, magnifies	**bury**	burying, buried, buries
cry	crying, cried, cries	**hurry**	hurrying, hurried, hurries
worry	worrying, worried, worries	**pry**	pitying, pitied, pities

Hard g or Soft g Sorting Mat
RallyCoach

Instructions: Copy one mat for each pair. Sort each word into the correct column according to the sound the g makes in the word.

Hard g Sound /g/	Soft g Sound /j/

Balanced Literacy • Fourth Grade • Skidmore & Graber

Hard *g* or Soft *g* Word Cards
RallyCoach

Instructions: Copy one set of cards for each pair. Cut apart.

Word Cards	Word Cards
gelatin	gardener
gadget	garlic
gala	gallery
gills	goblet
galaxy	galore
general	germs
gym	gawk
gatherings	gizmo
geckos	goalie
geography	gem
genie	gopher
guard	germinate

Hard *g* or Soft *g* Word Cards
RallyCoach

Instructions: Copy one set of cards for each pair. Cut apart.

Word Cards	Word Cards
given	generation
gown	guests
giants	guide
guys	guitar
giraffe	gene
gerbil	gentle
gutter	get
general	gorilla
gushed	gallon
gingerbread	game
guess	giggle
government	Germany

Hard g or Soft g Word Cards
RallyCoach

Instructions: Copy one set of cards for each pair. Cut apart.

Word Cards	Word Cards
pledge	burgers
argue	bridge
igloo	hedge
page	vinegar
magic	agree
sage	angry
bargain	dodge
cottage	marriage
tigers	Kindergarten
target	legal
Kangaroo	cottage
carriage	figure

SHOWDOWN ACTIVITY

Word Study Showdown

Teams play Showdown to practice prefixes, antonyms, synonyms, and homophones.

STRUCTURE
Showdown

Activity Steps

1. Team Cards are placed facedown in the middle of the team.
2. Each student holds Student Card Set in his or her hand.
3. Teacher selects one student to be the Showdown Captain for the first round.
4. Showdown Captain selects the top card from the middle and reads it aloud.
5. Working alone, students individually identify an answer from Student Card Set.
6. When finished, teammates signal they are ready.
7. Showdown Captain calls, "Showdown!"
8. Teammates show their answers at the same time.
9. Showdown Captain leads checking.
10. If correct, the team celebrates. If not, the teammates coach, then celebrate.
11. The person to the left of the Showdown Captain becomes the Showdown Captain for the next round.

Blacklines

- Prefixes: anti-, dis-, ex-, non-, under- (Team and Student Sets)................378–381
- Antonyms, Synonyms, Homophones (Team and Student Sets)................382–388

Prefixes
(anti-, dis-, ex-, non-, under-)
Showdown (Team Set)

Instructions: Copy one set of cards for each pair. Cut apart.

___resident	___press	___infect
___-president	___respect	___score
___like	___freeze	___cover
___bacterial	___arm	___skid

Prefixes
(anti-, dis-, ex-, non-, under-)
Showdown (Team Set)

Instructions: Copy one set of cards for each team. Cut apart.

____ stop	____ organized	____ current
____ claim	____ terrorism	____ dairy
____ loyal	____ foot	____ go
____ social	____ carriage	____ profit

Prefixes
(anti-, dis-, ex-, non-, under-)
Showdown (Team Set)

Instructions: Copy one set of cards for each pair. Cut apart.

___ sense	___ belief	___ conformist
___ obey	___ pass	___ side
___ satisfied	___ charge	___ clothes
___ histamine	___ existent	___ standard

Prefixes
anti-, dis-, ex-, non-, under-
Showdown (Student Set)

Note: This page has cards for two students. Copy, cut apart, and give each student one set of prefix cards.

Prefixes: anti-, dis-, ex-, non-, under- Student Set	Prefixes: anti-, dis-, ex-, non-, under- Student Set	Prefixes: anti-, dis-, ex-, non-, under- Student Set	Prefixes: anti-, dis-, ex-, non-, under- Student Set	Prefixes: anti-, dis-, ex-, non-, under- Student Set
anti-	dis-	ex-	non-	under-
anti-	dis-	ex-	non-	under-

Antonyms, Synonyms, Homophones
Showdown (Team Set)

Instructions: Copy one set of cards for each team. Cut apart.

Antonyms, Synonyms, Homophones — Team Set

interesting

boring

Antonyms, Synonyms, Homophones — Team Set

flexible

rigid

Antonyms, Synonyms, Homophones — Team Set

wise

foolish

Antonyms, Synonyms, Homophones — Team Set

public

private

Antonyms, Synonyms, Homophones — Team Set

shiny

dull

Antonyms, Synonyms, Homophones — Team Set

messy

tidy

Antonyms, Synonyms, Homophones
Showdown (Team Set)

Instructions: Copy one set of cards for each team. Cut apart.

Antonyms, Synonyms, Homophones — Team Set	Antonyms, Synonyms, Homophones — Team Set	Antonyms, Synonyms, Homophones — Team Set
cheap expensive	brave cowardly	save waste
remember forget	nothing everything	energized exhausted

Antonyms, Synonyms, Homophones
Showdown (Team Set)

Instructions: Copy one set of cards for each team. Cut apart.

Antonyms, Synonyms, Homophones — Team Set	Antonyms, Synonyms, Homophones — Team Set	Antonyms, Synonyms, Homophones — Team Set
defeat beat	famished starving	pair couple
evil wicked	expensive costly	antique ancient

Antonyms, Synonyms, Homophones
Showdown (Team Set)

Instructions: Copy one set of cards for each team. Cut apart.

Antonyms, Synonyms, Homophones — Team Set	Antonyms, Synonyms, Homophones — Team Set	Antonyms, Synonyms, Homophones — Team Set
waste **squander**	**magnificent** **superb**	**wild** **undomesticated**
awful **terrible**	**order** **sequence**	**delighted** **pleased**

Antonyms, Synonyms, Homophones
Showdown (Team Set)

Instructions: Copy one set of cards for each team. Cut apart.

Antonyms, Synonyms, Homophones — Team Set

board
bored

Antonyms, Synonyms, Homophones — Team Set

heard
herd

Antonyms, Synonyms, Homophones — Team Set

chews
choose

Antonyms, Synonyms, Homophones — Team Set

patience
patients

Antonyms, Synonyms, Homophones — Team Set

wade
weighed

Antonyms, Synonyms, Homophones — Team Set

root
route

Antonyms, Synonyms, Homophones
Showdown (Team Set)

Instructions: Copy one set of cards for each team. Cut apart.

Antonyms, Synonyms, Homophones — Team Set	Antonyms, Synonyms, Homophones — Team Set	Antonyms, Synonyms, Homophones — Team Set
peace / **piece**	**links** / **lynx**	**mind** / **mined**
Antonyms, Synonyms, Homophones — Team Set	Antonyms, Synonyms, Homophones — Team Set	Antonyms, Synonyms, Homophones — Team Set
paced / **paste**	**oar** / **ore**	**aloud** / **allowed**

Antonyms, Synonyms, Homophones
Showdown (Student Set)

Note: This page has cards for two students. Copy, cut apart, and give each student one set of cards.

Antonyms, Synonyms, Homophones—Student Set	Antonyms, Synonyms, Homophones—Student Set	Antonyms, Synonyms, Homophones—Student Set
antonyms	**synonyms**	**homophones**

Antonyms, Synonyms, Homophones—Student Set	Antonyms, Synonyms, Homophones—Student Set	Antonyms, Synonyms, Homophones—Student Set
antonyms	**synonyms**	**homophones**

NUMBERED HEADS TOGETHER Activity

Word Wall Spelling

After spelling the word themselves, teammates put their "heads together" to ensure all members can correctly spell the word wall word. The teacher then calls a number and all students with that number share their team's spelling.

STRUCTURE
Numbered Heads Together

Note:
The Word Wall Cards on the following pages are not used for this activity. They are provided for your convenience to post on your word wall. However, before you begin this activity, make sure you take down word wall words students will spell.

Activity Steps

1. Students number off in small groups.
2. Teacher reads a selected word from the Word List.
3. Students privately write the word on a markerboard or on a piece of paper.
4. Teacher says, "Heads Together!" and students lift up from their chairs to put their heads together, show their answers, and discuss until they reach consensus on the word spelling.
5. Everyone clears their boards and sits down when they agree.
6. The teacher calls out a number. All students with that number write the agreed-upon spelling of the word on their markerboards.
7. All students with their number selected hold up their boards simultaneously. The teacher writes each group's spelling on the overhead.
8. The teacher leads the class in a discussion of each spelling by asking questions such as "Which way looks right?" "How do you know?" or "What was the tricky part or familiar part?"
9. Teammates celebrate or correct spelling on boards.
10. The process is repeated for each new word.

Note: "Additional Word Wall Words" provide extra word choices.

Blacklines

- Fourth Grade Word List 390–391
- Fourth Grade Word Wall Cards 392–397
- Fourth Grade Additional Word Wall Cards 398–404
- Fourth Grade Blank Word Wall Cards 405

Fourth Grade Word List
Numbered Heads Together

Instructions: Words to be used with Word Wall Spelling.

a	are	boy	does	fish	has	inside	live
about	around	brought	done	five	have	into	lived
above	as	but	don't	food	he	is	living
across	asked	by	door	for	head	it	long
add	at	called	down	form	hear	its	look
after	away	came	during	found	help	it's	made
again	back	can	each	four	her	just	make
against	be	car	early	from	here	keep	man
ago	became	change	earth	front	high	kind	many
air	because	children	eat	gave	him	know	may
all	been	city	end	get	himself	land	me
almost	before	close	enough	give	his	large	men
along	began	cold	even	go	home	last	might
also	being	come	every	going	house	later	money
always	below	could	example	good	how	learn	more
am	best	country	face	got	however	learned	morning
American	better	course	family	great	I	left	most
an	between	cut	far	ground	idea	let	mother
and	big	day	father	group	if	life	move
animal	black	did	feet	had	I'll	light	much
another	body	didn't	few	half	I'm	like	must
answer	book	different	find	hand	important	line	my
any	both	do	first	hard	in	little	name

Fourth Grade Word List
Numbered Heads Together

Instructions: Words to be used with Word Wall Spelling.

near	out	saw	still	three	usually	work
need	over	say	story	through	very	world
never	own	school	study	time	want	would
new	page	sea	such	to	was	write
next	paper	second	sun	today	water	year
night	part	see	sure	together	way	young
not	people	seen	table	told	we	your
nothing	picture	sentence	take	too	well	
now	place	set	tell	took	went	
number	plants	several	than	top	were	
of	play	she	that	toward	what	
off	point	short	the	tree	when	
often	put	should	their	trust	where	
old	read	show	them	try	which	
on	really	side	then	turn	while	
once	red	since	there	turned	white	
one	remember	small	these	two	who	
only	right	so	they	under	whole	
open	room	some	thing	United States	why	
or	run	something	think	until	will	
order	sad	soon	this	up	with	
other	said	sound	those	upon	without	
our	same	space	thought	use	words	

Fourth Grade
Word Wall Cards

Instructions: Use the cards provided to create a Word Wall.

are	because	between	body
about	above	across	always

Fourth Grade Word Wall Cards

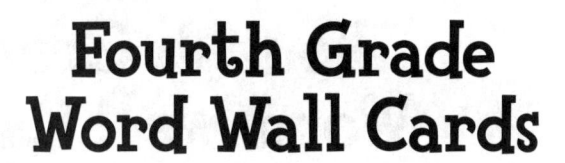

Instructions: Use the cards provided to create a Word Wall.

| during | early | every | example |
| brought | children | close | does |

Fourth Grade Word Wall Cards

Instructions: Use the cards provided to create a Word Wall.

Fourth Grade Word Wall Cards	Fourth Grade Word Wall Cards	Fourth Grade Word Wall Cards	Fourth Grade Word Wall Cards
know	money	near	nothing
few	however	idea	important

Fourth Grade
Word Wall Cards

Instructions: Use the cards provided to create a Word Wall.

remember	said	should	their
often	once	people	picture

Fourth Grade Word Wall Cards

Instructions: Use the cards provided to create a Word Wall.

usually	where	which	while
there	together	toward	use

Fourth Grade Word Wall Cards

Instructions: Use the cards provided to create a Word Wall.

- would
- write
- young
- your
- whole
- why
- without
- world

Fourth Grade Additional Word Wall Cards

Instructions: Use the cards provided to create a Word Wall.

- area
- instead
- finally
- heavy
- become
- shown
- built
- kept

Fourth Grade Additional Word Wall Cards

Instructions: Use the cards provided to create a Word Wall.

- special
- person
- notice
- either
- although
- hour
- bottom
- friend

Fourth Grade Additional Word Wall Cards

Instructions: Use the cards provided to create a Word Wall.

- English
- hundred
- piece
- understand
- carefully
- fact
- happened
- language

Fourth Grade Additional Word Wall Cards

Instructions: Use the cards provided to create a Word Wall.

- weather
- question
- among
- surface
- problem
- system
- possible
- suddenly

Fourth Grade Additional Word Wall Cards

Instructions: Use the cards provided to create a Word Wall.

| easy | perhaps | voice | animals |
| whether | beautiful | quite | heart |

Fourth Grade Additional Word Wall Cards

Instructions: Use the cards provided to create a Word Wall.

pattern	field
least	poor
road	everyone
carry	leaves

Fourth Grade Additional Word Wall Cards

Instructions: Use the cards provided to create a Word Wall.

- gone
- themselves
- tiny
- alone
- certain
- complete
- probably
- round

Fourth Grade Blank Word Wall Cards

Instructions: Use the cards to add additional words.

Balanced Literacy

Comprehension
Word Study
Fluency ✓
Writing

Fluency

Fluency

Fluency is a part of an effective reading program. When a reader is fluent, energies are automatically channeled into comprehending the text instead of decoding words.

Reading fluency includes the following components:
- expression (stress, pitch, volume, clarity)
- phrasing (pauses, word groups)
- rate (just the right speed)
- accuracy (correct words and punctuation)

The fluency resources and materials at the beginning of this section are designed to be used in the suggested order to scaffold the learner and ensure understanding (*aloud* and *shared*). The remainder of the activities in this section are designed to provide fluency practice (*guided* and *independent*).

Table of Fluency Resources

Page(s)	Resources	Balanced Literacy				
		Aloud	Shared	Guided	Independent	Literature Circles
412	Fluency Resource/Materials Descriptions					
413	Fluency Bookmarks	●	●	●	●	●
414	Fluency Graphics/Note Taking	●	●	●	●	●

Table of Fluency Activities

Balanced Literacy

Page(s)	Activities	Blacklines	Aloud	Shared	Guided	Independent	Literature Circles
416	**RallyCoach Activities**						
417	Expression	• Rubric and Graph	●	●	●	●	●
418	Phrasing	• Rubric and Graph	●	●	●	●	●
419	Accuracy	• Rubric and Graph	●	●	●	●	●
420	Rate	• Rubric and Graph	●	●	●	●	●
421	Fluency	• Continuum Worksheet	●	●	●	●	●
422	**Poems for Two Voices Activities**						
423	Tropical Rainforests	• Copy of Poem		●	●		
425	Human Body Riddles	• Copy of Poem		●	●		
427	Blank Form	• Blank Worksheet		●	●		
428	**Quiz-Quiz-Trade Activity**						
429	Fluency Sentences	• Sentence Cards		●	●	●	

Balanced Literacy • Fourth Grade • Skidmore & Graber
Kagan Publishing • 1 (800) 933-2667 • www.KaganOnline.com

Fluency Resources

Fluency Resources

Resources/Materials Descriptions

Fluency Bookmark (p. 413)
Fluency is automatic and accurate recognition of words in a text while using phrasing and expression in a way that makes reading sound like spoken language. The Fluency Bookmark is a visual prompting tool for students to use as they learn and practice the components of fluent reading.

Fluency Graphics/Note Taking (p. 414)
This fluency page provides flexible instructional uses. The teacher may have students attach their own labels, graphics, or notes to build mental connections as they become fluent readers.

Fluency Rubrics and Graphs (pp. 417–420)
The broad fluency components of expression, phrasing, rate, and accuracy have been defined through the rubric continuum to increase students' fluency knowledge, self-awareness, and monitoring of progress.

Students must be given opportunities to reread and practice if fluency is going to improve. The graph below each rubric provides students with a visual record for charting their own progress as they practice with a partner or individually.

Together, these two tools provide data for reflection and conversation between students and between student and teacher.

Fluency Continuum (p. 421)
After using the Rubrics and Graphs described above to create a solid understanding of fluency, the Fluency Continuum becomes another self-monitoring option for students.

Student Bookmarks

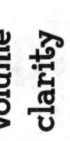

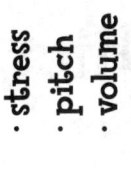

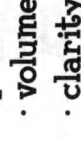

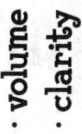

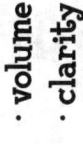

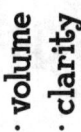

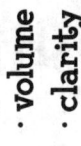

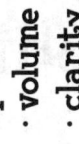

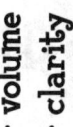

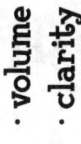

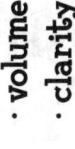

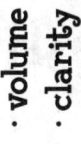

Fluency Expression

expression 
- stress
- pitch
- volume
- clarity

phrasing 
- pauses
- word groups

rate 
- speed (just right)

accuracy 
- right words
- correct pronunciation

Fluency Expression

expression   
- stress
- pitch
- volume
- clarity

phrasing
- pauses
- word groups

rate 
- speed (just right)

accuracy
- right words
- correct pronunciation

Fluency Expression

expression 
- stress
- pitch
- volume
- clarity

phrasing 
- pauses
- word groups

rate
- speed (just right)

accuracy 
- right words
- correct pronunciation

Fluency Expression

expression 
- stress
- pitch
- volume
- clarity

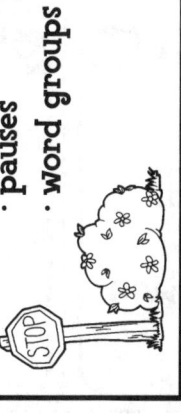

phrasing 
- pauses
- word groups

rate 
- speed (just right)

accuracy
- right words
- correct pronunciation

Balanced Literacy • Fourth Grade • Skidmore & Graber
Kagan Publishing • 1 (800) 933-2667 • www.KaganOnline.com

Fluency Graphics/ Note Taking

Instructions: Copy for each student.

Fluency Graphics/Note Taking
expression
- stress
- pitch
- volume
- clarity

Fluency Graphics/Note Taking

Fluency Graphics/Note Taking
phrasing
- pauses
- word groups

Fluency Graphics/Note Taking

Fluency Graphics/Note Taking
rate
- speed (just right)

Fluency Graphics/Note Taking

Fluency Graphics/Note Taking
accuracy
- right words
- correct pronunciation

Fluency Graphics/Note Taking

Fluency Activities

RALLYCOACH Activity

Fluency Scoring

Students read a text passage to a partner. The partner uses a rubric to score the reading on one dimension. Students practice reading the same passage to improve their fluency and chart their progress.

Activity Steps

1. There are four rubrics provided to work on different dimensions of fluency. Each student receives a rubric sheet.

2. Partner A reads the text passage while Partner B listens carefully, paying special attention to the rubric scoring.

3. Partner B uses the rubric to score Partner A's reading. Partner B colors in the score in the "1st time" column of the graph. Then Partner B describes the score and how Partner A can improve.

4. Partner B then reads while Partner A listens.

5. Partner A scores the reading by filling in the graph and provides feedback to Partner B.

6. The process is repeated multiple times with the same text passage to improve fluency. There are five columns on the graph provided so students can graph their progress.

STRUCTURE
RallyCoach

Hint:
Tell students in advance that they will be scoring each other on their reading. The scores are used only as a way for students to provide each other constructive feedback and chart their progress.

Blacklines

- Expression Rubric and Graph..417
- Phrasing Rubric and Graph..418
- Accuracy Rubric and Graph...419
- Rate Rubric and Graph 420
- Fluency Continuum 421

Fluency Blackline

Expression Rubric
RallyCoach

Instructions: Copy for each student.

Score	1	2	3	4
Expression • Stress • Pitch • Volume • Clarity	No Voice change	Voice changes sometimes	Voice changes most of the time when needed	Voice changes when needed

Expression Graph
RallyCoach

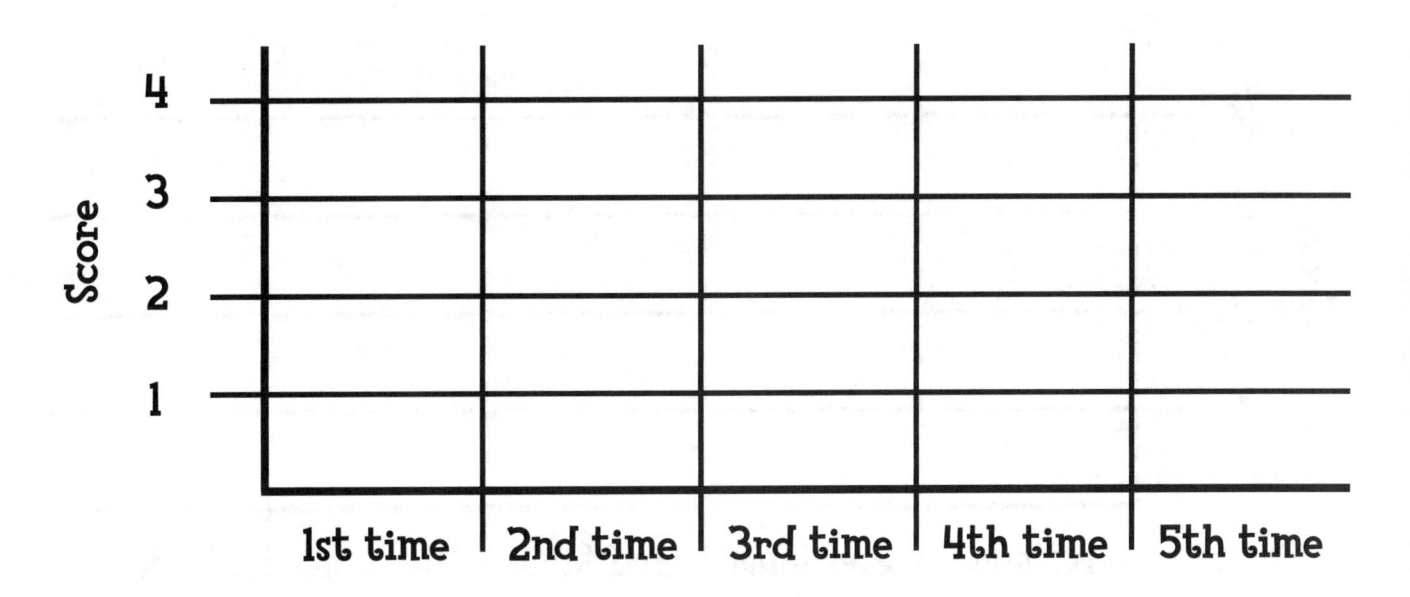

Score (4, 3, 2, 1) vs. 1st time, 2nd time, 3rd time, 4th time, 5th time

Name _____

Balanced Literacy • Fourth Grade • Skidmore & Graber
Kagan Publishing • 1 (800) 933-2667 • www.KaganOnline.com

Phrasing Rubric
RallyCoach

Instructions: Copy for each student.

Score	1	2	3	4
Phrasing • Pauses • Word Groups	Reads word by word and does not stop at punctuation	Reads in small chunks and sometimes stops at punctuation	Reads in larger chunks and usually stops at punctuation	Reads in long chunks and stops at punctuation

Phrasing Graph
RallyCoach

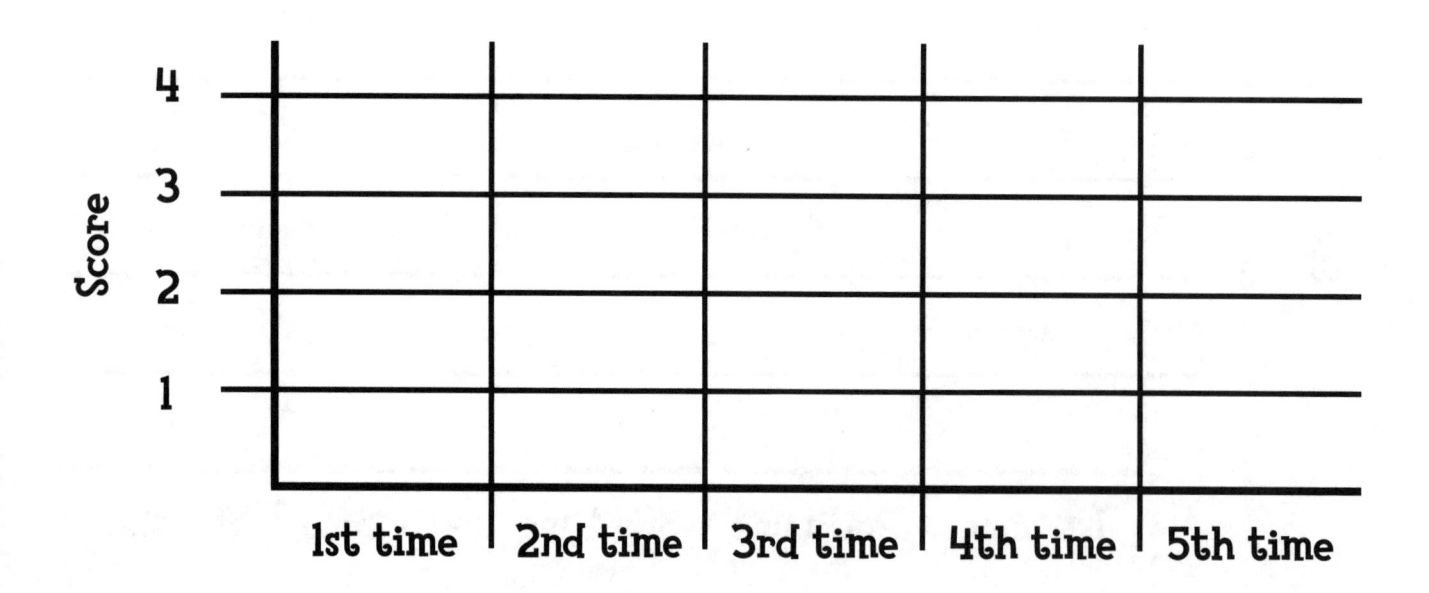

Score (4, 3, 2, 1) vs. 1st time, 2nd time, 3rd time, 4th time, 5th time

Name _____

Accuracy Rubric
RallyCoach

Instructions: Copy for each student.

Score	1	2	3	4
Accuracy • Right Words • Correct Pronunciation	Many errors	Errors, which sometimes change the meaning	Some errors, which do not change the meaning	Very few or no errors Words correctly pronounced

Accuracy Graph
RallyCoach

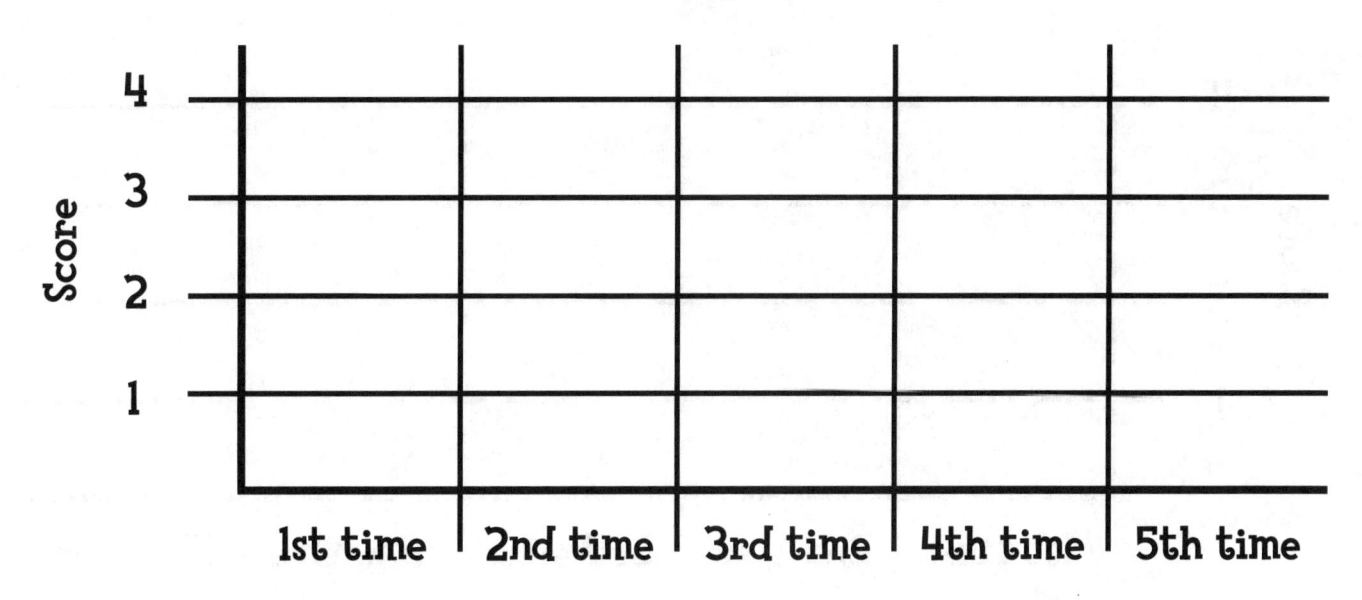

Score (4, 3, 2, 1) vs. 1st time, 2nd time, 3rd time, 4th time, 5th time

Name _____

Rate Rubric

RallyCoach

Instructions: Copy for each student.

Score	1	2	3	4
Rate • Speed (Just Right)	Reads too fast or too slow Hard to understand	Reads too fast or too slow sometimes	Reads "just right" most of the time	Keeps speed steady and "just right"

Rate Graph

RallyCoach

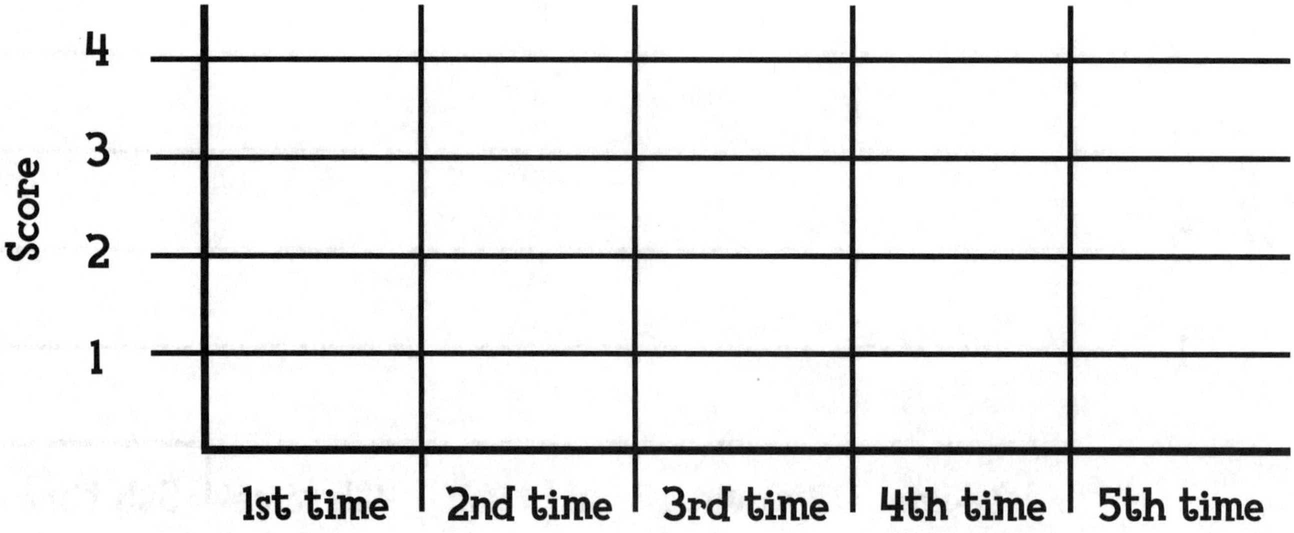
Score
4
3
2
1
1st time
2nd time
3rd time
4th time
5th time

Name ______________________________

Fluency Continuum
RallyCoach

Instructions: Copy for each student.

Fluency Continuum
expression
- stress
- pitch
- volume
- clarity

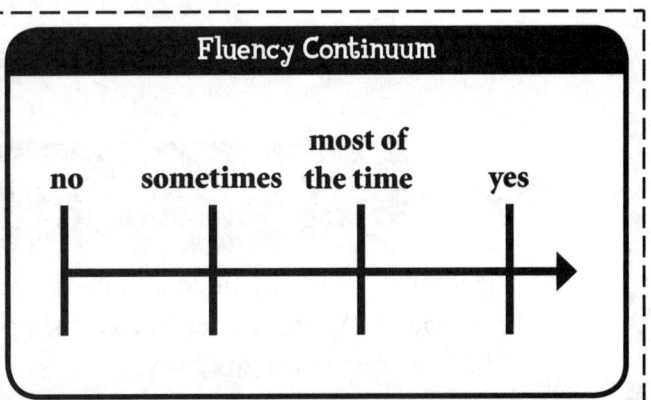

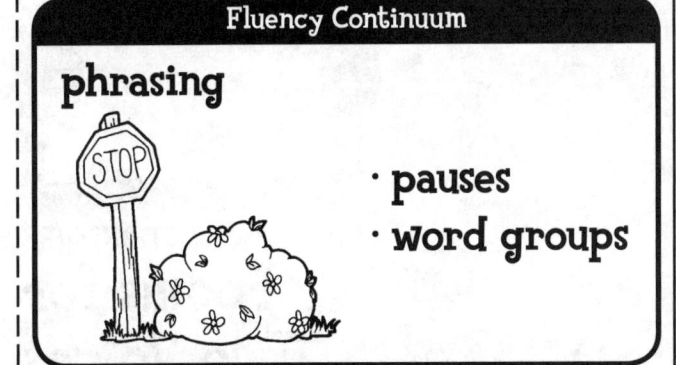

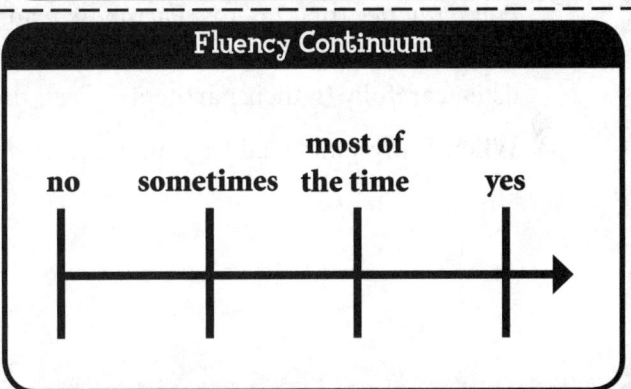

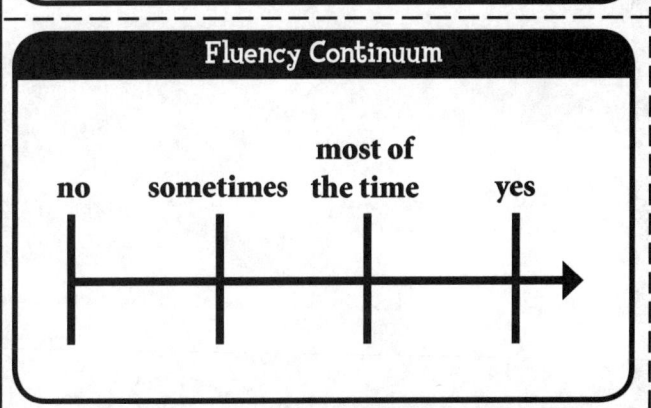

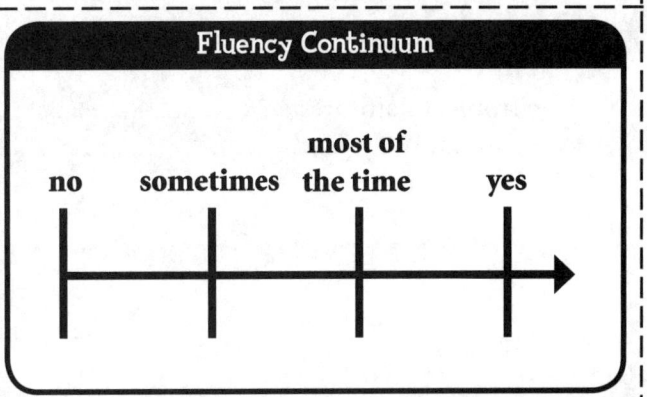

Fluency Continuum
no | sometimes | most of the time | yes

Fluency Continuum
phrasing
- pauses
- word groups

Fluency Continuum
no | sometimes | most of the time | yes

Fluency Continuum
rate
- speed (just right)

Fluency Continuum
no | sometimes | most of the time | yes

Fluency Continuum
accuracy
- right words
- correct pronunciation

Fluency Continuum
no | sometimes | most of the time | yes

Balanced Literacy • Fourth Grade • Skidmore & Graber
Kagan Publishing • 1 (800) 933-2667 • www.KaganOnline.com

POEMS FOR TWO VOICES Activity

Fluency Poems

Partners present a poem—recited at times by one partner, the other partner, or both.

Activity Steps

1. The teacher provides students a poem. The poem has some lines labeled "A," some lines labeled "B," and some lines labeled "AB." The teacher assigns pairs.

2. Pairs practice their poems. Partner A reads the A lines. Partner B reads the B lines. They read the AB lines in unison. Students listen carefully to their partners to keep the flow.

3. When ready, pairs read their poem to another pair.

STRUCTURE
Poems for Two Voices

Blacklines

- Tropical Rainforests 423–424
- Human Body Riddles 425–426
- Blank Form 427

Tropical Rainforests

Poems for Two Voices

Instructions: Copy for each student or pair.

AB	Tropical Rainforests
A	Found in a belt around Earth's equator
B	In South America, Central America, Africa, Southeast Asia, and Australia
AB	Dense, warm, wet forests
A	Receiving over 80 inches of water a year
B	Never freezing and never getting very hot
AB	Greatest plant and animal diversity in the world
A	From the tops of the tallest trees
AB	Emergent strata
B	To the upper parts of the trees
AB	Canopy
A	To the dark, cool area under the leaves of the trees, but over the ground...
AB	Understory
B	Down to the ground...
AB	Forest floor

Tropical Rainforests (continued)

Poems for Two Voices

Instructions: Copy for each student or pair.

A	Howler monkeys, apes, chimpanzees, orangutans
B	Ocelots, jaguars, tigers
A	Toucans, parrots
B	Frogs, lizards, turtles
A	Anacondas, boas
AB	Millions of mammals, amphibians, reptiles, birds, and insects
A	Important to Earth's ecosystem
B	Recycle and clean water
A	Generate much of Earth's oxygen
B	Remove carbon dioxide from the atmosphere
A	Slow global warming and greenhouse effect
B	Provide plants used in new drugs to fight disease
AB	Tropical Rainforests

Human Body Riddles
Poems for Two Voices

Instructions: Copy for each student or pair.

A   Let's work together on guessing the answers to these riddles about the human body.

B   I'm ready for the first one!

AB   Let's begin.

A   I cover and protect you, from the top of your head to the bottoms of your feet. Think of me as a giant candy wrapper, that keeps in the water and keeps out harmful germs and dirt. What am I?

B   Skin.

A   That's exactly right!

B   I give you shape and hold you up. Giving protection to soft parts inside you is also my job. Think of me as the frame of a house. What am I?

A   Bones.

B   Good for you!

A   I help you do heavy work. You need me for every single move you make. Think of me as a crane, that helps you lift and pull. What am I?

B   Muscles.

A   You've got the idea of this guessing game.

B   I help you breathe in the oxygen your body needs. Think of me as being like two balloons, expanding when you breathe in and shrinking when you breathe out.

A   Lungs.

B   Exactly.

Human Body Riddles (continued)
Poems for Two Voices

Instructions: Copy for each student or pair.

A	I am found inside your head. I organize and store information. Another of my jobs is to send messages to other parts of your body, telling them what to do and how to feel. Think of me as a computer, that you take with you wherever you go. What am I?
B	Brain.
A	Right again!
B	I am your body's strongest muscle. Think of me as a squeeze bottle. When I am squeezed, blood flows out to every part of your body. What am I?
A	Heart.
B	You really know these riddle answers.
A	Squishing and squeezing the food you eat is my job whenever you swallow. Think of me as a blender. What am I?
B	Stomach.
A	Once again, you got it.
AB	Each part of our bodies has an important job.
A	Skin and bones
B	Muscles and lungs
A	Brain, heart, and stomach
AB	Together they make up our wonderful bodies!

Blank Form
Poems for Two Voices

Names: _____

_____

Our Poem Is About: _____

Instructions: Copy for each pair of students.

A _____

B _____

A _____

B _____

AB _____

A _____

B _____

A _____

B _____

AB _____

QUIZ-QUIZ-TRADE Activity

Fluency Sentences

Partners play Quiz-Quiz-Trade for repeated practice on fluency.

Activity Steps

1. Each student receives a fluency sentence card with the same sentence on the front and back. The sentence on the back is so the partner can also see the sentence.

2. Students stand up, put a hand up, and pair up with another student.

3. Partner A asks Partner B to read the sentence on the card.

4. Partner B reads for fluency.

5. Partner A praises if the student read it well or reads it to demonstrate improved fluency.

6. Partner B now quizzes Partner A, Partner A reads, and Partner B praises or demonstrates correct inflection.

7. Partners trade cards and find a new partner to quiz. The activity continues for multiple rounds, allowing students to quiz and get quizzed multiple times.

STRUCTURE
Quiz-Quiz Trade

Front

Fluency Sentences

Read this sentence. Remember phrasing and expression.

I am so excited to go to the movie with you!

Back

Fluency Sentences

Answer

I am so excited to go to the movie with you!

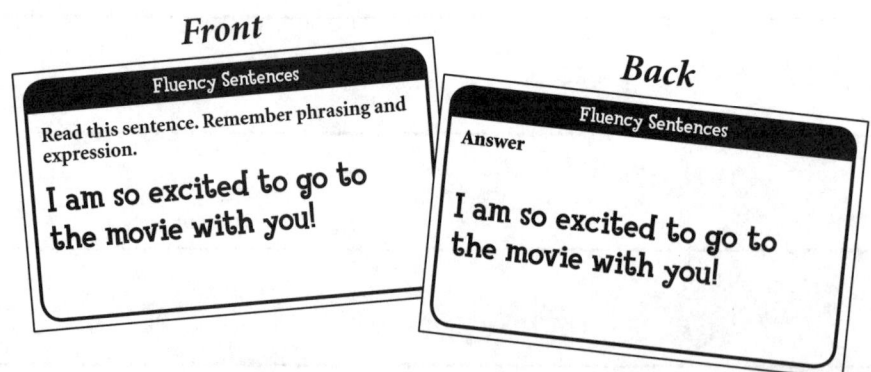

Blacklines

• Fluency Sentence Cards...429–436

Fluency Sentences
Quiz-Quiz-Trade

Instructions: Copy enough cards so each student has one card. Cut on dotted lines and fold in half.

Fluency Sentences

Read this sentence. Remember phrasing and expression.

I **NEVER** want to go on that ride again!

Fluency Sentences

Answer

I **NEVER** want to go on that ride again!

Fluency Sentences

Read this sentence. Remember phrasing and expression.

"Are you coming to the party tonight?" inquired Brenda.

Fluency Sentences

Answer

"Are you coming to the party tonight?" inquired Brenda.

Fluency Sentences

Read this sentence. Remember phrasing and expression.

I'm so excited to go to the movie with you!

Fluency Sentences

Answer

I'm so excited to go to the movie with you!

Fluency Sentences

Read this sentence. Remember phrasing and expression.

"Happy Birthday to you. Happy Birthday to you," we sang to our teacher.

Fluency Sentences

Answer

"Happy Birthday to you. Happy Birthday to you," we sang to our teacher.

Fluency Sentences
Quiz-Quiz-Trade

Instructions: Copy enough cards so each student has one card. Cut on dotted lines and fold in half.

Fluency Sentences

Read this sentence. Remember phrasing and expression.

"The ball is coming to you, Jordan," called Chris. "It's your catch."

Fluency Sentences

Answer

"The ball is coming to you, Jordan," called Chris. "It's your catch."

Fluency Sentences

Read this sentence. Remember phrasing and expression.

"Cheer up, Jack," said Dad, as we drove home.

Fluency Sentences

Answer

"Cheer up, Jack," said Dad, as we drove home.

Fluency Sentences

Read this sentence. Remember phrasing and expression.

"Hey, that was a great game," complimented Mom. "You should feel proud of yourself."

Fluency Sentences

Answer

"Hey, that was a great game," complimented Mom. "You should feel proud of yourself."

Fluency Sentences

Read this sentence. Remember phrasing and expression.

Long ago, the howling of a wolf could often be heard. But today, those howls are seldom heard.

Fluency Sentences

Answer

Long ago, the howling of a wolf could often be heard. But today, those howls are seldom heard.

Fluency Sentences
Quiz-Quiz-Trade

Instructions: Copy enough cards so each student has one card. Cut on dotted lines and fold in half.

Fluency Sentences

Read this sentence. Remember phrasing and expression.

The gray wolf is the largest of the wolf family.

Fluency Sentences

Answer

The gray wolf is the largest of the wolf family.

Fluency Sentences

Read this sentence. Remember phrasing and expression.

Oh, how wonderful! I can't believe how pretty the mountains look!

Fluency Sentences

Answer

Oh, how wonderful! I can't believe how pretty the mountains look!

Fluency Sentences

Read this sentence. Remember phrasing and expression.

Large areas of the world's oceans remain unexplored—deep, dark, and very mysterious.

Fluency Sentences

Answer

Large areas of the world's oceans remain unexplored—deep, dark, and very mysterious.

Fluency Sentences

Read this sentence. Remember phrasing and expression.

The biggest monster of the deep sea, and definitely a real monster, is the giant squid.

Fluency Sentences

Answer

The biggest monster of the deep sea, and definitely a real monster, is the giant squid.

Fluency Sentences
Quiz-Quiz-Trade

Instructions: Copy enough cards so each student has one card. Cut on dotted lines and fold in half.

Fluency Sentences

Read this sentence. Remember phrasing and expression.

The jellyfish has long, stinging tentacles and is very dangerous.

Fluency Sentences

Answer

The jellyfish has long, stinging tentacles and is very dangerous.

Fluency Sentences

Read this sentence. Remember phrasing and expression.

"I don't ever want to hold a snake," Lilly exclaimed to Tarrah.

Fluency Sentences

Answer

"I don't ever want to hold a snake," Lilly exclaimed to Tarrah.

Fluency Sentences

Read this sentence. Remember phrasing and expression.

A group of kangaroos is called a mob, while a group of lions is called a pride.

Fluency Sentences

Answer

A group of kangaroos is called a mob, while a group of lions is called a pride.

Fluency Sentences

Read this sentence. Remember phrasing and expression.

"Sarah, Jill, and Jane will be coming soon," I told Mom as she came through the door.

Fluency Sentences

Answer

"Sarah, Jill, and Jane will be coming soon," I told Mom as she came through the door.

Fluency Sentences
Quiz-Quiz-Trade

Instructions: Copy enough cards so each student has one card. Cut on dotted lines and fold in half.

Fluency Sentences

Read this sentence. Remember phrasing and expression.

"Oh, no! That can't be the bus already!"

Fluency Sentences

Answer

"Oh, no! That can't be the bus already!"

Fluency Sentences

Read this sentence. Remember phrasing and expression.

"Let's whisper so she doesn't hear us," whispered Jan to Julie.

Fluency Sentences

Answer

"Let's whisper so she doesn't hear us," whispered Jan to Julie.

Fluency Sentences

Read this sentence. Remember phrasing and expression.

Bang! Crash! Bang! "An opossum must be getting into the garbage can again," exclaimed Dad.

Fluency Sentences

Answer

Bang! Crash! Bang! "An opossum must be getting into the garbage can again," exclaimed Dad.

Fluency Sentences

Read this sentence. Remember phrasing and expression.

"Are you as frightened of the thunder as I am?" asked Molly.

Fluency Sentences

Answer

"Are you as frightened of the thunder as I am?" asked Molly.

Fluency Sentences
Quiz-Quiz-Trade

Instructions: Copy enough cards so each student has one card. Cut on dotted lines and fold in half.

Fluency Sentences

Read this sentence. Remember phrasing and expression.

Don't push me! I'm going as fast as I can!

Fluency Sentences

Answer

Don't push me! I'm going as fast as I can!

Fluency Sentences

Read this sentence. Remember phrasing and expression.

If this train doesn't hurry, I'll be late!

Fluency Sentences

Answer

If this train doesn't hurry, I'll be late!

Fluency Sentences

Read this sentence. Remember phrasing and expression.

January 20, 1995, is my birthday.

Fluency Sentences

Answer

January 20, 1995, is my birthday.

Fluency Sentences

Read this sentence. Remember phrasing and expression.

Sharks have excellent hearing, sharp eyes, and a keen sense of smell.

Fluency Sentences

Answer

Sharks have excellent hearing, sharp eyes, and a keen sense of smell.

Fluency Sentences
Quiz-Quiz-Trade

Instructions: Copy enough cards so each student has one card. Cut on dotted lines and fold in half.

Fluency Sentences

Read this sentence. Remember phrasing and expression.

Basketball, skates, and a CD player are things I have listed on my birthday list.

Fluency Sentences

Answer

Basketball, skates, and a CD player are things I have listed on my birthday list.

Fluency Sentences

Read this sentence. Remember phrasing and expression.

"Where should we go on vacation?" asked Dad. "Do you want to go to the ocean?"

Fluency Sentences

Answer

"Where should we go on vacation?" asked Dad. "Do you want to go to the ocean?"

Fluency Sentences

Read this sentence. Remember phrasing and expression.

"Look out for cars!" warned my mom, as I raced across the street.

Fluency Sentences

Answer

"Look out for cars!" warned my mom, as I raced across the street.

Fluency Sentences

Read this sentence. Remember phrasing and expression.

Wheeeeeee! Aren't roller coasters the best!

Fluency Sentences

Answer

Wheeeeeee! Aren't roller coasters the best!

Fluency Sentences
Quiz-Quiz-Trade

Instructions: Copy enough cards so each student has one card. Cut on dotted lines and fold in half.

Fluency Sentences

Read this sentence. Remember phrasing and expression.

Rainforest birds, such as the macaw and the toucan, are brilliantly colored.

Fluency Sentences

Answer

Rainforest birds, such as the macaw and the toucan, are brilliantly colored.

Fluency Sentences

Read this sentence. Remember phrasing and expression.

Hurry up! It's almost time for the movie to start.

Fluency Sentences

Answer

Hurry up! It's almost time for the movie to start.

Fluency Sentences

Read this sentence. Remember phrasing and expression.

"Are you going to wear that **again**!" my mom asked, as I came down the stairs.

Fluency Sentences

Answer

"Are you going to wear that **again**!" my mom asked, as I came down the stairs.

Fluency Sentences

Read this sentence. Remember phrasing and expression.

"Brrrrr! My hands feel like icicles," I exclaimed as I came inside.

Fluency Sentences

Answer

"Brrrrr! My hands feel like icicles," I exclaimed as I came inside.

Balanced Literacy

Comprehension
Word Study
Fluency
Writing

Writing

Writing Overview

Authors use four main text types to convey meaning in print:

- **Narrative**—to entertain
- **Expository**—to inform
- **Technical**—to tell how to...
- **Persuasive**—to convince

This writing section is organized into two parts. In the first part, sequential lessons will guide students in producing an expository piece of writing through a cooperative group learning process. In the second part, students will be guided through the steps of writing a persuasive writing piece. The goal is for students to apply what they have learned through group work to their individual writing.

Expository writing is a great starting place for students. Children naturally write in expository form, informing us of what they know or are learning from their experiences. Many states are testing students' proficiency in comprehending expository text, which is often more challenging for students. Therefore, the first part of this writing section focuses on writing an expository piece with the goal of strengthening both expository reading and writing.

Persuasive writing is used to convince or influence the reader. Writing and reading persuasive text are skills we use throughout our lives. As readers we are influenced by writers trying to convince us to take their point of view. As writers we have the capabilities to encourage others to agree with us or to take a certain course of action. The activities in the second part of this writing section will strengthen the connection between reading persuasive text and writing persuasively.

Note: The teacher should have his or her own ongoing piece of writing that is used for modeling in each lesson.

Table of Expository Writing Resources

Page(s)	Resources	Balanced Literacy				
		Aloud	Shared	Guided	Independent	Literature Circles
446	Expository Writing Resource Descriptions					
447	Expository Writing Model	●	●	●	●	
448	Expository Writing Steps	●	●	●	●	
449	Six Trait Checklist for Expository Writing	●	●	●	●	

Table of Expository Writing Activities

Page(s)	Activities	Blacklines	Balanced Literacy				
			Aloud	Shared	Guided	Independent	Literature Circles
452	Expository Writing Stages	• Teacher Resource Lesson Guide					
453	**Inside-Outside Circle Activity**							
454	Prewriting Circles	• Prewriting Question Cards	●		●		
455	**Jot Thoughts Activity**							
456	Brainstorming Ideas	• Brainstorming Mat	●			●	
457	**RoundTable Consensus Activity**							
458	Sorting Ideas	• Sorting Mat	●	●	●		
459	**Solo Activities**							
460	Paragraph Writing	• Sample Topic Sentence Form • Sample Detail Sentence Form • Topic Sentence Form • Detail Sentences Form	●			●	
466	**RoundRobin Activity**							
467	Improving Details	• Six Ways to Improve Details • Detail Improvement Form	●	●	●	●	
469	**CenterPiece Activities**							
470	Word Choice Practice	• Word Choice—Powerful Verbs • Word Choice—Powerful Verbs (Possible Answers) • Word Choice—Powerful Adjectives • Word Choice—Powerful Adjectives (Possible Answers) • Word Choice—Similes • Word Choice—Describing a Noun • Word Choice Form	●	●	●	●	

Table of Expository Writing Activities (continued)

Page(s)	Activities	Blacklines	Balanced Literacy					
			Aloud	Shared	Guided	Independent	Literature Circles
478	**RallyCoach Activity**						
479	Sentence Writing Practice	• Sentence Mechanics • Revising Sentences Form					
484	**Team Stand-N-Share Activity**						
485	Hooks and Endings	• Hook Examples • Ending Examples • Hook and Ending Form—Sample • Hook and Ending Form	●	●	●	●	
489	**Two-Partner Edit Activity**						
489	Six Trait Feedback	• Six Trait Checklist			●	●	
490	**Mix-Pair-Share Activity**						
490	Sharing Final Drafts				●		

Balanced Literacy • Fourth Grade • Skidmore & Graber
Kagan Publishing • 1 (800) 933-2667 • www.KaganOnline.com

Table of Persuasive Writing Resources

| Page(s) | Resources | Balanced Literacy |||||
		Aloud	Shared	Guided	Independent	Literature Circles
492	Persuasive Writing Resource Descriptions					
494	Topics for Persuasive Writing	●	●	●	●	
495	Persuasive Writing Model	●	●	●	●	
496	Persuasive Writing Form	●	●	●	●	
497	Student Persuasive Writing Plan (Forms A, B, C)	●	●	●	●	
500	Student Persuasive Writing Plan Examples (Forms A, B, C)	●				
505	Persuasive Writing Six Trait Checklist	●	●	●	●	

Table of Persuasive Writing Activities

Page(s)	Activities	Blacklines	Balanced Literacy Aloud	Shared	Guided	Independent	Literature Circles
508	Persuasive Writing Stages	• Teacher Resource Lesson Guide					
509	**Inside-Outside Circle Activity**						
510	Prewriting Circles	• Prewriting Question Cards	●	●	●		
511	**Corners/RoundRobin Activity**						
511	"For" or "Against"	• Persuasive Writing Plan (Form A)	●	●	●	●	
512	**RoundTable/RallyTable Activity**						
512	Reasons for Opinion	• Persuasive Writing Plan (Form B)	●	●	●	●	
513	**RoundRobin Consensus/RallyCoach Activity**						
513	Supporting Details	• Persuasive Writing Plan (Form B)	●	●	●	●	
514	**Solo Activities**						
514	Restatement of Opinion and Main Reasons	• Persuasive Writing Plan (Form C)	●	●	●	●	
515	Adding an Ending	• Persuasive Writing Plan (Form C)	●	●	●	●	
516	**Jot Thoughts Activity**						
516	Hook Examples		●	●	●	●	
517	**Inside-Outside Circle Activity**						
517	Choosing a Hook		●	●	●	●	
518	**Solo Activity**						
518	Final Copy					●	

Table of Persuasive Writing Activities (continued)

Page(s)	Activities	Blacklines	Balanced Literacy – Aloud	Shared	Guided	Independent	Literature Circles
519	RallyCoach Activity–Transitional Words						
520	Transitional Words	• Transitional Word List • Transitional Word Passages	●	●	●	●	
523	Two-Partner Edit Activity–Six Trait Feedback						
523	Six Trait Feedback	• Six Trait Checklist			●	●	
524	Mix-Pair-Share Activity–Sharing Final Drafts						
524	Sharing Final Drafts				●		

Expository Writing Resources

Expository Writing Resources

Writing Resource Descriptions

One key to scaffolding instruction is the inclusion of modeling. **The teacher should have his or her own ongoing piece of writing that is used for modeling in each lesson.** This permits the students to see the skill being used, creates a better understanding of what is expected, and allows for more effective application of the skill.

Expository Writing Model (p. 447)
The hook, fish, and tail graphics are visuals that can be used to increase the students' understanding of the parts of an expository writing piece.
- **Hook** = beginning sentence(s) that engage the reader and make him or her want to continue reading
- **Fish (Mighty Middle)** = the topic sentences and supporting details that provide the information and facts relating to the topic
- **Tail End** = the ending gives the writing natural closure

Expository Writing Steps (p. 448)
The organization of expository writing is necessary to move the reader through the text: hook, mighty middle, and ending. As you notice, the writer will start with the informational part of the piece first (mighty middle). Once the writer has organized his or her information, the teacher will use focus lessons to help students revise to produce a quality writing piece. The beginning hook comes next. The writer will create a hook that will draw the reader in and make him or her want to continue reading. Because the writer has already written the mighty middle and knows the information he or she is presenting to the reader, it will be easier for him or her to write an appropriate hook. The tail end comes last. The purpose of the ending is to bring the writing to a satisfying closure, tying up loose ends for the reader.

Six Trait Checklist for Expository Writing (p. 449)
Ideas, organization, voice, word choice, sentence fluency, and conventions are six trait writing components used to evaluate the student's writing performance. In this section, a six trait checklist is provided to increase student awareness of qualities that make up each component. After students complete their writing, the students can evaluate their writing by placing an "X" on the line indicating the qualities used in their writing. This visual will help students realize which areas they need to work on for improvement. Once the students have experience self-evaluating and have a clear understanding of the characteristics that make up each trait, the teacher can move students from a checklist to a rubric.

Expository Writing Model

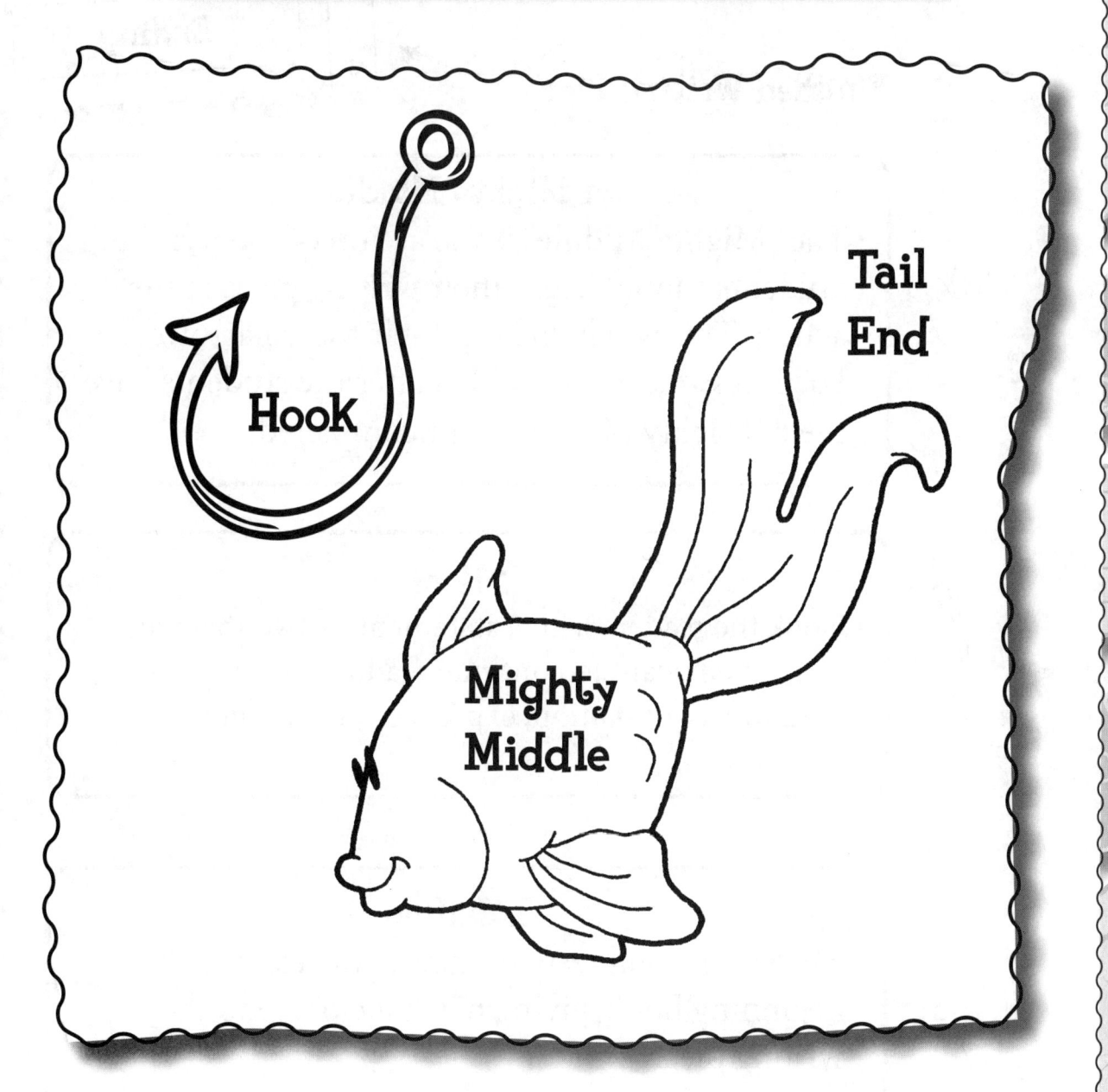

Hook

Tail End

Mighty Middle

Expository Writing Steps

Finished Writing Piece →

[Hook | Mighty Middle | Ending]

1. Mighty Middle
- The "Mighty Middle" is the action of the writing.
- Students should begin their writing piece at the action. This will help keep their topic narrowed.
- Focus lessons will be added after the students have their "Mighty Middle" draft completed.

2. Hook
- Hook the readers with a statement or two that will make them want to continue reading: use a question, bold words, quotation, expression, riddle, etc.

3. Ending
- The ending will restate, answer, or relate to the beginning hook, giving natural closure to the writing piece.

Six Trait Checklist for Writing

Name_____ Date_____

Instructions: The teacher determines how many of the six traits to evaluate. The student and/or teacher can evaluate a piece of writing by placing an *X* on each line indicating the skill(s) being used to strengthen each trait. Copy for each student.

Voice

___ My writing sounds like me. It does not sound like it is copied from a book.

___ My writing uses words that show my feelings.

___ My writing shows that I care about the topic.

___ My writing is appropriate for my audience.

___ My writing answers questions that readers might have.

Conventions

___ My writing uses spaces between words.

___ My writing uses capital letters correctly.

___ My writing uses end marks correctly. (Only light editing is needed for internal punctuation.)

___ My writing has been checked for spelling (or my best try at spelling).

___ My writing starts a new paragraph when new information is presented.

Organization

___ My writing has a strong beginning hook that makes the reader want to continue.

___ My writing focuses on a few main reasons/ideas and uses supporting details.

___ My writing uses transitional words to connect ideas.

___ My writing follows a logical sequence.

___ My writing has an ending that brings it to a natural closure.

Sentence Fluency

___ My writing uses sentences that are easy to read aloud.

___ My writing has some sentences that can be read expressively.

___ My writing uses sentences that begin in different ways.

___ My writing flows logically from sentence to sentence.

___ My writing flows logically from sentence to sentence.

Ideas

___ My writing is focused and sticks to the topic.

___ My writing has a purpose: to inform, to entertain, to persuade or convince, or to explain/tell how to . . .

___ My writing uses supporting details/sensory details.

___ Main idea(s) stand out.

___ My writing gives enough information to make it interesting. It tells things that not everyone knows.

Word Choice

___ My writing uses new words.

___ My writing uses strong verbs, specific nouns, and describing words.

___ My writing lets the reader picture (visualize) what is happening.

___ My writing does not repeat the same words too many times.

___ My writing uses literary devices: comparison, simile, dialogue, humor, suspense, onomatopoeia, _____ (circle ones used).

Balanced Literacy • Fourth Grade • Skidmore & Graber
Kagan Publishing • 1 (800) 933-2667 • www.KaganOnline.com

Expository Writing Activities

Expository Writing Stages

The following writing activities are sequenced to take students through the stages of writing an expository piece. Some of the activities are short and you can do multiple activities in one day. Other will take longer. There are also practice activities and forms integrated in this section to help students develop their expository writing skills. Below is an overview of the stages of writing and the activities included.

(Since students will be brainstorming and sorting ideas in teams, it will be helpful if they are grouped in teams by writing topics the first time the expository writing model and accompanying cooperative learning structures are used. Once students have worked through the expository writing process, the teacher will be able to make adaptations allowing students to choose individual topics. The teacher may decide to substitute some cooperative learning pair structures for team structures.)

Prewriting (pp. 453–458)
- **Prewriting Circles**—Students ask partners prewriting questions to focus them on their writing topic.
- **Brainstorming Ideas**—Students brainstorm ideas related to their writing topic.
- **Sorting Ideas**—Students sort ideas into categories that will be developed into complete sentences.

Writing (pp. 459–463)
- **Paragraph Writing**—Students develop their ideas into a topic sentence and supporting detail sentences. (Students will put several paragraphs together to form their expository writing piece.)

Editing & Rewriting (pp. 466–488)
- **Improving Details**—Students learn six ways to improve their detail sentences and then work to improve their own detail sentences.
- **Word Choice Practice**—Students practice word choice and then work to improve the word choice in their expository writing.
- **Sentence Writing Practice**—Students practice rewriting sentences for mechanics and fluency.
- **Hooks and Endings**—Students write beginning hooks and endings to their expository writing pieces.

Peer Feedback (p. 489)
- **Six Trait Feedback**—Students get feedback from peers, focusing on the six traits.

Sharing (p. 490)
- **Sharing Final Drafts**—Students share their final drafts with peers as an audience.

PREWRITING Activity

Prewriting Circles

The amount of writing that students produce is in proportion to the amount of talking and processing that they get to do before they write. In this activity, students form two concentric circles so that pairs face each other. Using the questions provided, students ask their partner a question. The circles rotate multiple times so students share with multiple partners. This activity helps students focus on their topic, expand their writing ideas, and write in complete sentences.

STRUCTURE
Inside-Outside Circle

Activity Steps

1. Students are given time to choose a topic and read about their topic.
2. Students form pairs and each student is given one Prewriting Question Card.
3. One student from each pair moves to form one large circle.
4. Remaining students find and face their partners. (The class now stands in two concentric circles.)
5. The Inside Circle students ask the Outside Circle students the question on their question card. The Outside Circle students respond.
6. Partners switch roles: Outside Circle students ask the questions and Inside Circle students respond.
7. Students trade cards, then the Inside Circle students rotate clockwise to face a new partner to ask and answer a new prewriting question.

Blackline

- Prewriting Question Cards 454

Prewriting Question Cards
Inside-Outside Circle

Instructions: Make enough copies of this blackline so that each student has one card. Cut out the question cards and give each student one card. Students use cards to ask partners prewriting questions during Inside-Outside Circle.

Prewriting Questions

What topic are you planning to write about?

Prewriting Questions

What do you already know about this topic?

Prewriting Questions

What questions do you still have about this topic?

Prewriting Questions

What is the most important idea to get across to your readers?

Prewriting Questions

Where could you find more information about this topic?

Prewriting Questions

What will readers find interesting about this topic?

Prewriting Questions

What does this topic remind you of?

Prewriting Questions

If you could add a photograph to your writing about this topic, what would it be?

Prewriting Questions

What information about this topic will you not include in your writing?

Prewriting Questions

How can you present the topic so that it is not boring to read?

Prewriting Questions

What words do you want to include in your writing about this topic?

Prewriting Questions

What would be a good title for your writing? Why?

Balanced Literacy • Fourth Grade • Skidmore & Graber
Kagan Publishing • 1 (800) 933-2667 • www.KaganOnline.com

PREWRITING Activity

Brainstorming Ideas

Students brainstorm in teams using Jot Thoughts. They write one word, phrase, or sentence about their topic, read it aloud to the team, then place the idea on a mat with the topic in the center of the table. This process frees students' minds to generate information without worrying about organization. Creative and varied responses are encouraged as students read their ideas aloud to spark additional ideas.

STRUCTURE
Jot Thoughts

Activity Steps

1. Each team gets a Brainstorming Mat. They write the writing topic in the center of the mat. Students each have sticky notes and a pen.

2. Students write the ideas that come to mind on the sticky note, and place it on the mat. They announce their idea to the team.

3. The team tries to completely cover the mat with ideas about the topic.

Sample Brainstorming Mat

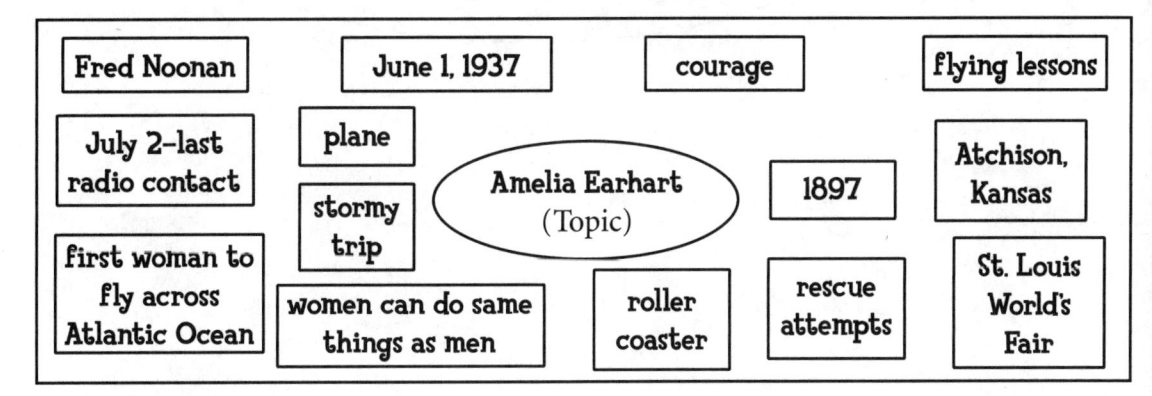

Fred Noonan	June 1, 1937	courage	flying lessons
July 2–last radio contact	plane		Atchison, Kansas
	stormy trip	Amelia Earhart (Topic)	1897
first woman to fly across Atlantic Ocean	women can do same things as men	roller coaster	rescue attempts	St. Louis World's Fair

Blackline

- Brainstorming Mat 456

Brainstorming Mat
Jot Thoughts

Instructions: Write your writing topic in the center of this mat. As a team, brainstorm ideas relating to the topic on sticky notes and place them on the mat. Announce your idea to teammates as you place it on the mat. (Make one copy per team.)

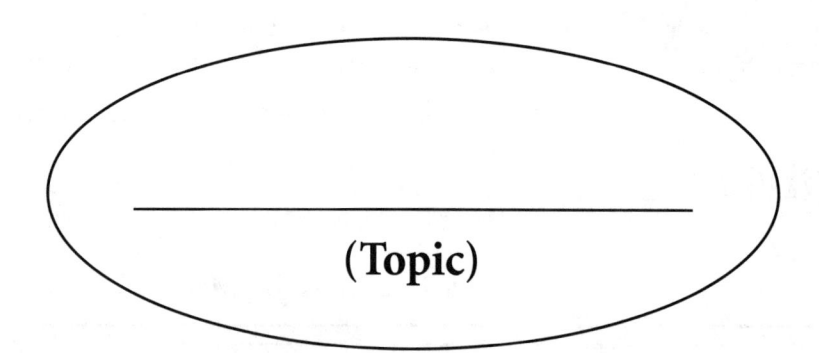

_____
(Topic)

PREWRITING Activity

Sorting Ideas

After students have generated numerous ideas relating to the topic, they use RoundTable Consensus to physically sort the ideas into categories on a sorting mat. The concrete aids help students organize expository information into groups that are later developed into paragraphs.

Activity Steps

1. Each team gets a Sorting Mat and their ideas generated from the previous activity.

2. The first student selects a sticky note, places the note on the Sorting Mat, and announces the possible category or reason for sorting.

3. Teammates show agreement or lack of agreement with thumbs up or thumbs down.

4. If there is agreement, the team celebrates and the next student places the next idea on the sorting mat. If there is not consensus, students discuss the idea until they reach agreement.

5. When all items are sorted, students take turns labeling each category, checking for consensus before writing.

STRUCTURE
RoundTable Consensus

Sample Sorting Mat

Childhood	Adult Life	Accomplishments
Atchison, Kansas	flying lessons	Fred Noonan
roller coaster	plane	stormy trip
St. Louis World's Fair	first woman to fly across Atlantic Ocean	June 1, 1937
1897		courage
		July 2–last radio contact
		rescue attempts

Blackline

- Sorting Mat 458

Balanced Literacy • Fourth Grade • Skidmore & Graber
Kagan Publishing • 1 (800) 933-2667 • www.KaganOnline.com

Sorting Mat
RoundTable Consensus

Instructions: Students take turns sorting ideas into like categories. Once all ideas are sorted, students label categories. (Make one copy per team.)

WRITING Activity

Paragraph Writing

Now that students have their ideas sorted into categories, they are ready to develop each category into a paragraph. To do this, they independently write the topic sentence of a paragraph, followed by supporting detail sentences.

Activity Steps

1. Copy the Topic Sentence Form on light-colored paper and the Detail Sentences Form on a different light-colored paper. Give both sheets to each student.

2. Using the Sample Topic Sentence Form, model for students how to fill out the Topic Sentence Form using one category from the Sorting Mat example.

3. Students complete their Topic Sentence Form by writing the 1) Topic, 2) Question, and 3) Topic Sentence for one of the categories on their Sorting Mat. Then they cut out the topic sentence for later use.

4. Next, model for students how to turn the ideas from one labeled category on the Sorting Mat into complete written sentences using the Sample Detail Sentences Form.

5. Students select three individual sticky notes from one category of their Sorting Mat and write them as three complete detail sentences on the form (one detail for each box).

6. Students cut the three detail sentences (boxes) apart and select their favorite sequence. Then they tape the sentences together in the preferred sequence and tape the topic sentence on top. This forms one of the paragraphs of their expository writing piece.

7. Students follow the same procedure for the remaining categories on their Sorting Mat. (They will need an additional copy of the Topic Sentence Form and the Detail Sentence Form for each category on their Sorting Mat.) Each category will become one paragraph.

8. These paragraphs are then taped together in a logical order to form the "Mighty Middle" of their writing piece.

STRUCTURE
Solo

Blacklines

- Sample Topic Sentence Form...460
- Sample Detail Sentences Form..461
- Topic Sentence Form..462
- Detail Sentences Form...463

Balanced Literacy • Fourth Grade • Skidmore & Graber
Kagan Publishing • 1 (800) 933-2667 • www.KaganOnline.com **459**

Sample Topic Sentence Form

Instructions: Use this form to model how to develop a topic sentence.

Topic

Amelia Earhart's Childhood

Question

What was different about Amelia Earhart's childhood?

Topic Sentence

Amelia Earhart had an interesting childhood.

Sample Detail Sentences Form

WRITING Blackline

Instructions: Use this form to model how to develop detail sentences.

#__1__ Amelia Earhart was born in Atchison, Kansas, in 1897.

#__2__ When Amelia was seven years old, her family took a trip to the St. Louis World's Fair where she rode on a roller coaster.

#__3__ Amelia had so much fun at the fair that when she got home, she had relatives help her build a type of roller coaster off the roof of the shed in the backyard. Amelia felt like she was flying!

WRITING Blackline

Topic Sentence Form

Instructions: Write your paragraph topic in the box below. Then write the topic as a question. Then write the question as a topic sentence. Cut out your topic sentence. (Make 3–4 copies per student—one for each paragraph.)

Topic

_____

Question

_____
_____

Topic Sentence

_____
_____
_____

Detail Sentences Form

Instructions: Write a detail sentence in each box below. Cut them out, then sequence them in the best order. Number the sentences in order from 1–3. Tape them together in the sequence you like. Then tape your Topic Sentence (page 462) on top. (Make 3–4 copies per student—one for each paragraph.)

#_____ _____

#_____ _____

#_____ _____

Editing and Rewriting Activities

EDITING & REWRITING ACTIVITY

Improving Details

Students have each written several paragraphs about the topic. Now, their task is to improve their paragraphs by adding details to text. The teacher models how to improve details. Students work independently to add details and share their improvements with teammates.

Activity Steps

1. Using the Six Ways to Improve Details form, share with students the various ways they can improve their writing.

2. Students select one detail sentence they have written. They select which of the six methods they plan to use to improve the information (page 467). The Detail Improvement Form on page 468 is used to record the improvements.

3. Students then share the new and improved sentence with teammates.

4. Teammates hold up 1–6 fingers to guess which idea for improvement their teammate used. The student informs the team which method he or she used and congratulates students who guessed correctly.

5. They repeat the process for several sentences, choosing different ways to improve their other sentences.

STRUCTURE
RoundRobin

Blacklines

- Six Ways to Improve Details..................................467
- Detail Improvement Form......................................468

Editing & Rewriting Blackline

Six Ways to Improve Details

Instructions: Use this form to share with students six ways to write and improve detail sentences.

Comparison

Monkeys and apes are alike in many ways.

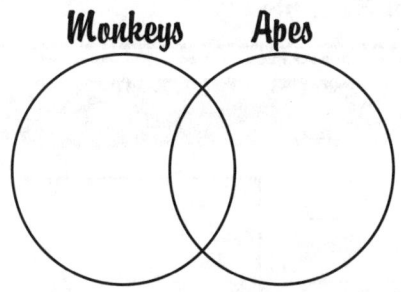

Monkeys Apes

Personal Experience

When I went to the beach last summer, I found a sand dollar in the sand after the tide went out. My sand dollar has a star on the top.

Number Word

Bullfrogs can jump as far as 6 feet. The longest jump for a frog is 11 feet.

Description

Manatees have rounded, wrinkled faces. Their front flippers look like short, blunt arms, and their tails look like ping-pong paddles.

Text Feature

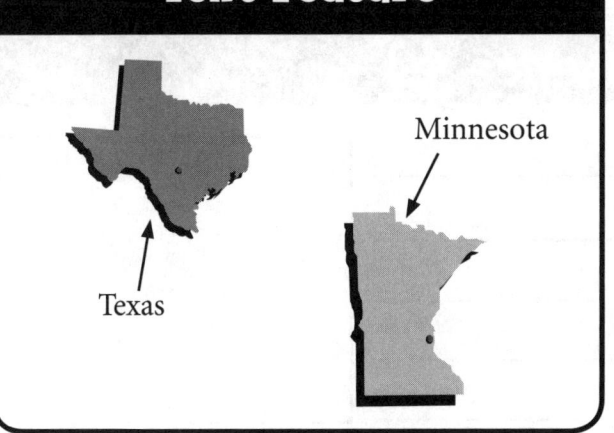

Texas

Minnesota

Specific Name or Example

Painted Ladies and **Silvery Blues** are brightly colored butterflies.

Detail Improvement Form

Instructions: Choose three different detail sentences from within your paragraph writing. Rewrite each of the sentences below. For each sentence, pick one of the six ideas for improvement. Write the idea for improvement number in the circle. If needed, use the box to add text features. Share one sentence at a time with teammates and see if they can pick which idea for improvement you used.

Six Ways to Improve My Sentences

1. Comparison
2. Personal Experience
3. Number Word
4. Description
5. Text Feature (graph, diagram, chart, definition, picture)
6. Specific Name or Example

Detail Sentence #1

Detail Sentence #2

Detail Sentence #3

EDITING & REWRITING Activity

Word Choice Practice

Students continue to improve their writing by adding descriptive language to engage the reader. Students brainstorm and share word choice ideas. Blacklines are included to practice verb choice, adjective choice, similes, and describing nouns.

STRUCTURE
CenterPiece

Activity Steps

1. Each team is given five items, focusing on the same word choice skill. For example, to practice verb choice, each team is given five verb cards (call, meet, fly, hold, see).

2. Students each get one card and one card is placed in the center of the team table (the centerpiece).

3. Students brainstorm one alternate word choice for their word card, write the new word on the card, and exchange their card with the centerpiece. For example, for the word *call*, examples may include *declare, explain, cry,* etc.

4. Students continue brainstorming and trading their papers with the centerpiece until time is up or until they cannot think of additional ideas.

5. Share additional word choices with students (blacklines provided).

6. After practicing word choice, students revise their paragraphs to improve word choice.

7. This process is repeated with other word choice topics (e.g., adjectives, similes).

Blacklines

- Word Choice—Powerful Verbs 470
- Word Choice—Powerful Verbs (Possible Answers) 471
- Word Choice—Powerful Adjectives 472
- Word Choice—Powerful Adjectives (Possible Answers) 473
- Word Choice—Similes 474–475
- Word Choice—Describing a Noun 476
- Word Choice Form 477

Word Choice—Powerful Verbs
CenterPiece

Instructions: Cut out cards. Each teammate gets one card and one is the centerpiece. Brainstorm one powerful verb, write it on your card, and then trade your card with the centerpiece. Continue brainstorming, writing, and trading to generate many alternatives for each word.

call

meet

fly

hold

see

Word Choice—Powerful Verbs
Possible Answers

Instructions: Share these possible word choices with students after they generate their own.

call

announce	command	holler	summon	lure
ask	remark	shout	order	bellow
exclaim	name	speak	plead	invite
request	label	cry	appeal	declare

meet

encounter	congregate	rendezvous	assemble
face	rally	convene	
join	organize	gather	
confront	greet	converge	

fly

glide	sail	mount	flap	flutter
swoop	soar	rise	dive	float
swirl	ascend	circle	drift	
float	climb	take wing	dip	

hold

grasp	control	possess	press	support
retain	contain	enfold	squeeze	keep
constrain	clasp	hug	bear	
grip	embrace	own	carry	

see

look	examine	spot	detect	follow	glimpse
watch	monitor	witness	spy	observe	
view	notice	survey	inspect	glare	
study	note	identify	stare	glance	

Word Choice—Powerful Adjectives
CenterPiece

Instructions: Cut out cards. Each teammate gets one card and one is the centerpiece. Brainstorm one powerful adjective, write it on your card, and then trade your card with the centerpiece. Continue brainstorming, writing, and trading to generate many alternatives for each word.

slow

fast

smooth

rough

light

Word Choice—Powerful Adjectives
Possible Answers

Instructions: Share these possible word choices with students after they generate their own.

slow

sluggish	easy	inactive	easygoing	listless	tiresome
unhurried	pokey	painstaking	thorough	dragging	tedious
relaxed	deliberate	lethargic	crawling	dawdling	
laid-back	leisurely	lazy	precise	casual	

fast

quick	hurried	flying	high-speed	jet-propelled
hasty	fleeting	timely	immediate	rushed
rapid	sudden	punctual	swift	expeditious
speedy	brisk	instant	prompt	

smooth

velvety	polished	glassy	even	fluent	unwrinkled
shiny	fluid	glossy	level	silky	unnotched
uncreased	slick	flat	satiny	lustrous	
sleek	slippery	waxy	straight	flowing	

rough

bumpy	toothed	jagged	potholed	pocked	rocky
dented	uneven	spiky	rutted	broken	mountainous
pointy	coarse	patchy	hilly	cracked	knobby
prickly	sharp	crooked	notched	puckered	
unequal	irregular	textured	serrated	rugged	

light

gleaming	radiant	intense	glowing	luminous	dramatic
shimmering	vivid	glinting	beaming	stunning	vibrant
sunlit	sparkling	shiny	clear	illuminated	incandescent
brilliant	glossy	dazzling	bright	sunny	floodlit

Word Choice — Similes
CenterPiece

Instructions: Cut out cards. Each teammate gets one card and one is the centerpiece. Brainstorm one simile, write it on your card, and then trade your card with the centerpiece. Continue brainstorming, writing, and trading to generate as many similes as you can.

fresh as ...

straight like ...

excited as ...

golden like ...

rough as ...

EDITING & REWRITING
Blackline

Word Choice — Similes
CenterPiece

Instructions: Cut out cards. Each teammate gets one card and one is the centerpiece. Brainstorm one simile, write it on your card, and then trade your card with the centerpiece. Continue brainstorming, writing, and trading to generate as many similes as you can.

sleepy like ...

quiet as ...

noisy like ...

busy as ...

strange like ...

Balanced Literacy • Fourth Grade • Skidmore & Graber
Kagan Publishing • 1 (800) 933-2667 • www.KaganOnline.com

Word Choice—Describing a Noun
CenterPiece

Instructions: Cut out cards. Each teammate gets one card and one is the centerpiece. Brainstorm one adjective to describe the noun, write it on your card, and then trade your card with the centerpiece. Continue brainstorming, writing, and trading to generate as many adjectives as you can.

race car

spider

blanket

raccoon

tree

Word Choice Form
CenterPiece

Instructions: Use this form to create more word choice activities. Write the word in the blank provided. Students brainstorm alternatives on the card.

EDITING & REWRITING Activity

Sentence Writing Practice

Students practice rewriting sentences in pairs. Blacklines are provided to practice mechanics, substituting words, adding words, deleting words, and using descriptive language. A form is provided for the teacher to create additional practice sentences.

Activity Steps

1. Each pair receives a set of sentence strips. They place the sentence strips facedown between them.

2. Partner A turns over the first sentence strip and reads it aloud. He or she then describes how he or she is going to rewrite the sentence.

3. Partner B is the coach. The coach makes suggestions or approves the rewriting plan.

4. Partner A rewrites the sentence.

5. Partners switch roles for each sentence strip so they both get practice rewriting and offering suggestions.

6. After practicing rewriting sentences, students revisit their writing again to see if they can improve it with new skills.

STRUCTURE
RallyCoach

Blacklines

- Sentence Mechanics...479–480
- Revising Sentences..481–482
- Revising Sentences Form..483

Sentence Mechanics
RallyCoach

Instructions: Cut out sentence strips. Place them facedown between you and your partner. Partner A turns over the first one, reads it, and describes how to rewrite the sentence. Partner B offers suggestions or agrees. Partner A then rewrites the sentence. Switch roles for each sentence strip.

Sentence Mechanics

1. i wish the wind would stop blowing so hard exclaimed mom

Sentence Mechanics

2. excellent job cheered mrs clark

Sentence Mechanics

3. come back spot yelled pam

Sentence Mechanics

4. that poem was funny laughed the twins

Sentence Mechanics

5. i think ill have a burger and fries decided penny

Sentence Mechanics

6. time for bed yawned pete

Sentence Mechanics

7. dont let the tiger see you whispered alex

Sentence Mechanics
RallyCoach

Instructions: Cut out sentence strips. Place them facedown between you and your partner. Partner A turns over the first one, reads it, and describes how to rewrite the sentence. Partner B offers suggestions or agrees. Partner A then rewrites the sentence. Switch roles for each sentence strip.

Sentence Mechanics

8. ive injured my arm moaned dale

Sentence Mechanics

9. this assignment is too hard whined the student

Sentence Mechanics

10. that book had interesting information about zebras lions and elephants noted tim

---

Sentence Mechanics

11. remember your coat reminded dad

Sentence Mechanics

12. who tipped over the vase demanded ms smith

Sentence Mechanics

13. im better at football than you bragged steve

Sentence Mechanics

14. we need bread peanut butter and jelly for our sandwiches jeff exclaimed

Revising Sentences
(Substitute, Add, or Delete Words for More Descriptive Writing)

RallyCoach

Instructions: Cut out sentence strips. Place them facedown between you and your partner. Partner A turns over the first one, reads it, and describes how to rewrite the sentence. Partner B offers suggestions or agrees. Partner A then rewrites the sentence. Switch roles for each sentence strip.

Revising Sentences

1. The girl sat on the chair.

Revising Sentences

2. The giant walked through the forest.

Revising Sentences

3. The thunder made noise in the sky.

Revising Sentences

4. The bear moved down the hillside.

Revising Sentences

5. Kent ran in the race.

Revising Sentences

6. We saw the snow on the ground.

Revising Sentences

7. The rain came down.

Revising Sentences
(Substitute, Add, or Delete Words for More Descriptive Writing)
RallyCoach

Instructions: Cut out sentence strips. Place them facedown between you and your partner. Partner A turns over the first one, reads it, and describes how to rewrite the sentence. Partner B offers suggestions or agrees. Partner A then rewrites the sentence. Switch roles for each sentence strip.

Revising Sentences

8. A kite went up in the sky.

Revising Sentences

9. The cat waited in the grass.

Revising Sentences

10. We liked the present Mom gave us.

Revising Sentences

11. The book made a noise when it fell.

Revising Sentences

12. Ted is glad he will go on vacation.

Revising Sentences

13. Mattie climbed the tree.

Revising Sentences

14. John got a fish on his pole.

Revising Sentences Form

Instructions: Use this blackline to create your own sentence strips for partners to practice revising.

Revising Sentences

Revising Sentences

Revising Sentences

Revising Sentences

Revising Sentences

Revising Sentences

Revising Sentences

EDITING & REWRITING Activity

Hooks and Endings

Students learn to write paragraph openers to "hook" the reader and endings to give the writing a natural closure. Teams investigate other writing samples and share what hooks and endings writers use.

Activity Steps

1. Students look through expository magazines, such as *National Geographic Kids* and *Ranger Rick*, noticing different ways authors begin articles.
2. Using RoundTable, the team generates a list of hooks.
3. After teams have enough time to collect multiple ideas, the teacher asks the class to stand.
4. The teacher calls on a standing student.
5. The selected student states one idea from the team list.
6. The student in each team who is holding the team list either adds the item to the list, or if it is already listed, checks it off. The teacher also makes a master list of student ideas.
7. Teammates pass their team list one teammate clockwise.
8. Teams sit when all their items are shared. While seated they add each new item as it is stated using RoundTable. When all teams are seated, Team Stand-N-Share is complete.
9. The teacher may use the Hook Examples blackline to share additional hook ideas.
10. Students repeat the process examining and sharing endings.
11. Finally, students use the Hook & Ending Form to write a new hook and ending for their paper.

STRUCTURE

Team Stand-N-Share

Blacklines

- Hook Examples..485
- Ending Examples..486
- Hook & Ending Form—Sample..487
- Hook & Ending Form..488

Hook Examples

Instructions: Use this form to share effective writing hooks with students.

- **Question**
  Have you used courage lately? Read to find out about someone who used courage to accomplish her dreams.

- **Riddle**
  This woman loved to fly. She set many flying records. Who was she?

- **Exclamation**
  What an amazing woman!

- **Onomatopoeia**
  "Weee!" Amelia loved going fast!

- **Alliteration**
  Courageous, confident, and carefree are words that describe Amelia Earhart.

- **Exaggeration**
  Amelia spent so much time in the air that she could have been a bird.

- **Description**
  Endless blue sky and billowy white clouds was the view that Amelia loved the most.

Ending Examples

Instructions: Use this form to share effective writing endings with students.

- **Answer to Beginning Question**
  As you can see, Amelia Earhart used courage as she pursued her dreams.

- **Reference Back to Riddle**
  After reading you now know that Amelia Earhart was the woman who loved to fly and who set many flying records.

- **Generalization**
  Amelia Earhart was a fascinating and courageous woman.

- **Personal Comment**
  I have learned many interesting facts about this amazing woman.

- **Restatement of Main Idea**
  Amelia Earhart was definitely a fascinating and courageous woman, who followed her dreams and learned to fly.

- **Challenge to the Reader**
  Find out more about Amelia Earhart for yourself by searching the Web. You may even find a photograph of her plane.

Hook & Ending Form—Sample

Instructions: Use this form to write a new hook and ending.

Type of Hook <u>Alliteration</u>

Hook
Courageous, confident, and carefree are words that describe Amelia Earhart.

⬇

Middle

⬇

Type of Ending <u>Restatement of Main Idea</u>

Ending
Amelia Earhart was definitely a fascinating and courageous woman, who followed her dreams and learned to fly.

Hook & Ending Form

Instructions: Use this form to write a new hook and ending.

Type of Hook _____

Hook

Middle

Type of Ending _____

Ending

PEER FEEDBACK ACTIVITY

Six Trait Feedback

Students share their writing with peers and receive feedback on six specific traits of their writing.

Activity Steps

1. Students complete a polished draft.
2. Students stand up, put a hand up, and pair up with a classmate.
3. The pair sits down at a table, each with their Six Trait Checklist (page 449).
4. Partner A reads his or her writing.
5. Partner B provides feedback on one of the six traits by reading each statement under the trait, discussing it, and putting a plus or minus by the statement.
6. Students switch roles and Partner A provides feedback to partner B.
7. Students thank each other and then pair up with another partner to examine the next trait. The process continues for six pairings, each focusing on a different trait.
8. After receiving feedback, students write a final draft.

STRUCTURE
Two-Partner Edit

Blacklines
- Six Trait Checklist....................449

SHARING Activity

Sharing Final Drafts

Students share their writing with peers and receive feedback on their writing.

Activity Steps

1. Each student takes his or her final draft, stands up, puts a hand up, and mixes in the classroom.

2. The teacher calls, "Pair."

3. Students pair up with the person closest to them, who is not from their team, and give a high five.

4. Students take turns sharing their expository writing pieces by reading them to their partners using RallyRobin. Students provide feedback to their partners. The feedback can be:
   - Open-ended reactions
   - Praise
   - Response to a provided gambit: "From your writing, I learned…"
   - Copycat gambit: Students repeat after the teacher a flattering phrase such as "Your expository writing was well written and tremendously informative!"

5. Students can do multiple rounds of peer sharing.

STRUCTURE
Mix-Pair-Share

Persuasive Writing Resources

Persuasive Writing Resources

Writing Resource Descriptions

Learning to write persuasively is a skill children will use throughout their lives. In persuasive writing the goal of the writer is to convince or influence the reader to agree with the writer. The writer takes a position "for" or "against" an issue and attempts to persuade the reader that a particular point of view or course of action is the best. Persuasive writing is often used in advertisements, book reviews, editorials, letters to the editor, movie critiques, and political campaign literature. As teachers, we know that reading and writing are reciprocal processes—each reinforcing the skills learned. Many states are testing students' proficiency in comprehending persuasive text. Using the following writing lessons will help students apply the persuasive characteristics in their writing that they have been learning and noticing in their reading.

One key to scaffolding instruction is the inclusion of modeling. The teacher continually models each step of the persuasive writing process using his or her own individual writing. This permits the students to see the skill being used, creates a better understanding of what is expected, and allows for more effective application of the skill. Because the persuasive writing topic is already so narrow, it may be valuable for the teacher to pick a different persuasive topic from the students. The teacher will be able to model the techniques and still allow students to create their own pieces.

Students are motivated by the authenticity of assignments, so the teacher is encouraged to provide students with an audience for their persuasive writing. Perhaps their work can be published in a school newsletter, mailed to the appropriate audience, or hand delivered and personally read to an interested party.

Topics for Persuasive Writing (p. 494)

This page gives a list of possible topics for the persuasive writing process outlined in this writing section. The first time that the persuasive writing model and accompanying cooperative learning structures are used, it will be helpful to have the class choose the same writing topic. Students will be sharing ideas in teams and pairs. Having the same topic will facilitate the process and allow for more effective coaching. Early in the writing process, students will have a choice as they choose to be "for" or "against" an issue. Once students have worked through the persuasive writing lessons, the teacher will be able to make adaptations allowing for students to choose different persuasive writing topics. For example, he or she may decide to substitute some cooperative learning pair structures for team structures.

Persuasive Writing Resources (continued)

Writing Resource Descriptions

Persuasive Writing Model (pp. 495-496)
The diagram of the persuasive writing model can be made into a chart or overhead transparency to increase students' understanding of the parts of a persuasive writing piece. The blank form provides an opportunity for the teacher to add labels step-by-step to the persuasive writing model, as they are introduced to the students, modeled, and practiced.

- **Opening** = Hook (begins the piece and catches the reader's attention)
  = Opinion Statement (lets the reader know the topic and sets the purpose for the piece)
- **Reasons** = Reasons (each states a solid basis to back the stated opinion)
  = Supporting Details (elaborate on the chosen reasons using facts and examples)
- **Closing** = Restatement of Opinion/Main Reasons (restates the opinion addressed in the piece and summarizes the reasons for the argument)
  = Ending (brings the writing to a natural closure, often with a personal statement or call to action)

Blank forms are provided for students to use as they plan their own persuasive pieces.

Student Persuasive Writing Plan Examples (Forms A, B, and C) (pp. 497-504)
These three forms provide students with a sequential plan for creating their own persuasive writing piece. A persuasive writing format is necessary in order for the writer to move the reader through developed arguments supporting his or her viewpoint. These forms will be utilized throughout the persuasive writing lessons and provide examples for teacher modeling.

Persuasive Writing Six Trait Checklist (p. 505)
Ideas, organization, voice, word choice, sentence fluency, and conventions are six trait writing components used to evaluate the student's writing performance. In this section, a six trait checklist is provided to increase student awareness of qualities that make up each component. After students complete their writing, the students can evaluate their writing by placing an X on the line indicating the qualities used in their writing. This visual will help students realize which areas they need to work on for improvement. Once the students have experience self-evaluating and a clear understanding of the characteristics that make up each trait, the teacher can move students from a checklist to a rubric.

Topics for Persuasive Writing

General Topics
- Uniforms in school
- Pets in the classroom
- Fast food in the cafeteria
- Homework in the summer
- Boys and girls in separate schools
- Homework
- Drinking more water and less soda
- Eating in the classroom
- Wearing hats in school
- Longer school day
- Protecting endangered animals
- Protecting rainforests
- Required seatbelts
- Curfews for children under 18
- Rating movies
- Monitoring students on the Internet
- Recycling
- Animals in zoos
- Longer recess

Personal Topics
- Unlimited TV viewing
- Staying up late
- Allowances
- Best season of the year
- Body piercing

Persuasive Writing Model

Instructions: Make into a chart or overhead transparency to guide students in persuasive writing.

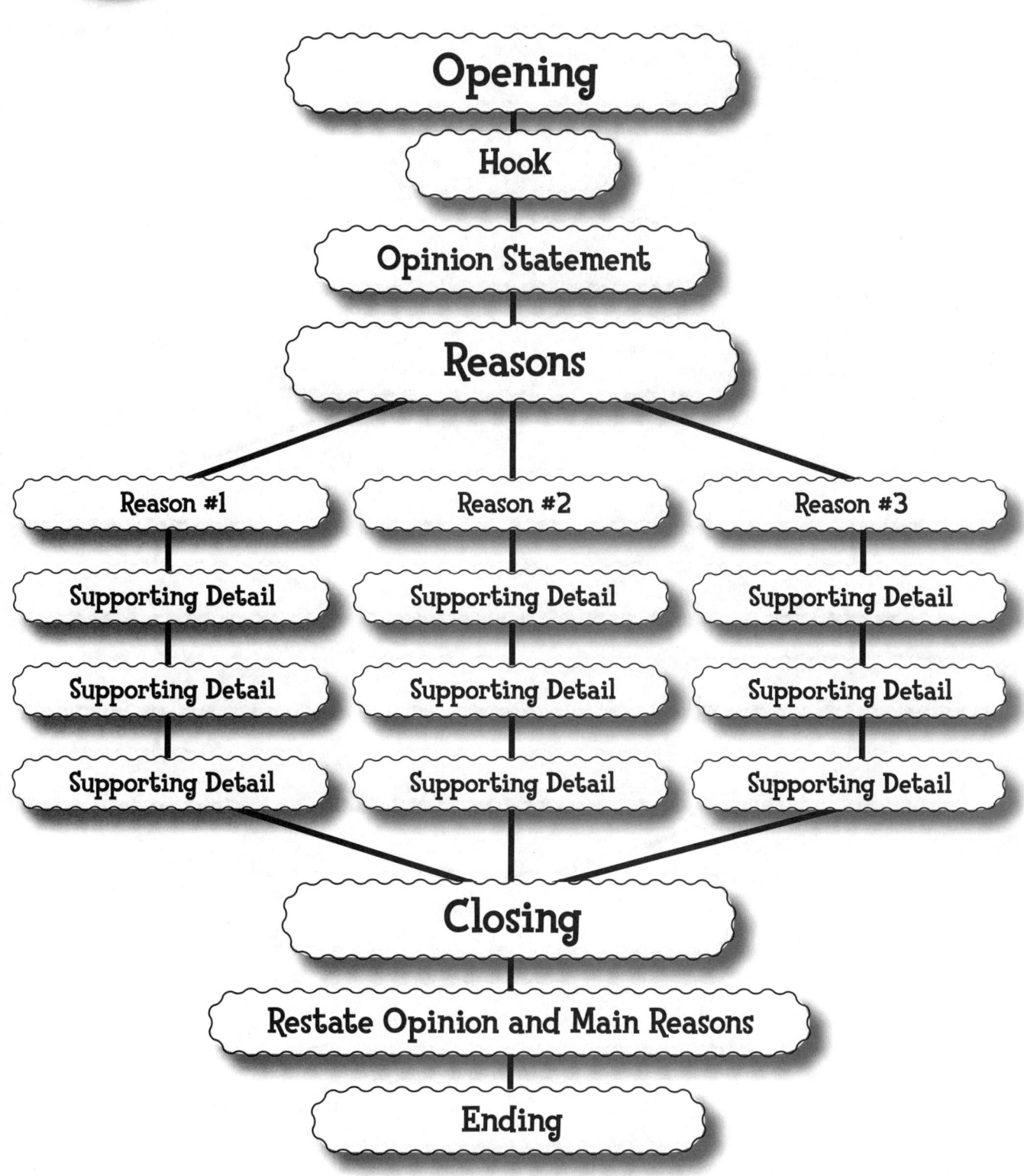

- **Opening**
  - Hook
  - Opinion Statement
- **Reasons**
  - Reason #1
    - Supporting Detail
    - Supporting Detail
    - Supporting Detail
  - Reason #2
    - Supporting Detail
    - Supporting Detail
    - Supporting Detail
  - Reason #3
    - Supporting Detail
    - Supporting Detail
    - Supporting Detail
- **Closing**
  - Restate Opinion and Main Reasons
  - Ending

Persuasive Writing Model Form

Instructions: Make into a chart or overhead transparency. The teacher may add labels—step by step—throughout the persuasive writing process.

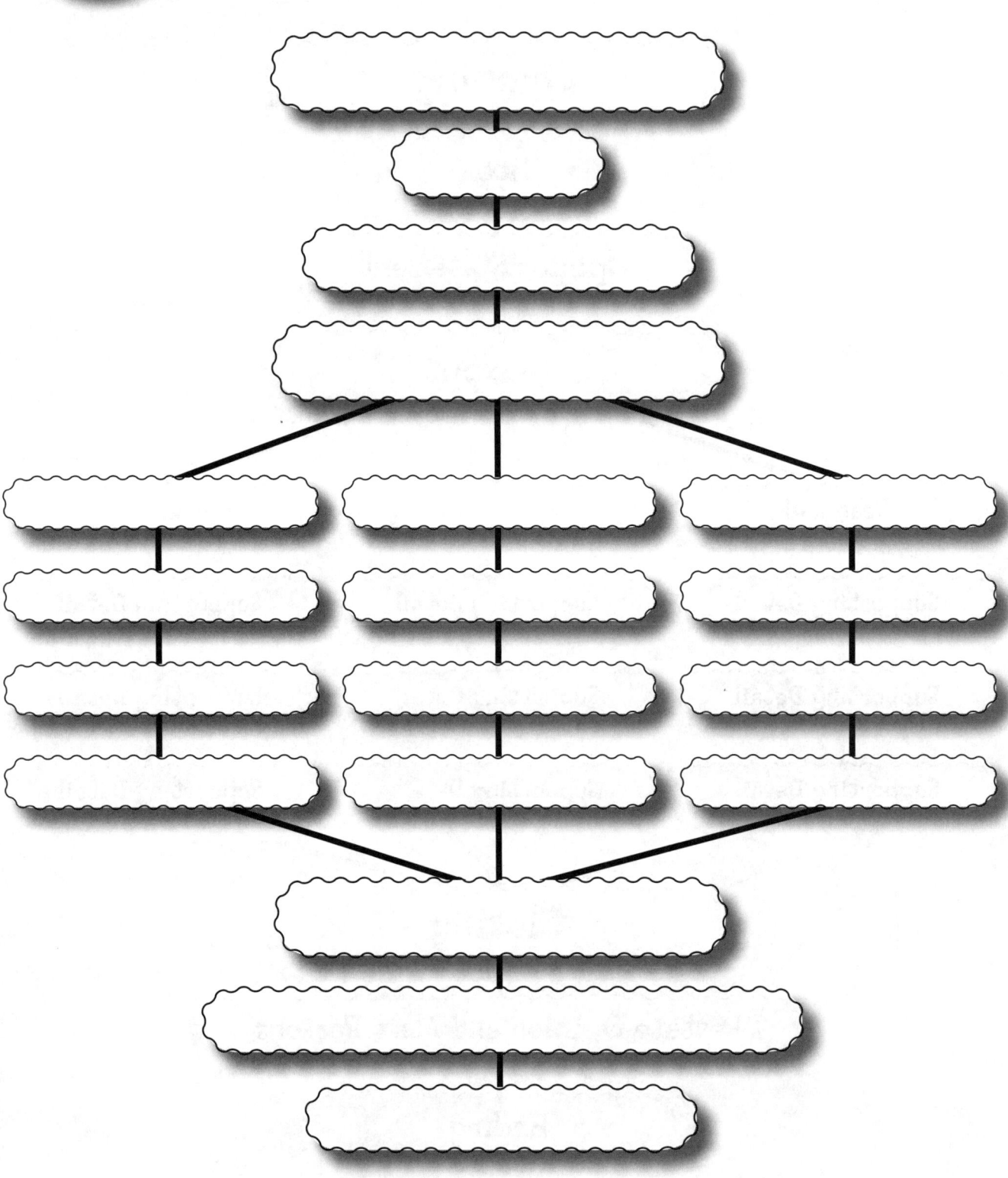

Student Persuasive Writing Plan
Form A

Instructions: Make one copy for each student.

#1 Topic:

_____

_____

❏ For ❏ Against

Opening:

Hook Examples:

❏ question

❏ unusual detail

❏ quotation

❏ fact/statistic

❏ hyperbole (exaggeration)

❏ _____

#9 Hook: (grab reader's attention)

_____

_____

_____

_____

_____

#2 Opinion Statement:

It is my opinion/I think _____

_____

_____

_____

_____

Student Persuasive Writing Plan
Form B

Instructions: Duplicate this page at least three times (one page for each reason).

#3 Reason # _____ :

_____

_____

_____

Detail Suggestions:

❏ real-life example

❏ personal example

❏ numbers

❏ research facts

❏ table/chart/diagram

❏ analogy

❏ comparison

❏ _____

#4 Supporting Detail

#5 Supporting Detail

#6 Supporting Detail

Student Persuasive Writing Plan
Form C

Instructions: Make one copy for each student.

Closing:

#7 (restate opinion and main reasons)

_____
_____
_____
_____
_____
_____
_____
_____

Ending Suggestions:

- ❏ prediction
- ❏ cause-effect
- ❏ question
- ❏ recommendation
- ❏ call to action
- ❏ quotation
- ❏ universal ending
- ❏ humor
  (play on words/personification)
- ❏ reference for additional information
- ❏ _____

#8 (add ending)

_____
_____
_____
_____
_____
_____
_____
_____

Student Persuasive Writing Plan
Form A—Example Sheet

#1 Topic:
Class Pet (Hamster)

☒ For ☐ Against

Opening:

Hook Examples:
- ☐ question
- ☐ unusual detail
- ☐ quotation
- ☐ fact/statistic
- ☐ hyperbole (exaggeration)
- ☒ advertisement

#9 Hook: (grab reader's attention)
WANTED:
- one small creature to love
- very quiet worker
- little space needed

#2 Opinion Statement:
It is my opinion / (I think) a hamster is just what our class needs.

Student Persuasive Writing Plan
Form B—Example Sheet

#3 Reason # __1__:

It will teach us responsibility.

Detail Suggestions:

- ❏ real-life example
- ❏ personal example
- ❏ numbers
- ❏ research facts
- ☒ table/chart/diagram
- ❏ analogy
- ❏ comparison
- ☒ problem-solution

#4 Supporting Detail

Problem-Solution:
We will have a bake sale at the school carnival to raise money for hamster supplies (food, cage, litter, etc.).

#5 Supporting Detail

We will take turns:
Hamster Responsibilities

NOVEMBER

1 John	2 Ted	3 Mary	4 Sue	5 Kate	6 Pete	7 Tim
8 Matt	9 Jill	10 Chloe	11 Melinda	12 Hannah	13 Micah	14 Sharon

#6 Supporting Detail

Student Persuasive Writing Plan
Form B—Example Sheet

#3 Reason # __2__:

It will be a learning experience.

Detail Suggestions:

- ☒ real-life example
- ☒ personal example
- ☐ numbers
- ☐ research facts
- ☐ table/chart/diagram
- ☐ analogy
- ☐ comparison
- ☐ _____

#4 Supporting Detail

<u>Personal Example:</u>
We will learn from a real hands-on experience.
- Hands-on experiences are when I learn the most (field trips, making things, etc.).

#5 Supporting Detail

<u>Real-Life Example:</u>
We will tie our learning about hamsters into:
- science projects
- research
- writing reports
- writing chapters for class book on hamsters

#6 Supporting Detail

Student Persuasive Writing Plan
Form C—Example Sheet

#3 Reason # __3__:

It will give everyone in the class experience with pets.

Detail Suggestions:
- ❏ real-life example
- ❏ personal example
- ☒ numbers
- ❏ research facts
- ❏ table/chart/diagram
- ❏ analogy
- ❏ comparison
- ❏ _____

#4 Supporting Detail

Numbers:
- 15 out of 25 students do not have a pet at home.
- Everyone will have a turn to take the hamster home for a weekend.

#5 Supporting Detail

#6 Supporting Detail

Student Persuasive Writing Plan
Form C—Example Sheet

~~~ Closing: ~~~

#7 (restate opinion and main reasons)

I think our class should have a pet hamster because it will teach us responsibility, it will be a learning experience, and it will give everyone experience with a pet.

Ending Suggestions:
- ☐ prediction
- ☐ cause-effect
- ☐ question
- ☐ recommendation
- ☐ call to action
- ☐ quotation
- ☒ universal ending "everyone"
- ☐ humor
  (play on words/personification)
- ☐ reference for additional information
- ☐ _____

#8 (add ending)

Everyone should have the opportunity to experience taking care of and loving a pet...including Room #14 at Jefferson Elementary.

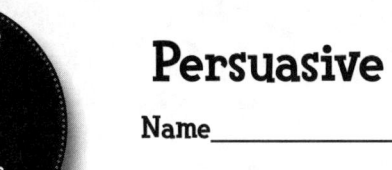

Persuasive Writing Six Trait Checklist

Name_____ Date_____

Instructions: The teacher determines how many of the six traits to evaluate. The student and/or teacher can evaluate a piece of writing by placing an *X* on each line indicating the skill(s) being used to strengthen each trait. Copy for each student.

Voice
___ My writing sounds like me. It does not sound like it is copied from a book.
___ My writing uses words that show my feelings.
___ My writing shows that I care about the topic.
___ My writing is appropriate for my audience.
___ My writing answers questions that readers might have.

Conventions
___ My writing uses spaces between words.
___ My writing uses capital letters correctly.
___ My writing uses end marks correctly. (Only light editing is needed for internal punctuation.)
___ My writing has been checked for spelling (or my best try at spelling).
___ My writing starts a new paragraph when new information is presented.

Organization
___ My writing has a strong beginning hook that makes the reader want to continue.
___ My writing focuses on a few main reasons/ideas and uses supporting details.
___ My writing uses transitional words to connect ideas.
___ My writing follows a logical sequence.
___ My writing has an ending that brings it to a natural closure.

Sentence Fluency
___ My writing uses sentences that are easy to read aloud.
___ My writing has some sentences that can be read expressively.
___ My writing uses sentences that begin in different ways.
___ My writing uses both long and short sentences.
___ My writing flows logically from sentence to sentence.

Ideas
___ My writing is focused and sticks to the topic.
___ My writing has a purpose: to inform, to entertain, to persuade or convince, or to explain/tell how to…
___ My writing uses supporting details/sensory details.
___ Main idea(s) stand out.
___ My writing gives enough information to make it interesting. It tells things that not everyone knows.

Word Choice
___ My writing uses new words.
___ My writing uses strong verbs, specific nouns, and describing words.
___ My writing does not repeat the same words too many times.
___ My writing uses literary devices: comparison, simile, dialogue, humor, suspense, onomatopoeia, _____ (circle ones used).

Balanced Literacy • Fourth Grade • Skidmore & Graber
Kagan Publishing • 1 (800) 933-2667 • www.KaganOnline.com

Persuasive Writing Activities

Persuasive Writing Stages

The following twelve sequenced lessons take the writer through the stages required to write a persuasive piece. Flexibility with the time for each lesson will be needed. Some lessons may require several days.

Prewriting (Lessons 1 and 2) (p. 509)
The amount of writing that the students produce is in direct relation to the amount of talking they do before they write. The pre-writing lessons are designed to create an atmosphere for talking and formulating "for" or "against" opinions with key points on a specific topic before they begin putting their ideas on paper.

Writing (Lessons 3–9) (pp. 512-518)
Teacher modeling, research, and cooperative learning structures lead students through the process of formulating the parts of a persuasive writing piece (opening, reasons, closing, hook).

Revising and Editing (Lesson 10) (pp. 519-522)
A focus lesson is utilized to improve students' writing. After the focus lesson instruction, students return to their work for revisions. They revise by adding transitional words. Students edit for conventions and sentence fluency.

Feedback (Lesson 11) (p. 523)
A structure provides situations for feedback from peers that will guide polishing of the writing piece.

Sharing (Lesson 12) (p. 524)
Students have been writing for a specific purpose. This stage gives them an opportunity to share their work with an audience.

PREWRITING Activity

Prewriting Circles

The amount of writing that students produce is in proportion to the amount of talking and processing that they get to do before they write. In this activity, students form two concentric circles so that pairs face each other. Using the questions provided, students ask their partner a question. The circles rotate multiple times so students share with multiple partners. This activity helps students focus on their topic, expand their writing ideas, and write in complete sentences.

Activity Steps

1. Students are given time to choose a topic and read about their topic.
2. Students form pairs and each student is given one Prewriting Question Card.
3. One student from each pair moves to form one large circle.
4. Remaining students find and face their partners. (The class now stands in two concentric circles.)
5. The Inside Circle students ask the Outside Circle students the question on their question card. The Outside Circle students respond.
6. Partners switch roles: Outside Circle students ask the questions and Inside Circle students respond.
7. Students trade cards, then the Inside Circle students rotate clockwise to face a new partner to ask and answer a new prewriting question.

STRUCTURE
Inside-Outside Circle

Blackline

• Prewriting Question Cards 510

Prewriting Question Cards
Inside-Outside Circle

Instructions: Make enough copies of this blackline so that each student has one card. Cut out the question cards and give each student one card. Students use cards to ask partners prewriting questions during Inside-Outside Circle.

Prewriting Questions
What topic are you planning to write about?

Prewriting Questions
What do you already know about this topic?

Prewriting Questions
What is your opinion about this topic?

Prewriting Questions
What is the most important idea to get across to your readers?

Prewriting Questions
What supporting detail(s) is important for you to share with the reader?

Prewriting Questions
What will readers find interesting about this topic?

Prewriting Questions
What personal interest do you have in this topic?

Prewriting Questions
If you could add a text feature to your writing about this topic, what would it be?

Prewriting Questions
What data, facts, or experiences support your view?

Prewriting Questions
How can you present the topic so that it is not boring to read?

Prewriting Questions
What words do you want to include in your writing about this topic?

Prewriting Questions
Which reason will you need to spend more time researching?

PREWRITING Activity

"For" or "Against"

For prewriting, students decide whether they are for or against an issue. They go to a corner of the room marked with their choice and interact with others with same corner choice using RoundRobin.

Activity Steps

1. Teacher labels two corners of the room (#1—For; #2—Against).

2. Each student completes Box #1 on the "Student Persuasive Writing Plan (Form A)."

3. Each student takes his or her Form A and goes to the corner corresponding to the For/Against choice using RoundRobin. *(These become the working teams for the remainder of the persuasive writing project.)*

4. Optional: Students may share and paraphrase across corners.

STRUCTURE
Corners with RoundRobin

Blackline

• Persuasive Writing Plan (Form A) 497

WRITING Activity

Reasons for Opinion

Students will begin to formulate reasons, which will be used to support their opinions.

Activity Steps

1. Students are organized into teams or partners according to the "For" or "Against" views.
2. The teacher asks students to list reasons supporting their opinion about the topic.
3. In teams or partners, students take turns passing a paper and pencil, each writing one reason to support their view.

Each student needs two to three copies of "Student Persuasive Writing Plan (Form B)." The teacher models choosing reasons to support his or her topic and opinion, while verbally sharing decision-making thoughts. Consensus is used to decide on two to three reasons to support their opinion. One reason is written per page in Box #3 of Form B. Using consensus, teams order and number their reasons, starting with Reason #1 being the strongest reason to support their opinion.

STRUCTURE
RoundTable/ RallyTable

Blackline

- Persuasive Writing Plan (Form B) 498

WRITING Activity

Supporting Details

After teacher modeling and student research, students are ready to choose the best detail(s) to support each reason for their opinion. In teams or pairs, students take turns orally sharing to support the reason for their opinion.

Activity Steps

1. The teacher uses specific examples to explain the effective use of supporting details. *Detail suggestions are listed next to Box #4 on the "Student Persuasive Writing Plan (Form B)."* The teacher may choose examples from:
   - *nonfiction magazine articles such as* Ranger Rick *or* National Geographic Kids
   - *newspaper, Internet, nonfiction books, etc.*
   - *student work from previous years*

   The teacher returns to her or his own writing piece to model the use of details that support each previously modeled reason.

2. Research time is given to allow students to gather more information to use as supportive details. Students will need to take notes to refer to later.

3. The teacher has each team start working with Reason #1 and its supporting details.

4. In teams, students respond orally, each taking turns listing a supporting detail taken from personal experience or text (referring to research notes as needed).

5. Continue until all details for Reason #1 have been shared.

6. Students discuss each detail and decide by consensus which detail(s) to use to support Reason #1.

7. When consensus is reached, each student returns to Form B and records the agreed upon detail(s) in Boxes #4, #5, and #6.

8. Repeat Steps 2 through 5 for Reason(s) #2 and #3.

Students may check the details used in the Detail Suggestion Box on "Student Persuasive Writing Plan (Form B)".

STRUCTURE
RoundRobin Consensus/ RallyCoach

Blackline

- Student Persuasive Writing Plan (Form B) 498

WRITING Activity

Restatement of Opinion and Main Reasons

After the teacher models, students are ready to write a statement restating their opinion and the main reasons for the opinion.

Activity Steps

1. The teacher models her thinking as she formulates a restatement of her opinion and main reasons on Form C—Box #7. (Use Form A—Box #2 and Form B—Boxes #3 to formulate the restatement.)

2. Students individually write their restatements using "Student Persuasive Writing Plan (Form C)" Box #7.

STRUCTURE
Solo

Blacklines

- Student Persuasive Writing Plan (Form A) 497
- Student Persuasive Writing Plan (Form B) 498
- Student Persuasive Writing Plan (Form C) 499

Writing Activity

Adding an Ending

Students research ending techniques that will bring their persuasive writing piece to a satisfying closure.

STRUCTURE
Solo

Activity Steps

1. The teacher displays a large poster with labeled categories for types of endings (e.g., *prediction, cause-effect, question, recommendation, call to action, quotation, universal ending, reference for additional information, humor*).

2. Students individually look through nonfiction magazines, books, and other texts searching for examples of ending techniques. Sticky notes should be used to mark and label the endings.

3. Students are numbered in teams. The teacher spins the spinner and calls on the student from each team with that number to share any ending examples previously located.

4. As each student shares an ending, the class identifies the category of each example. (The teacher may tally or make brief notes on the poster under each category heading to be used as a reference for students.)

5. Time is given to allow students to individually choose an ending for their persuasive writing piece and record it in Box #8 on "Student Persuasive Writing Plan (Form C)." Students identify the type of ending chosen by checking the box next to the appropriate category in the Ending Suggestions Box on Form C.

Blackline

- Student Persuasive Writing Plan (Form C) 499

WRITING Activity

Hook Examples

Jot Thoughts allows students to note possibilities for hooks used by various authors. The examples generated from Jot Thoughts will be used as a class resource when students begin their persuasive writing.

Activity Steps

1. Students look through magazines for beginning hooks.

2. Students write one hook on each blank sentence strip and announce the example to the team, as it is displayed in the middle of the team.

3. When the allotted time is up, students work together to sort the hooks into like categories (examples: question, exclamation, onomatopoeia, riddle, data, unusual detail, quotation, hyperbole, fact/statistic, etc.)

4. The teacher calls on a team to give a hook category. The teacher writes the title of the mentioned hook category on a large piece of poster paper. Each team is given discussion time to pick their top two hook examples for that category. The teacher uses the spinner to select a member from each team to read the hook examples and glue them to the poster.

5. Continue the same procedure for the remaining hook categories and examples.

STRUCTURE
Jot Thoughts

Blackline

- Student Persuasive Writing Plan (Form A) 497

WRITING Activity

Choosing a Hook

Now that the students have completed their persuasive writing piece, they are ready to add a beginning hook to their writing.

Activity Steps

1. Each student writes two or three different hook possibilities on a blank piece of paper.
2. Students take their hook example page with them and form two concentric circles with inside/outside partners facing each other.
3. Inside circle partners share their writing hooks with outside circle partners.
4. Outside Circle partner offers feedback and praises.
5. Partners switch roles. Outside Circle partners share. Inside Circle partner offers feedback and praises.
6. The teacher has the inside circle rotate clockwise to find a new partner. (The teacher may call rotation numbers: "Rotate three ahead.")
7. Continue sharing using Steps 3 through 6.
8. The teacher models the use of several hooks using her own writing piece. Through teacher think-aloud, the teacher verbalizes the thought processes involved in deciding on the most appropriate hook choice.
   - Which hook best fits my audience?
   - Which hook will grab the readers's attention?
   - Which hook will make the reader want to continue reading?
   - Which hook best ties into what I want to talk about?
9. Students are given time to work on their hooks. They will then write their chosen hook in Box #9 on "Student Persuasive Writing Plan (Form A)." Students also check the box indicating the category of the chosen hook.

STRUCTURE
Inside-Outside Circle

Blackline

- Student Persuasive Writing Plan (Form A).........................497

WRITING Activity

Final Copy

Students use their writing plan forms to draft their persuasive writing piece.

Activity Steps

1. Students use "Student Persuasive Writing Plan" Forms A, B, and C as a guide for writing their persuasive writing piece. The following format can be followed, as students rewrite the ideas from each box into complete sentences from their writing plan sheets.

> **Persuasive Writing Piece**
> **(Organizational Structure)**
>
> Paragraph 1. **Hook**
> Paragraph 2. **Opinion Statement**
> Paragraph 3. **Reason #1 and Supporting Details**
> Paragraph 4. **Reason #2 and Supporting Details**
> Paragraph 5. **Reason #3 and Supporting Details**
> Paragraph 6. **Restatement of Opinion and Main Reasons**
> Paragraph 7. **Ending**

STRUCTURE
Solo

Suggestion: Revising will be easier if students write on lined paper, skipping every other line. This will provide space for revisions.

REVISING ACTIVITY

Transitional Words

Students practice using transitional words, then use transitional words to improve their own persuasive writing.

Activity Steps

1. The teacher will need to model how to add transitional words into his or her writing. The think-aloud may include thoughts such as:
   - I need to use special words to help the reader know where I am at in my thinking." (first, next, finally, the last thing...)
   - "I need to alert the reader when I'm about to say something important." (consequently, as a result, for instance, otherwise, however...)
   - "I need to let the reader know when I'm going to use information to support my opinion." (according to, as _____ said, as well as, for example, for this reason...)

2. Each pair receives a set of cut-apart Transitional Word Passages and a Transitional Word List.

3. The passages are placed facedown between partners.

4. Partner A turns over the first passage, reads it, and chooses an appropriate transitional word(s) to fill in the blank. Partner A rereads the passage.

5. Partner B watches and listens, checks, and praises.

6. Partner B chooses a new passage, and the process continues.

7. The teacher gives each student a copy of the Transitional Word List to use as a reference, as he or she returns to the persuasive writing piece to add transitional words.

STRUCTURE
RallyCoach

Blacklines
- Transitional Word List...520
- Transitional Word Passages..521–522

Transitional Word List
RallyCoach

Instructions: Copy one list for each pair of students.

Transitional Word List	Transitional Word List
• for instance • on the other hand • as a result • finally • last • the last thing • first • second • next • consequently • a consequence • therefore • and so • frequently • in addition • for this reason • in fact • according to • along with • as well as • for example • although • otherwise • however • as I said	• for instance • on the other hand • as a result • finally • last • the last thing • first • second • next • consequently • a consequence • therefore • and so • frequently • in addition • for this reason • in fact • according to • along with • as well as • for example • although • otherwise • however • as I said

Transitional Word Passages
RallyCoach

Instructions: Cut out passages. Place them facedown between you and your partner. Partner A turns over the first one, reads it, and chooses a word(s) from the Transitional Word List to fill in the blank. Partner B praises or coaches. Switch roles.

Transitional Word Passages

Some cities limit the number of pets people may own. _____, I feel that people are able to give attention to more than one pet and properly take care of them.

Transitional Word Passages

There are many ways to cut down on your energy bill. _____, turn off lights when leaving a room and wash clothes when you have a full load.

Transitional Word Passages

It is important to follow the directions exactly as they are printed on the package. _____, your guests may be disappointed.

Transitional Word Passages

_____ a nationwide study, seat belts provide protection in numerous situations.

Transitional Word Passages

Ten cases of the West Nile Virus were reported in our county last year. _____, the same number was reported in the neighboring county.

Transitional Word Passages

Students should have longer lunch periods. _____, by the time a student gets through the lunch line, picks up a food tray, and finds a place to sit, there are only about ten minutes left to eat.

Transitional Word Passages
RallyCoach

Instructions: Cut out passages. Place them facedown between you and your partner. Partner A turns over the first one, reads it, and chooses a word(s) from the Transitional Word List to fill in the blank. Partner B praises or coaches. Switch roles.

Transitional Word Passages

By the mid-1800s, the United States was divided into the free states in the North and the slave states in the South. _____, slaves escaped along a series of routes to the North known as the "Underground Railroad."

Transitional Word Passages

I think "Hip Hoppers" would be an excellent name for our class book. _____ the book is about frogs, which move by hopping. _____, the book is about some really interesting creatures. _____ it's a catchy title that would make people want to read it.

Transitional Word Passages

Humans are cutting down forests. _____, pandas have fewer places to live and less to eat. _____, pandas are fighting for survival.

Transitional Word Passages

Pet size and characteristics are important considerations when selecting a pet. _____ these factors should be thought through carefully before a choice is made.

Transitional Word Passages

Many of our home products come from the rainforest. _____, cocoa, furniture polish, wax, and perfume are products you probably have in your home now.

PEER FEEDBACK ACTIVITY

Six Trait Feedback

Students share their writing with peers and receive feedback on six specific traits of their writing.

Activity Steps

1. Students complete a polished draft.
2. Students stand up, put a hand up, and pair up with a classmate.
3. The pair sits down at a table, each with their Six Trait Checklist (page 505).
4. Partner A reads his or her writing.
5. Partner B provides feedback on one of the six traits by reading each statement under the trait, discussing it, and putting a plus or minus by the statement.
6. Students switch roles and Partner A provides feedback to partner B.
7. Students thank each other and then pair up with another partner to examine the next trait. The process continues for six pairings, each focusing on a different trait.
8. After receiving feedback, students write a final draft.

STRUCTURE
Two-Partner Edit

Blackline

- Persuasive Writing Six Trait Checklist 505

SHARING Activity

Sharing Final Drafts

As a final sharing activity, students read their final drafts to multiple classmates and receive feedback.

Activity Steps

1. Each student takes his or her final draft, stands up, puts a hand up, and mixes in the classroom.
2. The teacher calls, "Pair."
3. Students pair up with the person closest to them, who is not from their team, and give a high five.
4. Students take turns sharing their persuasive writing pieces by reading them to their partners using RallyRobin. Students provide feedback to their partners. The feedback can be:
   - Open-ended reactions
   - Praise
   - Response to a provided gambit: "From your writing, I learned…"
   - Copycat gambit: Students repeat after the teacher a flattering phrase such as "Your persuasive writing was well written and tremendously informative!"
5. Students can do multiple rounds of peer sharing.

STRUCTURE

Mix-Pair-Share

Index of Structures for Balanced Literacy

Structure	Page(s)
CenterPiece	469–477, 526
Corners	511, 527
Fan-N-Pick	182–195, 528
Find My Rule	276, 278, 280, 282, 285–286, 288, 529
Find-the-Fiction	242–245, 530
Find Someone Who	291–296, 531
Inside-Outside Circle	453–454, 509–510, 517, 532
Jot Thoughts	228–230, 455–456, 516, 533
Listen-Sketch-Draft	221–223, 534
Mix-Pair-Share	490, 524, 535
Numbered Heads Together	179–181, 389–405, 536
Poems for Two Voices	422–427, 537
Quiz-Quiz-Trade	83–178, 297–355, 428–436, 538–539
RallyCoach	215–220, 238–241, 274–275, 277–287, 289–290, 356–376, 416–421, 478–483, 513, 519–522, 540–541
RallyRobin	511, 542
RallyTable	512, 543
RoundRobin	466–468, 511, 544
RoundRobin Consensus	513, 544
RoundTable	49, 512, 545
RoundTable Consensus	204–214, 457–458, 546
Showdown	50–82, 377–388, 547
Solo	215–220, 459–463, 514–515, 518, 548
Talking Chips	196–203, 549
Team Stand-N-Share	484–488, 550
Timed Pair Share	46–49, 224–227, 551
Traveling Heads Together	231–237, 552
Two-Partner Edit	449, 489, 523, 553

Structure

CenterPiece

Students brainstorm ideas, always trading their paper with the centerpiece.

Setup

• Five pieces of paper per teams of four (one per person and one in the center)

Steps

1. Teacher assigns a brainstorming topic.

2. Students generate items. They write one idea at a time and trade their paper with the one in the center.

3. Students continue brainstorming items, each time trading their paper with the centerpiece.

CenterPiece Activities and Blacklines

- Word Choice Practice 469
- Word Choice—Powerful Verbs 470–471
- Word Choice—Powerful Adjectives 472–473
- Word Choice—Similes 474–475
- Word Choice—Describing a Noun 476
- Word Choice Form 477

Structure

Corners

Students move to different corners of the room to express their preferences and then interact with classmates with similar preferences, and they listen to ideas of those with different perspectives.

Steps

1. Teacher announces three or more corners.
2. Students think about, then write down their corner selection.
3. Students move to their corners.
4. Teacher provides interaction question.
5. Pairs are formed within each corner.
6. Pairs share using Timed Pair Share or RallyRobin.
7. Teacher calls on students from each corner to share reasons with the class.
8. Students may be asked to paraphrase reasons of those from other corners using RallyRobin.

Corners Activity and Blackline

- "For" or "Against" Sentence Writing Practice 511

Structure

Fan-N-Pick

Students play a card game to respond to questions.

Setup

- *Each team receives a set of question cards.*

Steps

1. Student #1 holds question cards in a fan and says, "Pick a card, any card!"

2. Student #2 picks a card, reads the question aloud, and allows five seconds of Think Time.

3. Student #3 answers the question.

4. Student #4 responds to the answer:
   - For right or wrong answers, Student #4 checks and then either praises or tutors.
   - For higher-level thinking questions that have no right or wrong answer, Student #4 does not check for correctness, but praises and paraphrases the thinking that went into the answer.

5. Students rotate roles, one person clockwise for each new round.

Fan-N-Pick Activities and Blacklines

- Pick a Card, Any Card 182
- Fan-N-Pick Mat (used for all of the activities) 183
- Metacognitive Awareness Strategies 184–185
- Text Features 186–188
- Story Elements (Fiction) 189–193
- Previewing Before Reading (Nonfiction) 194–195

Structure

Find My Rule

Students induce a rule from examples provided by the teacher.

Steps

1. Teacher places one item in each area of the category frame.
2. Teacher asks, "What is my rule for placing items?" and provides think time.
3. Students RallyRobin with their shoulder partners to generate possible rules the teacher is using.
4. Teacher places two more objects in the category frame.
5. Teacher again says, "What is my rule?" and provides think time.
6. Students RallyRobin with their face partners to generate possible rules.
7. Teacher places more objects in the category frame, each time having teams discuss possible rules.
8. Teacher says, "Don't tell me your rule. Name an item that fits in each category," and calls a number. Students with that number stand to share their items. The teacher confirms correct answers.
9. When most students seem to know the rule, the teacher calls on one student to verbalize the rule for the class.
10. Teacher confirms the rule.
11. Teacher presents new items one at a time, each time calling for students to hold up fingers indicating the category for the item.
12. Teacher congratulates the class.

Find My Rule Activities and Blacklines

- Sorting 276, 280, 285
- Making Words Teacher Transparency Form 278, 282, 286
- Find My Rule Mat 288

Structure

Find-the-Fiction

Students pick out the fictitious statement from a set of three statements.

Steps

1. Teammates write three statements: two true, one false.
2. One student on each team stands, then reads his or her statements to teammates.
3. Without consulting teammates, each student writes down his or her own best guess as to which statement is false.
4. Teammates RoundRobin and defend their "best guess." (Note: Teacher may or may not ask teams to attempt to reach consensus.)
5. Teammates announce their guess(es).
6. The standing student announces the false statement.
7. Students celebrate: The standing student congratulates teammates who guessed correctly. Teammates who were fooled congratulate the standing student.
8. The next teammate stands to share. The process is repeated from Step 2.

Find-the-Fiction Activities and Blacklines

- Idiom Cards—True or False?..242
- Idiom Cards—True or False?..243–245

Structure

Find Someone Who

Students mix about the room, finding others who help them learn content or skills.

Setup
- The teacher prepares a worksheet or questions for students.

Steps

1. Students mix in the class, keeping a hand raised until they find a new partner that is not a teammate.
2. In pairs, Partner A asks a question from the worksheet; Partner B responds. Partner A records the answer on his or her own worksheet.
3. Partner B checks and initials the answer.
4. Partner B asks a question. Partner A responds. Partner B records the answer on his or her own worksheet.
5. Partner A checks and initials the answer.
6. Partners shake hands, part, and raise a hand again as they search for a new partner.
7. Students repeat Steps 1–6 until their worksheets are complete.
8. When their worksheets are completed, students sit down; seated students may be approached by others as a resource.
9. In teams, students compare answers; if there is disagreement or uncertainty, they raise four hands to ask a team question.

Find Someone Who Activities and Blacklines

- Who Knows?..291
- All About Prefixes..292
- Skill Review..293–295
- Find Someone Who Form..296

Structure

Inside-Outside Circle

In concentric circles, students rotate to face new partners and answer questions.

Setup

- The teacher prepares questions or question cards for students. Students form pairs.

Steps

1. One student from each pair moves to form one large circle in the class.
2. Remaining students find and face their partners. (The class now stands in two concentric circles.)
3. Inside circle students ask a question from their question card; outside circle students answer. Inside circle students praise or coach. (Alternative: The teacher asks a question and indicates inside person or outside person to share with their partner).
4. Partners switch roles.
5. Partners trade question cards.
6. Inside circle students rotate clockwise to a new partner. (The teacher may call rotation numbers: Rotate Three Ahead. The class may do a choral count as they rotate.)

Note: When played with cards, Steps 3–6 become Quiz-Quiz-Trade.

Inside-Outside Circle Activities and Blacklines

- Prewriting Circles 453, 509
- Prewriting Question Cards 454, 510
- Choosing a Hook 517

Structure

Jot Thoughts

Teammates cover the table with ideas on slips of paper.

Setup

- Give multiple slips of paper (e.g., precut sticky notes, note pad) to each team.

Steps

1. The teacher names a topic and sets a time limit.
2. Students announce and write as many ideas as they can in the allotted time, one idea per slip of paper.
3. Students attempt to cover the table with ideas (no slips are to overlap).

Jot Thoughts Activities and Blacklines

- Sort It Out 228
- Recall Mat 229
- Sorting Mat 230
- Brainstorming Ideas 455
- Brainstorming Mat 456
- Hook Examples 516

Structure

Listen-Sketch-Draft

Students sketch content chunk by chunk, create and compare main idea statements, and finally draft a summary statement.

Steps

1. Students listen while teacher presents the first chunk of information.
2. Teacher stops presenting and calls for each student to sketch the most important details.
3. Students share sketches using:
   - RoundRobin
   - Timed Pair Share
4. Students draft a main idea statement, based on the information shared in Step 1. While students draft their main ideas, teacher circulates and monitors.
5. The process is repeated for the next chunk.
6. When all chunks have been presented, students draft a summary statement.
7. Students compare their summaries with a partner or teammates praising ideas.

Listen-Sketch-Draft Activity and Blacklines

- Sketching for Comprehension 221
- Listen-Sketch-Draft Sample Form 222
- Listen-Sketch-Draft Form 223

Structure

Mix-Pair-Share

Students pair with classmates to discuss questions posed by the teacher.

Setup

- Teacher prepares discussion questions to ask students.

Steps

1. Students silently mix around the room.
2. Teacher calls, "Pair."
3. Students pair up with the person closest them and give a high five. Students who haven't found a partner raise their hands to find each other.
4. Teacher asks a question and gives think time.
5. Students share with their partners using:
   - Timed Pair Share
   - RallyRobin
   - RallyCoach

Mix-Pair-Share Activity

- Sharing Final Drafts...490, 524

Structure

Numbered Heads Together

Teammates work together to ensure all members understand; one is randomly selected to be held accountable.

Setup

• Teacher prepares questions or problems to ask teams.

Steps

1. Students number off.
2. Teacher poses a problem and gives think time. (Example: *Everyone think about how rainbows are formed.*)
3. Students privately write their answers.
4. Students lift up from their chairs to put their heads together, show answers, and discuss and teach.
5. Students sit down when everyone knows the answer or has something to share.
6. Teacher calls a number. The student with that number from each team answers simultaneously using:
   • Slate Share
   • Choral Practice
   • Finger Responses
   • Chalkboard Responses
   • Response Cards
   • Manipulatives
7. Teammates praise students who responded.

Numbered Heads Together Activities and Blacklines

- Which Definition? 179
- Vocabulary Definitions 180–181
- Word Wall Spelling 389
- Fourth Grade Priority Word List 390–391
- Fourth Grade Priority Word Wall Cards 392–397
- Fourth Grade Additional Word Wall Cards 398–404
- Blank Word Wall Cards 405

Structure

Poems for Two Voices

Partners present a poem—recited at times by one partner, the other partner, or both.

Setup

- The teacher prepares a poem with lines labeled A, B, or AB.

Steps

1. Teacher explains and assigns students A and B roles.

2. Students read their labeled line, listening carefully to their partners to keep the flow.

Note: Students may progress through three stages:

1. Teacher provides poem and AB scripting.
2. Teacher provides poem and students provide AB scripting.
3. Students create or select poem and script it.

Poems for Two Voices Activity and Blacklines

- Fluency Poems 422
- Tropical Rainforests 423–424
- Human Body Riddles 425–426
- Blank Form 427

Structure
Quiz-Quiz-Trade

Students quiz a partner, get quizzed by a partner, and then trade cards to repeat the process with a new partner.

Steps

1. Stand Up, Hand Up, Pair Up.
2. Partner A quizzes.
3. Partner B answers.
4. Partner A praises or coaches.
5. Switch roles.
6. Partners trade cards.
7. Repeat Steps 1–6 a number of times.

*Text type, text structure, and figurative language **resources** are included in the Comprehension Resource Section pages.

Quiz-Quiz-Trade Activities and Blacklines

- Comprehension Quizzes 83
- Text Types—Definitions 84–87
- Text Types—Author's Purpose 88–95
- Text Types—Examples 96–102
- Determining Author's Purpose and Text Types 103–111
- Text Structures—Definitions, Signal Words, and
  Graphic Organizers 112–118
- Text Structure Passages 119–123
- Cause and Effect 124–131
- Text Features 132–135
- Homophone Definitions 136–142
- Figurative Language 143–148
- Homophone Sentences 149–156

(continued on next page)

Structure
Quiz-Quiz-Trade (continued)

Students quiz a partner, get quizzed by a partner, and then trade cards to repeat the process with a new partner.

Quiz-Quiz-Trade Activities and Blacklines

- Word Meanings 157–163
- Possesive Nouns 164–170
- Present and Past Tense Verbs 171–178
- Partner Word Study Practice 297
- Contractions 298–304
- Silent Letters 305–311
- Letter Patterns (ar, er, ir, or, ur) 312–318
- Letter Patterns (au, aw, ou, ow) 319–326
- Letter Patterns (ie, ei) 327–333
- Prefixes (anti-, dis-, ex-, non-, under-) 334–341
- Prefixes (anti-, dis-, ex-, non-, under-)
   Suffixes (-en, -ful, -less, -ment, -ness) 342–348
- Their, There, They're 349–355
- Fluency Sentences 428
- Fluency Sentences Cards 429–436

Structure

RallyCoach

Partners take turns, one solving a problem while the other coaches.

Setup

- One set of high-consensus problems and one pencil per pair

Steps

1. Partner A solves the first problem.
2. Partner B watches and listens, checks, and praises.
3. Partner B solves the next problem.
4. Partner A watches and listens, checks, and praises.
5. Repeat starting at Step 1.

Note: RallyCoach may be used with worksheet problems, oral problems provided by the teacher, or manipulatives.

RallyCoach Activities and Blacklines

- Anticipation Guide 215
- Anticipation Guide Sample 216–219
- Anticipation Guide Form 220
- Idiom Meanings 238
- Idiom Mat 239
- Idiom Cards (Set 1) 240
- Idiom Cards (Set 2) 241
- Making Words 274–275, 277, 280–281, 284–285
- Transfer 277, 281, 285
- Making Words Teacher Transparency Form 278, 282, 286
- Making Words Planning Form 289
- Making Words Student Form 279, 283, 287, 290
- Coach Me 356

(continued on next page)

Structure

RallyCoach (continued)

Partners take turns, one solving a problem while the other coaches.

RallyCoach Activities and Blacklines

- Prefix Cube, Worksheet, and Answer Sheet
  (anti-, dis-, ex-, non-, under-) 357–359
- Suffix Cube, Worksheet, and Answer Sheet
  (-ful, -en, -less, -ment, -ness) 360–364
- Antonym-Synonym Cube, Worksheet and Answer Sheet 365–367
- Spinner and Worksheet (Contractions) 368–369
- Spinner, Worksheet, and Answer Sheet (Adding Endings) 370–372
- Sorting Mat and Word Cards (Hard *g*/Soft *g*) 373–376
- Fluency Scoring 416
- Expression Rubric and Graph 417
- Phrasing Rubric and Graph 418
- Accuracy Rubric and Graph 419
- Rate Rubric and Graph 420
- Fluency Continuum 421
- Sentence Writing Practice 478
- Sentence Mechanics 479–480
- Revising Sentences 481–482
- Revising Sentences—Form 483
- Supporting Details 513
- Transitional Words 519
- Transitional Word List 520
- Transitional Word Passages 521–522

Structure

RallyRobin

In pairs, students alternate generating oral responses.

Steps

1. Teacher poses a problem to which there are multiple possible responses or solutions.

2. In pairs, students take turns stating responses or solutions.

RallyRobin Activity and Blacklines

- "For" or "Against" Sentence Writing Practice..511

Structure

RallyTable

In pairs, students alternate generating written responses or solving problems.

Setup

- One paper and one pencil per pair

Steps

1. Teacher poses a task to which there are multiple possible responses.//
2. In pairs, students take turns passing the paper and pencil or pair project, each writing one answer or making a contribution.

   Variation: Simultaneous RallyTable. Students may each have their own piece of paper. Each writes at the same time and then trades at the same time.

RallyTable Activity and Blacklines

- Reasons for Opinion 512

Structure

RoundRobin

In teams, students take turns responding orally.

Steps

1. Teacher assigns a topic or question with multiple possible answers.
2. In teams, students respond orally, each in turn taking about the same amount of time.

RoundRobin Activity and Blacklines

- Improving Details 466
- Six Ways to Improve Details 467
- Detail Improvement Form... 468
- "For" or "Against" Sentence Writing Practice...................................... 511

RoundRobin Consensus Activity and Blacklines

- Supporting Details Details 513

544 Balanced Literacy • Fourth Grade • Skidmore & Graber
Kagan Publishing • 1 (800) 933-2667 • www.KaganOnline.com

Structure

RoundTable

In teams, students take turns—generating written responses, solving problems, or making a contribution to the team project.

Setup

- One piece of paper and one pencil per team

Steps

1. Teacher provides a task to which there are multiple possible responses.

2. In teams, students take turns passing a paper and pencil or a team project, each writing one answer or making a contribution.

RoundTable Activities and Blacklines

- Lou Gehrig, the Luckiest Man Shared Read Aloud..................49
- Reasons for Opinion..................512

Structure

RoundTable Consensus

In teams, students take turns answering questions or placing cards, checking for consensus each time.

Steps

1. Teacher provides or students generate question cards or (manipulatives.)
2. One student answers using manipulatives, if necessary.
3. The student checks for consensus.
4. The teammates show agreement or lack of agreement with thumbs up or down.
5. If there is agreement, the students celebrate and the next student responds. If not, teammates discuss the response until there is agreement and then they celebrate. If no agreement is reached, the card is set aside to be discussed later.
6. Play continues with the next student answering.

RoundTable Consensus Activities and Blacklines

- Spinning Vocabulary 204
- Vocabulary Spinner 205
- Sentence Cards for Vocabulary Spinner 206
- Blank Sentence Cards 207
- Comprehension Puzzles 208
- Retelling (Fiction) Puzzle Pieces and Puzzle Mat 209–210
- Retelling (Nonfiction) Puzzle Pieces and Puzzle Mat 211–212
- Text Feature (Nonfiction) Puzzle Pieces and Puzzle Mat 213–214
- Sorting Ideas 457
- Sorting Mat 458

Structure

Showdown

Students answer questions without help. Teams then share, check, and coach.

Setup

- Teams each have a set of question cards stacked facedown in the center of the table.

Steps

1. Teacher selects one student on each team to be the Showdown Captain for the first round.
2. Showdown Captain draws the top card and reads the question.
3. Working alone, all students write their answers.
4. When finished, teammates signal when they are ready.
5. The Showdown Captain calls, "Showdown."
6. Teammates show and state their answers.
7. Showdown Captain leads the checking.
8. If correct, the team celebrates; if not, teammates coach, then celebrate.
9. The person to the left of the Showdown Captain becomes the Showdown Captain for the next round.

*Metacognitive and Text Structure resources are included in the Comprehension Resource Section on pages 10–13, 35–40.

Showdown Activities and Blacklines

- Comprehension Showdown 50
- Metacognitive Terms and Definitions (Team and Student Set Cards) 51–54
- Text Types—Author's Purpose (Team and Student Set and Answer Key) ... 55–57
- Text Structures—Definitions, Signal Words, Graphic Organizers 58–64
- Text Structures and Paragraphs (Team and Student Set Cards) 65–68
- Text Structures—Signal Words (Team and Student Set Cards) 69–75
- Fact or Opinion (Team and Student Set Cards) 76, 82
- Word Study Showdown 377
- Word Card Prefixes (anti-, dis-, ex-, non-, under-)
  (Team Set and Student Set Cards) 378–381
- Antonyms, Synonyms, Homophones
  (Team Set and Student Set Cards) 382–388

Balanced Literacy • Fourth Grade • Skidmore & Graber
Kagan Publishing • 1 (800) 933-2667 • www.KaganOnline.com

Structure

Solo

Students write, read, draw, solve problems, or practice something on their own.

Steps

1. Teacher provides problem or activity for students.
2. Students engage in activity alone.

Solo Activities and Blacklines

- Anticipation Guide 215
- Anticipation Guide Sample 216–219
- Anticipation Guide Form 220
- Paragraph Writing 459
- Sample Topic Sentence Form 460
- Sample Detail Sentences Form 461
- Topic Sentence Form 462
- Detail Sentences Form 463
- Restatement of Opinion and Main Resources 514
- Adding an Ending 515
- Final Copy 518

Structure

Talking Chips

Students place a chip in the center of the table each time they talk.

Setup

- Teams have talking chips (*maximum: two chips each*)

Steps

1. Teacher provides a discussion topic.

2. Any student begins the discussion, placing one of his or her chips in the center of the table.

3. Any student with a chip continues discussing, using his or her chip.

4. When all chips are used, teammates each collect their chips and continue the discussion using their talking chips.

Talking Chips Activity and Blacklines

- Comprehension Cube 196
- Nonfiction Comprehension Question Cube (Before Reading) 197
- Nonfiction Comprehension Question Cube (Reflection) 198
- Fiction Comprehension Question Cube (Reflection) 199
- Questioning Cube 200
- Metacognitive Cube (After Reading) 201
- Literature Circle Discussion Cube #1 (After Reading) 202
- Literature Circle Discussion Cube #2 (After Reading) 203

Structure

Team Stand-N-Share

Teams stand to share their answers with the class.

Setup

- Teams need a list of items to share

Steps

1. All students stand near their teammates.
2. Teacher calls on a standing student.
3. Selected student states one idea from the team list.
4. The student in each team, who is holding the team list, either adds the item to the list, or if it is already listed, checks it off.
5. Students pass their team list one teammate clockwise.
6. Teams sit when all their items are shared. While seated they add each new item as it is stated using RoundTable. When all teams are seated, Team Stand-N-Share is complete.

Team Stand-N-Share Activity and Blacklines

- Hooks and Endings 484
- Hook Examples 485
- Ending Examples 486
- Hook & Ending Form—Sample 487
- Hook & Ending Form 488

Structure

Timed Pair Share

In pairs, students share with a partner for a predetermined time while the partner listens. Then partners switch roles.

Steps

1. The teacher announces a topic, states how long each student will share, and provides think time.
2. In pairs, Partner A shares; Partner B listens.
3. Partner B responds with a positive gambit.
4. Partners switch roles.

Hint: The teacher provides positive response gambits to use in Step 3:

Copycat response gambits
- *"Thanks for sharing!"*
- *"You are interesting to listen to!"*

Complete the sentence gambits
- *"One thing I learned listening to you was…."*
- *"I enjoyed listening to you because…."*
- *"Your most interesting idea was…."*

Timed Pair Share Activities and Blacklines

- *Lou Gehrig, the Luckiest Man* Shared Read Aloud 46–49
- Story Predictions 224
- Prediction Mat 225
- Blank Story Element Cards for Prediction Mat 226
- Story Element Cards for Prediction Mat 227

Structure

Traveling Heads Together

Students travel to new teams to share their team answer.

Setup

- Teams have a list of items to share

Steps

1. Students number off in teams.
2. The teacher presents a problem and gives think time.
3. Teammates stand up and put their heads together to discuss and teach each other.
4. Students sit down when ready.
5. The teacher calls a number and says how many teams to rotate ahead.
6. The student called rotates to the new team.
7. Students who rotated share their original team's answer with their new team.
8. If correct, teammates praise the visitor. If not, they correct and coach.

Alternative: Rather than rotating a specific number, One Stray may be used.

Traveling Heads Together Activity and Blacklines

- Idioms and Morals 231
- Idioms 232–234
- Idioms Answer Sheet 235
- Fable Morals 236–237

Structure

Two-Partner Edit

After writing, students discuss and edit their work with a partner, then again with a second partner.

Steps

1. Students write alone on a topic.
2. When complete, students go to a predetermined area of the room to find another student who has finished writing.
3. Students pair up and find a place to sit, shoulder to shoulder.
4. In each pair, Student A reads his or her writing.
5. Students discuss the writing while Student A makes edits.
6. Students switch roles: Student B reads and makes edits.
7. Students thank their shoulder partner.
8. Students Stand Up, Hand Up, Pair Up.
9. With their new partner, students each read, discuss, and re-edit their papers.

Two-Partner Edit Activity and Blacklines

- Six Trait Feedback 489, 523
- Six Trait Checklist for Writing 449

Notes

Notes

Notes

Notes

Notes

Notes

Notes

Kagan

It's All About Engagement!

**Kagan is your source
for active engagement in the classroom.**

Check out Kagan's line of books, SmartCards, software, electronics, and hands-on learning resources—all designed to boost engagement in your classroom.

Books

SmartCards

Spinners

Learning Chips

Posters

Learning Cubes

KAGAN PUBLISHING

www.KaganOnline.com ★ 1(800) 933-2667

Kagan

It's All About Engagement!

Kagan is the world leader in creating active engagement in the classroom. Learn how to engage your students and you will boost achievement, prevent discipline problems, and make learning more fun and meaningful. Come join Kagan for a workshop or call Kagan to **set up a workshop for your school or district**. Experience the power of a Kagan workshop. **Experience the engagement!**

SPECIALIZING IN:

- ★ Cooperative Learning
- ★ Win-Win Discipline
- ★ Brain-Friendly Teaching
- ★ Multiple Intelligences
- ★ Thinking Skills
- ★ Kagan Coaching

KAGAN PROFESSIONAL DEVELOPMENT

www.KaganOnline.com ★ 1(800) 266-7576